REVIEWS FROM FORMER STUDENTS OF DR. GILBERTS

I very much enjoyed Dr. Gilbert's teaching.

I have a strong feeling that the things I learned I will take with me throughout the course of my life. I feel more prepared now than I ever have been to engage in an intimate relationship in the future.

Dr. Gilbert helped me share my views as well as grow as a person. He challenged me to seek Biblical truth and I feel more prepared for my future because of it.

The world we know today is odd, confused, and in serious need of sexual education.

Thank you Dr. G for your teaching and preparing me well for my future.

All that I can say is that before taking Dr. Gilbert's course I had no solid/logical reasoning behind my beliefs. Through this course, God revealed beautiful and intricate ways in which He designed us.

I loved taking this course because it opened my eyes to things in my life I thought were okay, but were not.

Through this course I have learned a deeper understanding of what sex is and how it works. I have also gained comfortability with topics pertaining to sex.

Dr. Gilbert is tough, but it teaches us what we never learned growing up. It isn't necessarily about knowing the textbook in and out, but more so getting to know yourself in and out.

Before I dove into Dr. Gilbert's teaching I was in an unhealthy sexual relationship. Every time I had sex I felt confused and worthless. This course reinforced the beauty that sex entails, and how God created sex to be inside the bounds of marriage. I am so thankful for the material I learned to help me become the type of sexual being God intended.

Dr. Gilbert helped to expand my knowledge, understanding, and comfort with many aspects of sexuality in a healthy, appropriate way and from a Biblical Worldview. I believe it will benefit me personally and vocationally throughout the rest of my life.

I think this course was very informative and it is a course that everyone should take by the time they are in college.

I think my favorite thing about learning from Dr. Gilbert was that I figured out my own beliefs about things related to sex, gender, marriage, etc. It was extremely enlightening. If you are in a relationship, or planning on being in a relationship – READ THIS BOOK.

This was my favorite class I took in college. I learned a lot and it was all practical to making me a better follower of Christ.

This course helps us understand the complex yet powerful experiences and images that God has provided us.

Dr. Gilbert's class reshaped the way I view not only sexual behavior, but also my own sexual behavior. I greatly appreciate his insight and passion to help others know God's design for us as sexual beings.

I think that everyone should take this course. We have not learned how to handle sexuality in a healthy way because Christians don't talk about sex well! I feel more comfortable and prepared to maturely discuss sex with friends, a spouse, and future children.

God can redeem every area of our sexual brokenness.

I struggled with my identity as a sexual being - it felt wrong to have these desires and feelings, but God designed me this way. I can now move forward proud of who I am and seek out God's best for me.

I think everyone needs to hear this stuff. I wish I hadn't had to wait until college to learn such necessary material so openly and bluntly. It was hard, but refreshing.

Dr. Gilbert challenged me to think about my sexuality from a biblical perspective. It was the best environment I've ever been in to talk openly about uncomfortable topics and learn a biblical perspective on many aspects of sexuality, dating, and marriage.

Dr. Gilbert helps unveil the true beauty and intimacy that sex can bring in a marriage.

I think everyone should be required to take a course like this!

I learned so much and was able to begin to form my theology of sexuality other than "just don't talk about it" that reflected a biblical knowledge of sexuality, marriage, and family.

I really appreciated the Biblical / Christian growth incorporated into the materials. I liked how the information was applied practically. I think this should be a required course!

This course was quite useful in pointing out fallacies in principles many people (including my parents) teach their kids in this society.

Dr. Gilbert really helped me figure out what a biblical sexual ethic really is.

I feel as though EVERY young adult (and teen) should take this course! It's being taught in a safe place. There is no reason we shouldn't use this resource to gain knowledge and insight.

I feel like Dr. Gilbert gave me permission to have these conversations and talk about sexuality and have it be a mature and deep conversation.

Dr. Gilbert challenged me intellectually. Being challenged to think through sexuality and my own sexuality has been extremely beneficial and I am glad that I took this course.

This course helped me examine areas of sexuality through a biblical worldview like never before. This course and Dr Gilbert were SO helpful.

I have learned more in Dr. Gilbert's course than any other course I have ever taken. I have and will continue to benefit from it greatly.

Dr. Gilbert really lowered my expectations about sex - I don't mean that in a negative way, it just really demystified it :)

GOING BEYOND "THE TALK!" A TEEN AND PRETEEN'S GUIDE

Going Beyond "The Talk!" A Teen and Preteen's Guide

Empowering YOU to Make Choices About Sexuality and Gender from a Biblical Sexual Ethic

DR. COREY GILBERT

HealingLives, LLC

HealingLives, LLC
drcoreygilbert.com

Going Beyond "The Talk!" A Teen and Preteen's Guide

Empowering YOU to Make Choices about Sexuality and Gender from a Biblical Sexual Ethic.

Published by HealingLives, LLC

HealingLives, LLC
Salem, OR

Photography by Angelina Buswell, Salem, OR

Print ISBN: 978-163877817-2
Ebook ISBN: 978-163877818-9
Printed in the United States of America

CONTENTS

This book is dedicated to YOU – the preteen and teenager that wants to honor God with the way you live. Now go change the world. God is faithful!

This book is also dedicated to my 3 experiments – my kiddos, Alex, Blaize, and Mylie. I would not be who I am without you. Thank you for your patience with me as your dad. You have a weird one. It is such an honor though – I love you a ton, I fail a lot, but I hope I have been teachable myself and taught you well. Make your mom and I proud.

ACKNOWLEDGMENTS

I want to thank my children, Alex, Blaize, and Mylie, who are key players in my life, my teaching, and my worldview. I thank God for allowing me to be your dad. It is an honor and privilege – both in the fun times and in difficult conversations.

I want to thank my parents, John and Jane, and Kelly's parents, Ken and Ginger, for being examples to us as parents and leaders that submitted themselves to God's will and plan for their lives. We know this was not always easy. Thank you for the example you set with your commitment to each other, your families, the local church, and the Lord.

I want to thank my counseling and coaching clients for their trust in me as we work towards difficult change and growth. God redeems!

I want to thank my college students over the years that have gone on to change the world through their passions, interests and gifting. I'm so proud of you and how you lead, what you stand for, and how you live out marriage and your family priorities. It is not easy as many of you have seen and experienced.

I want to thank Katlyn Gugger for your edits that were so encouraging and so helpful.

I want to thank Angelina Buswell for an amazing photoshoot and providing me with amazing photos for the cover - and for the 5 teens and preteens that were our models - THIS IS FOR YOU!

Finally, I must continue to pour out thanks to my wife and best friend, Kelly. You are amazing. I am so thankful for you and your dedication, care, and commitment to me and us. I would not be where I am without your love and support, not to mention your overwhelming care for me during my health crises.

| 1 |

Taking Ownership of Your Future

This is for you! Welcome teen or preteen to a book that will potentially change your life and future for the better – forever! Whether you were given this book to read, had it assigned to you to read against your will, or picked it up yourself, **I am proud of you for "going there."** This is not a lighthearted read. It is meant to be digested slowly, worked through, and prayed through diligently. My hope is that a plan will emerge that will drastically change your life. The topics covered here, I believe, are some of the most important topics of our day that are impacting lives, boundaries, and young men and women's futures in life-altering ways. Some of the most important decisions you will make are before you, including whether you will or will not follow Jesus in all you say and do and are. Whom you marry. How you live out sexual choices and boundaries. How you view yourself. Who God has made you as a male or female. How you manage technology, porn, and so many other powerful aspects. This book will cover all of this and more.

You, TODAY – have a story. **Everyone has a story.** Throughout this book I am going to be sharing stories from teenagers and families just like yours. I have sat with them in their living rooms and in my office and walked through the pain from choices that changed their lives forever. Your story may sound like stories you read here. Maybe it is a bit different. Let me start by telling you part of MY story.

My family, like so many other families, did not talk about these hard topics very often. I grew up in a great family that loved the Bible, Jesus, and all things ministry related. These hard topics were mentioned, but not to the extent we needed to hear them at. Harm still found its way in. Pornography and the "M" word were sources of shame and self-hatred. Trauma found its way into our family and wreaked havoc to my identity, self-esteem, and ability to see my future. Praise God that He is our redeemer! He restores.

In my teens and twenties, I was a hopeless romantic. I was sucked into the romantic comedy lie that when you find someone, you will live happily ever after with them. It was a rude awakening to enter marriage in my late 20's and realize that I still lacked the skills to manage conflict and deal with the daily stress of life well.

I, like many of you, was not prepared.

I want to prepare you to understand what goes on in your body, your brain, and in your heart when you start thinking about sexuality and relationships beyond friendships.

Let me share a few examples of teens and preteens that were not prepared:

Jeff was 15 and really wanted to be a Godly man. He had a secret that haunted him. At times, it seemed like a best friend, and at other times he knew it was betraying him. No one knew that he had been addicted to pornography since the age of 8.

Kim was 16 and had withdrawn from her family and favorite activities. A family friend molested her when she was 10. Since then, she has lost count of the number of guys she has slept with. She feels like she is going crazy. She has kept all of this a secret, but she is not sure how much longer she can keep up this facade. It is killing her.

Sam is 18 and eager to move out and start his life in the adult world. He worries that he will not live up to his parents' expectations because of his past. At 12, his parents caught him touching a friend's sister inappropriately. At age 13, he began watching graphic porn videos. He escaped life by playing video games. Now, everyone expects him to act as an adult, and he fears that he will not be able to kick his bad habits.

Tiffany is 13 and her friends are pressuring her to begin dating. They insist that she dress in certain ways and that "friends with benefits" is no big deal. She feels torn. She is afraid that if she doesn't listen to her school friends, she will lose their respect. However, if she listens to them, she worries about the effect it will have on the relationship with her parents and friends from church. What should she do?

Ken is 17 and feels called into ministry but is unsure how to handle the constant bombardment of attraction to other men. How can he be a good Christian and have these feelings? What is wrong with him? Is there anyone he can trust?

Cindy is 17 and tired of living a lie. As soon as she turns 18, she plans to claim her true identity and begin the transition to becoming a male. She has come out at school, but not to her parents. She fears what they will say and do. She has felt torn since the age of 10, when a young man from the neighborhood raped her.

Parents Frank and Tammy both came from difficult homes where all kinds of abuse was normal. They married later in life, and soon had three children. They were adamant that their children would never experience the life they had. They protected them at all costs. By the time their third child reached adulthood, they were heartbroken by the choices they were seeing their children make. Where had they gone wrong? What could they have done differently? What was missing?

Do any of these scenarios hit close to home?

Are you bombarded by sexual imagery and language that are impossible to avoid?

What should you do?

Should you give in to your desires and attractions?

Should you move to the middle of nowhere, by yourself, to protect your eyes, ears, and heart?

My goal is to prepare you to answer these questions. **You are NOT alone!** I want to help walk you through this stage of life so that you can make wise choices based on accurate medical and scientific information, and Biblical Truth.

If your parents have avoided addressing these hard topics with you, I am deeply concerned that you will not be **prepared** when faced with a difficult decision or temptation.

I have found in my conversations with parents that many say they DID have these talks and prepared their children. However, their children don't remember anything but "my mom tried to have 'the talk' with me." They may have had a few intentional talks with their kids, but the reality is, we need more than a talk or two to address the complicated issues of sex, sexuality, the opposite sex, attraction, and gender.

This leads to confused young people who question themselves and experiment in ways that harm themselves and others.

Statistics show that most children arrive at adulthood having ZERO conversations with their parents about sexuality and gender.

If you are one of the lucky few that have had meaningful conversations with your parents, be sure to tell them "Thank you!" If you haven't, I hope and pray that this book becomes a source for you to turn to. It will prepare you to be the man or woman God wants you to be.

The Lord instructs us in Deuteronomy 6:6–7:

> *"And you must commit yourselves wholeheartedly to these commands that I am giving you today. Repeat them again and again to your children. Talk about them when you are at home and when you are on the road, when you are going to bed and when you are getting up," (NLT).*

I want to encourage you to include the instruction and commands of God regarding sexuality, marriage, and gender in these constant, continuing conversations — these *micro-conversations* — with a trusted adult.

My name is **Dr. Corey Gilbert,**[1] or as my college students call me, Dr. G. I've been a Licensed Professional Counselor (LPC) for over twenty years and a professor of counseling psychology for over fifteen years. I could impress you with my long list of trainings and certifications – but I won't! Let's just say I have a lot of them. On the other side of that coin, I have never been a good student, had very poor grades in school, did horrible on the SAT, and have really struggled academically. The irony now to be a University Professor is not lost on me. God DOES have a sense of humor!

Today I work with college students, couples, families, sexual abuse victims, and church leaders. I see a common theme in all of these groups of people: **most don't feel prepared to address topics surrounding sexuality. They don't feel comfortable talking about it with others or in thinking about how it affects them personally.**

So, this is why I have decided to write this book for you, the preteen or teen that wants to have successful healthy relationships throughout your lifetime. If you are being forced to read this, hang in there with me. I hope this changes your life for the better as well.

I want **YOU** to be different because you have accurate information, make good decisions, and avoid common pitfalls.

Where does this start? It starts with a foundation I will call a Biblical Sexual Ethic.

Access more FREE resources, including video trainings and extra content at teenbook.healinglives.com

What is a Sexual Ethic?

I know that I cannot even begin to address all the issues that you are possibly facing. That would require volumes that change by the day, if not by the minute. **My goal is to empower you to stand up to peer pressure and participate in life from a Biblical Sexual Ethic.**

First let me define **"Sexual Ethic."** A **Sexual Ethic** is an understanding of the nature of our sexuality, the differences between male and female, the meaning of marriage, sex, divorce, and more. This is a belief system. We all have one, whether it is thought through or halfway pieced together.

So, here are some questions to think about:

Are there boundaries for sexual expression? Are there any boundaries in marriage? Is marriage only between one man and one woman?

It will be important that you define these boundaries, the purpose of marriage, the importance of God's design for gender, and God's purpose in how He designed your sexuality.

A "**Biblical Sexual Ethic**" is basing your answers to these questions on Biblical principles. This is the heart of the resource you hold in your hands. If anything presented in this book does not line up with Scripture, then it is wrong. I am more than happy to hear from you if you feel something in these pages is out of alignment with Scripture. Let's have a *micro-conversation.* Email me at questions@healinglives.com.

My goal is for you to think about what you believe about these issues based on knowledge of biology and Scripture, not what you saw on YouTube or heard from a friend. This will allow you to build a Sexual Ethic with confidence and clarity.

Living from a Biblical Sexual Ethic will impact your current decisions, future decisions, and your ability to – one day – enjoy a strong healthy marriage.

You will get the best results by actively engaging with the questions throughout this book. You can write your thoughts and answers in a journal or in the spaces provided. Write out your questions and look them up in Scripture. Take the time and space to think, plan, and prepare.

The Importance of this Book for YOU – Today – Right Now!

You need this book because you were not meant to do this alone. You need an ally who will honestly and openly talk about these tough topics with you. Your choice of friends and whom you choose to listen to will either give life or take it away. This includes family, friends, and leaders at the church you attend. Ideally, you would have allies in all these places. If you don't, I want to say that I am SORRY. We have failed to provide healthy dialogue and modeling of a Biblical Sexual Ethic. **I want to walk alongside you and help you be prepared.**

Let me outline what we will cover in this book.

Chapter 1 sets the stage regarding the importance of a sexual ethic (we all have one, whether it is thought through or not).

Chapter 2 introduces the differences between protection and preparation. Yes, we want both – but we CANNOT forget the preparation part. Silence is deadly to your future.

Chapter 3 will give you 3 things to do. I want you to dive into what is written here – to start – and continue to dive deeper with the WORKING QUESTIONS that follow each section and chapter. This is your time to think, pray, research, and think some more on who you are and who you want to be.

Chapter 4 is there to help you begin to think through your own beliefs regarding human sexuality in general, how God made you, what He says in Scripture, and the critical choice of whom you choose to listen to.

Chapter 5 deepens your understanding of sex, sexuality, how we idolize (and even worship) sexual things, and how this impacts us and our beliefs, ethics, and choices.

Chapter 6 includes a very important look at the design, importance, and value of marriage, sex in marriage, and the impact of divorce, growing up with a single parent, and/or a blended family.

Chapter 7 will use an interesting lens that, to me, unlocks a lot of the mysteries of why you were made the way you are made - looking at love, sex, and neuroscience.

Chapter 8 unpacks a basic anatomy of boys and girls and how these come together.

Chapter 9 takes a look at what you should have been taught from Birth to age 5 – going beyond "The Talk!" with age-appropriate conversations.

Chapter 10 moves us into the importance of the most shaping of ages – between the ages of 6 and10 – providing a critical list and overview of talking points that are uncovered in more depth later.

Chapter 11 gives an overview of key topics that are critical to cover and know about as a young 6- to 10-year-old. This is the critical beginning.

Chapter 12 finishes the age-appropriate conversations for those between the ages of 11 and 17. Here the stakes get much riskier and with greater consequences.

Chapter 13 looks at critical questions about gender, masculinity, and femininity and what to do now.

Chapter 14 takes the important, yet difficult, look into what is means to be transgender and how to lead and love well.

Chapter 15 addresses questions about homosexuality. A brief history is provided along with how to love and lead well, biblically.

Chapter 16 explains same-sex attraction, theology, and what to say and/or do, along with a biblical response filled with care, compassion, and biblical truth.

Chapter 17 takes us on a journey into understanding what Polyamory is, how it is growing in popularity, and a biblical response.

Chapter 18 takes the critical dive into porn and its impact on intimacy, how it corrupts, and the impact it has on relationships. Porn is way too widely accepted. It ought not to be so.

Chapter 19 aims to give you a refreshing new look into the relationship continuum and boundaries around dating so that you can do this well and successfully.

Chapter 20 will give you a deeper understanding of the "M" word and various ways to think through its pros and cons.

Chapter 21 unpacks bullying, social media, smartphones, tv, and movies and how these are being used to steal, kill, and destroy today's culture.

Chapter 22 takes a look at the impact of the things we put onto pedestals as idols – those that influence us. It is so important to learn how to say "no" to this common trend.

Chapter 23 brings all of this together under the term ETHOS. Your choices matter. You matter. The boundaries you learn to implement can be lifesaving. Be wise!

Chapter 24 goes into the hard stuff of our pasts that seem to continue to be present – our hurts, failures, and disappointments that keep clinging on to us. Forgiveness frees YOU to grow and experience incredible joy!

Chapter 25 will give you steps to break free of past trauma, build resilience, and inform and encourage you on what to do in the face of potential harm.

Chapter 26 is your final assignment to bring this all together into a living ETHOS.

Chapter 27 is about your plan of action and your next steps as a leader, an example, and a change agent.

Chapter 28 is my final plea to you – DO not ever attempt to do life alone! Remember it is ALL about stewardship, responsibility, and being proactive.

Chapter 29 finishes this journey with a critical look at the power and importance of COMMUNITY!

My Promise to You

I promise that if you study these topics and take the time to think through them, it will change your present and your future.

Let's return to the stories from earlier in this chapter:

Jeff needed to feel secure in his beliefs of who he is and who God is. His goal of being a man of God is good. He needed a safe person to confide in about his struggle with pornography. Porn addiction is rarely overcome on our own. Community is critical. Friends can be life giving, but that depends on who they are, what they stand for, and what they stand against. Mentors, counselors, and coaches are key people who can be lifesaving.

Kim needed hope. She felt trapped. The shame, guilt, questions and fears haunted her. The weight of being silent was overwhelming. Her sexual experience with multiple guys numbed her heart. She grew more disconnected from family and friends every day. Her parents had no idea of what she was going through. She needed an ally, a friend who could help her escape her torment. She desperately needed to have hope that her future wasn't ruined.

Sam will find a whole new world open up if he can address his past and set up boundaries to protect himself. He needs to verbalize his mistakes, fears, and failures to someone he trusts. He needs to replace his identity with one that Christ gives him and stop defining himself by the terrible things he has done. As things stand now, his ability to dream is limited. A trustworthy friend, coach, or counselor could be his best asset.

Tiffany is torn. We have all been there. She will have to choose between her friends' ethics or her parents' ethic. What should she do? It is critical that Tiffany knows what she believes and why she believes it. This will allow her to see beyond momentary pressures, attractions, and desires.

Ken is not broken. God has called him to change the world with the Gospel. It pains me to see teens wrestling with their sexuality and gender, which distracts them from all God has before them. He is placing too much weight on who he is attracted to, instead of recognizing it is simply data. This data should never have this kind of hold or power over us. Ken needs a Biblical Sexual Ethic to put attraction in its rightful place and remind him of how much God loves him.

God has a future full of hope planned for him. He needs an understanding of a biblical worldview on same-sex desires and God's design for sexuality. Ken is not broken. He gets the honor of learning to surrender, something we ALL must do in our own ways. There is an incredible beauty and power in surrendering and living from a Biblical Sexual Ethic.

Cindy is in a precarious place. She has bought into the lie that transitioning will solve all of her problems. It will not. Transitioning will be a temporary solution to a lifelong battle. Cindy's fear of how her parents will react is valid. It will be critical that she have a wise counselor. If she listens to a gender-affirming therapist, they will encourage her to do whatever makes her happy. If she listens to a counselor who holds a Biblical Sexual Ethic, they will guide her into addressing the trauma she faced that changed her life forever. Either path will be difficult. Addressing the trauma will lead to surrendering to a new identity and placing trust in God, even if she doesn't understand all that He is doing in and through her life.

Frank and Tammy raised adults that didn't learn how to manage a reality that was dramatically different from their sheltered home life. They were doing their best to love their children when they protected them from outside influences, but the lack of preparation for the "real world" left them defenseless.

I want you to be prepared for the "real world." This means you are going to have to go beyond "The Talk." "The Talk" is ineffective and almost useless if there are not multiple honest conversations with accurate information on each issue pertaining to sexuality and gender. **By multiple, I mean hundreds!** I propose a lifetime of ***micro-conversations.***

Writing Your Story

You matter. Your story matters. Your experiences, hurts, failures, mistakes, and traumas make you who you are. You will make key decisions based on these. I want you to be proactive in addressing your whole story – trauma and all. May you let God redeem these parts of you so that He can completely alter your future. This is found in a solid Biblical Sexual Ethic that is not hindered by our past hurts.

God invented sex. God loves sex. God did not mess it up — we did.

Your first assignment is to be honest with yourself about your own biases towards sex, sexuality, nudity, the male and female bodies, intercourse, orgasms, body types, gender expressions, etc.

If your reaction to the previous sentence is to hide, go silent, scowl, or pause, then we have some work to do. A key part of the foundation of a sexual ethic is your own story. The experiences we had as children and growing up shapes us. Thinking into the future - If your parents rarely talked about these subjects, you will be less likely to talk with your children in the future. If your experiences caused you pain, you are likely to overprotect when you should prepare your kids instead. The more severe the trauma is in your story, the more likely you will be to err on the side of extreme overprotection. This will manifest in you raising children that have no clue what to think or do and must make ALL their mistakes on their terms.

Your story becomes the foundation for what's to come. Bless you and all God has before you in this journey of preparation.

* * *

Working Questions – Now it is YOUR TURN:

What is a "Sexual Ethic?"

____

____

____

Define "Biblical Sexual Ethic":

____

____

____

What topics do you think parents should talk about with their kids, even if they are uncomfortable?

____

____

____

____

Do you have friends or family members that you are concerned about because of choices they are making or ideas they believe about sexuality and relationships?

____

____

____

____

Do you have questions that you would like a straight answer on from your parents or another trusted adult? Write them down here — get them out of your head and onto paper.

____

____

____

____

Read Deuteronomy 6:6–7

"And you must commit yourselves wholeheartedly to these commands that I am giving you today. Repeat them again and again to your children. Talk about them when you are at home and when you are on the road, when you are going to bed and when you are getting up" (NLT).

What are the Lord's instructions to the family in these verses?

____

____

____

____

Does the idea of talking to your parents about sex stress you out? That's okay - your parents have felt the same way and probably still do. It gets very personal. If your parents are trying to talk to you, consider yourself lucky. Few people can say that. If they aren't having these conversations, it may be because they are waiting for you to let them know that you have questions. If your parents are a safe place for you, go ahead and share some answers you wrote from this section. They'll be glad you did!

____

____

____

____

List opportunities that might arise during the week to talk to your parents or another trusted adult about a Biblical Sexual Ethic.

____

____

____

____

Excellent start. Well done. Keep up the good work.

This will be a journey well worth embarking on.

| 2 |

You Are Not Alone

A few years ago, a friend and I went on a backpacking trip with our two eleven-year-old sons. We were heading down from Clear Lake alongside the McKenzie River in the Cascades of Oregon. We arrived and took a shuttle to the top of the trail, about twenty miles from our parked car.

We began our journey with laughter and excitement. After eleven miles deep in the forest along the roaring river with gorgeous waterfalls, we were exhausted. We could not get to water or find any place to set up a tent due to the sharp lava rocks everywhere. We were achy and carrying a lot of weight. What did we do wrong? **We hadn't prepared well enough.** What did we do right? We had great gear that we had collected over years. We even had a water filter. But we were too high to access the river below us and could not get to the water to use our filters. This was a problem. Walking eleven miles in one day was a problem. Late that evening, we called it. We hitchhiked back to the car and drove back to the trailhead, camping near our car. Let me tell you, that was a great night's sleep! We went home the next morning.

This is similar to what most parents do. They dive in with all the gear and expensive things everyone says they need to have to be good parents: a crib and changing table, a stroller and a diaper genie, a bigger washing machine, and, yes, even a minivan. They rearrange their whole lives for this child coming to crash at their place. This time is full of excitement. However, in all of their planning, they can still easily forget one major detail. This little helpless baby will grow up. Do they give more than a passing thought to what comes next?

In my experience, and statistics from research, your parents did not take parenting classes, at least not in the beginning. **Most good parents quickly realize they have NO IDEA what they are doing!** I find it sad that the only time many parents get training is when it is court mandated because they are in trouble. Some churches offer parenting classes, but there aren't many, and they are poorly attended.

So, your parents are doing the best they can with the guidance they have been given. Some parents are intentionally trying to go into the hard conversations and address painful and personal topics. This is hard though. Many of them have their experienced trauma themselves. They are looking for help and it is my honor to come alongside them.

I have been where your parents are. When I was younger, I had a VERY difficult time talking about these things, but I see its importance now more than ever.

These pages are for you - the teen or preteen that wants to prepare themselves. I promise that there are others who feel the same way I do. Many just don't know how to begin the conversation, but their hearts are in the right place. For some of you, this person might be one (or both) of your parents. For others of you, you may have to look outside of your family and have these conversations with a trusted adult like your youth pastor, or even a friend's parent.

Your Parents Might Believe "I Can't Say That!"

Titus 2:3–5 says:

> *"Similarly, teach the older women to live in a way that honors God. They must not slander others or be heavy drinkers. Instead, they should teach others what is good. These older women must train the younger women to love their husbands and their children, to live wisely and be pure, to work in their homes, to do good, and to be submissive to their husbands. Then they will not bring shame on the word of God" (NLT).*

This scripture is the heart of this book. I am honored to **"Say That!"** I hope you will do so well, carefully, and in a manner that honors God!

I hope to encourage you, challenge you, and empower you as a teen or preteen to learn as much about these topics as you can. Reading this from a book, however, is not the best option. The best option is to read this book alongside your parents. I cannot sit down with everyone or fill my classroom with every teen that needs these complex conversations about sex, sexuality, gender, and pornography. Honestly, addressing these topics with my college students is disheartening since it often comes too late. I wish all parents had the confidence to **"Say That!"** – to GO THERE! – to talk about what the Bible says about homosexuality and gender; to talk about what abuse looks like and prepare their children to say "NO!"; to talk about the impact of pornography on your brain structure, hearts, and future; and even to suggest that their child should have limits on dating, relationships, and devices.

Young Ladies — you need to understand how a man is wired - their anatomy and desires - and how they can get out of order. You need to understand the critical importance of stewardship and boundaries.

Young Men — you must understand how a woman is wired - their anatomy and desires - which can be so different from yours. You need to understand the critical importance of stewardship and boundaries. Young men, you have the additional responsibility to demonstrate integrity and honor as you cherish and protect the women around you.

These pages are for you now but know that even if mistakes and trauma have occurred, it is within your reach to be a young man or woman that thrives in life. We may all differ in our definition of what "**thrives**" looks like. Is it a good marriage? Going to college? A great paying job? Just getting out of the house?

Dr. George Barna,[2] in his research on *Revolutionary Parenting* (2007), **found that parents who defined thriving as raising children who desired to be *"Champions for Christ"*** saw other ways others defined "thriving" fall into place. It reminds me of the Scripture in Matthew 6:33,

> *"But seek first the kingdom of God and His righteousness, and all these things shall be added to you (NKJV).*

I know many teens want to be "**Champions for Christ**", but they do not know how to achieve it. One of the key ingredients to achieving this success is found in having your **OWN Biblical Sexual Ethic**.

"Protection" Does not Equal "Preparation"

One way I have seen parents attempt to provide loving guidance and boundaries is to protect their kids from certain things. We love our children. We don't want you to experience pain and so we attempt to control and limit exposure to things that may cause pain. In this process though, many parents, out of love and care, cripple their children in adulthood.

We are much more aware of bullying in recent years, which has worsened because of the internet and social media. Many schools have become zero-tolerance zones and are extremely punitive — no questions asked. A few groups take a different view on bullying. They believe that standing up to bullies actually helps prepare children for adulthood. **Facing difficulty strengthens us.** The real world — the adult world — also has bullies.

Do you think your parents overprotect you? There are pros and cons to this.

The pros: hopefully there are things that could have happened to you that did not because of their protection.

The cons: a lack of preparation leads to uncertainty when you have to make decisions. Being led by our emotions and attractions, instead of deliberate choices, leaves you vulnerable.

Your protection needs to include preparation to make wise, informed decisions. Yes, the decisions I would expect a three-year-old to manage will differ greatly from my expectations for a fourteen-year-old. **Most teens, with a few exceptions, can handle more responsibility than we give them.** What do you need?

- You need tools to succeed in relationships – dating boundaries and how to steward attractions and desires.

- You need to be taught what online stewardship looks like as you have access to the whole world online, including pornography.

- You need to be taught how to steward your time. It is important that you get your work and responsibilities done first before you play.

- You need to be permitted to fail — so that you can learn to succeed.

FYI - you are meant to grow up, leave the nest, and fly! We just hope and pray you land on your feet.

"Silence" is Deadly – It Matters Who You Listen To

A danger I see in our culture and with families around me is **silence**. I have taught a human sexuality course to undergraduate students for over fifteen years. I survey them every year, and the data has been revealing, to say the least. One of the most telling truths I found in the research was that most of them had the desire to talk about this stuff with their parents, but they did not feel like it was welcome, and so they logically turned to friends, the internet, and porn for their education.

The truth is that your parents probably want to "go there", but they are just plain afraid or feel like they don't know enough. If you feel like this may be your parents, have them check out my book I wrote specifically for them at www.drcoreygilbert.com.

Be patient with them.

You need to have these conversations over and over with someone. Find safe people who will help you mature in your understanding of a Biblical Sexual Ethic. This book is meant to get the conversations and relationships started, but this should not be where they end.

I call these short conversations *micro-conversations.*

***Micro-conversations* are the brief teachable moments that come up daily. They can look like a Q and A session with engagement from both sides. They can also be more like mini lectures that plants seeds for you to think about. All of these moments pile onto past ones. Each time we hear the same idea or principle we add depth and perspective that we missed before.**

Let me ask you a personal question:

Who is teaching YOU about sexuality and gender? Who do you go to for advice when you have a question about dating or gender? Do you think this should come from just anyone? Does their sexual ethic matter? What is their worldview? Is it centered on a Biblical perspective or around pleasure and self? This is why it matters who your teachers are. If we don't intentionally think about it, we can easily find ourselves more influenced by Instagrammers, YouTubers, and Tik-Tok videos than anything else.

Be intentional about **WHO** helps you build and lay this foundation.

Silence is deadly. Who **YOU** listen to can be life or death.

Taking Your Future into Your Own Hands

Bill and Cara are a happily married Christian couple with three kids. They love their children. They want the best for them. They are very active in their kids' schools. Their children are on multiple athletic teams and thriving in these. They are very active in their church where their kids take part in AWANA[3], choir, and other events. On every visible level they are the ideal couple, raising perfect kids. Each of their three kids have made a profession of faith and been baptized.

Can you think of anything that could be wrong with what they are doing? Maybe not, but I would want to ask them a few questions before I decided. It is easy for behaviors to be deceiving. I would want to ask them if they are having conversations that get to the heart of issues and go beyond keeping up with appearances. I would challenge them to go deeper with their kids before someone else does.

These are the questions I would ask them – and they may step on YOUR toes too:

- Have you discussed the friends they have at school or on the team that identify as gay, lesbian, or trans?
- Do your kids know what the Bible teaches on both sexuality and loving our neighbors?
- When was the last time you discussed sex, sexuality, pornography, dating, nudity, marriage, homosexuality, masturbation, sexting, social media, friends with benefits, music, music videos, movies, or TV shows with your kids?
- Have you had an honest conversation about Uncle Bob and his affairs, or Aunt Sherry and her walking around the house with little to no clothing when she visits?

What if your parents had had these types of conversations - these *micro-conversations* when you were younger? Would those seeds planted in your heart then be influencing your decisions today? Think about that.

I have found that these topics are off limits for most parents because it terrifies them. And they are honestly waiting on YOU to ask questions. OUCH! NO! NO! NO! This means they are putting the ball in your court. It should not be this way.

I hope that this book will give you the confidence to start the conversation with your parents, or another trusted adult and get the ball back into their court.

* * *

Working Questions – Now it is YOUR TURN:

Read **Titus 2:3–5 again:**

"Similarly, teach the older women to live in a way that honors God. They must not slander others or be heavy drinkers. Instead, they should teach others what is good. These older women must train the younger women to love their husbands and their children, to live wisely and be pure, to work in their homes, to do good, and to be submissive to their husbands. Then they will not bring shame on the word of God" (NLT).

Reword this passage as a command to yourself. How does this apply to you, now, as a teenager?

____

____

____

____

How would you define "success" as an adult? What do you want your life to look like when you are an adult?

____

____

____

____

What do you think it means to be a "Champion for Christ" as a teenager? Would you say that you are a "Champion for Christ" now? How can adults be "Champions for Christ?"

____

____

____

____

Do you know anyone that is an example of being a "Champion for Christ?" What makes them stand out to you in this way?

____

____

____

____

Most parents want to protect their children from the evil in the world. What are some ways your parents (or other key influences) have protected you during your lifetime?

Parents also have a responsibility to prepare their children to live in a sinful broken world. How have your parents (or another trusted adult) attempted to prepare you to live well?

Are there any areas in which your parents may have failed to protect you? If you have not already shared this with them (and if they are safe), please do so.

Are there any areas in which you wish you were better prepared? Write them here and discuss them with your parents so you can come up with a plan.

____

____

____

____

Dr. Gilbert says that a key to being prepared on issues surrounding sexuality and gender is by having *micro-conversations.* What are *micro-conversations?*

____

____

____

____

Make a list of topics you wish you could talk about with your parents (or another trusted adult). Consider sharing this list with them.

____

____

____

____

| 3 |

Three Things TO DO

I'll say it again - I am so proud of you already for picking up a book like this, regardless of whether or not you were forced to! I hope it guides you into being a leader who influences others.

Who are your role models – those you are watching day in and day out?

For most of us, this list would begin with our parents or primary caregivers. They are our main examples for the first few years. In your elementary school years, you are learning about masculinity, femininity, marriage, sexuality, and how to treat the opposite sex from those role models. You pick all of this up without realizing the impact of these key figures in your life.

You are ALWAYS learning from those around you.

Since we are always learning from those around us, I want to challenge you to be intentional about who you put around you.

Romans 12:2 commands us,

> *"Do not conform to the pattern of this world, but be transformed by the renewing of your mind" (NIV).*

This is a biblical concept that is verified by science. For some of you, this may seem odd. I want to encourage you not to fear science. All research that has been done well points to God's perfect creation. What you think matters. What you think **about** matters even more.

Galatians 2:20 reminds us you can develop your spirit through the choices you make — in your mind — that are led by the Holy Spirit:

> *"My old self has been crucified with Christ. It is no longer I who live, but Christ lives in me. So I live in this earthly body by trusting in the Son of God, who loved me and gave himself for me" (NLT).*

I want you to **see yourself as a leader**. Why? Others are watching YOU! You have the role of a leader whether or not you want the role and no matter your age. Others are watching you. My hope is that you will use this time while you are reading this book to do **three key things:**

One: Learn, Learn, and Learn Some More

Be teachable.

Be open to thinking through your beliefs and asking hard questions.

Be willing to admit some of your beliefs may not be biblical and may need further examination.

Be willing to admit you do not know something and learn more about it.

This is a critical season for you. Remember that adults in their 20's, 30's, and even 40's and 50's are still learning and do NOT know it all. So – that being said – remain a young man or woman filled with humility, willing to listen, lean into another's opinion, learn, and grow. I ask this of everyone I talk with. I attempt to live this out myself. It is tough – yet life changing.

Two: Dream Big

I want you to want more for your life. This comes out of a bigger picture and vision for your life. Dream big!

I want you to want to respect others and yourself. This leads to growth, strength, self-respect, and a care for self and others.

I want you to want peace and a long-lasting love over momentary thrills or highs. Living for something bigger than myself, than today, and than what I can get in the here and now opens me up to stronger boundaries, confidence, and a much greater life.

I want that vision for your future to include others and how you can impact them versus what others can do for you.

A word of caution – hold these dreams loosely since God is ultimately the one that calls and leads and appoints.

Three: Search Through God's Word

Have a defense. Know God's Word.

First Peter 3:15 states:

> *"... always be ready to give a defense to everyone who asks you a reason for the hope that is in you, with meekness and fear" (NKJV).*

Do you want to know the most powerful superpower you can have?

It is to know that the Spirit of God teaches us truth and equips us to do what God has called us to do.

I Believe in You

It is an important reality check to understand that your choices TODAY will impact your life as an adult. Though you can be forgiven, and relationships can sometimes be restored, there are still consequences that can haunt you into adulthood that you cannot escape.

My goal is that you recognize that YOU hold the key to your future. You will find peace in placing boundaries around your sexual desires. The person you will be depends on your choice of guiding light. Is it greater than yourself – Christ? I hope so.

Where do we start? We could start with a list of questions to ask ourselves, or key topics that need further information. I come at this from a different angle. I believe in YOU and YOUR power to make WISE choices - if you have the right framework and ETHOS to work from. (Hint - it's the Bible!)

If you are intentional about giving serious thought to what's coming in these pages, you have the potential to be set free.

If you are struggling with pornography, sexual promiscuity, or your sexual identity, then this is the time and place to work through these things. And, as I have mentioned already, you should not try to do this alone.

Proverbs 14:15 says:

> *"The simple believe anything, but the prudent give thought to their steps." (NIV).*

Be the prudent one. Other translations of this passage word it this way:

"Only the simpletons believe everything they're told! The prudent carefully consider their steps" (NLT), or,

"is discreet and astute and considers well where he is going" (AMP), or,

"The simple believes every word, but the prudent considers well his steps" (NKJV).

Know where you are going. You can gain the skills and confidence here. I promise.

Two Discoveries From Science That Offer Hope

Your belief system – your ETHOS – is the place from which you will take every step in your life. This framework will guide you. This ETHOS will encourage you and challenge you to stand up for what is right when the pressures are to give in and/or to indulge. This ETHOS will be your strength. Your resolve. And it brings peace, lessening the turmoil and increasing your life potential.

I want to see your ETHOS guide you into the battle — even into the storms. I want you to be strong.

Recent discoveries in science enable us to worship our creator even more fully. One discovery that helps us gain perspective, hope, and perseverance in this endeavor toward a Biblical Sexual Ethic is that of ***neuroplasticity.***

The concept of **neuroplasticity** means that the brain is adaptable and moldable — we remain teachable. Our brain is always changing and rewiring itself every single moment of every day and night.

A second concept that gives us hope is that of ***epigenetics.***

Epigenetics teaches that our thoughts affect how our genes express themselves. Genetics do not have to be a doomsday reality. We turn them on and off based on our thoughts and the choices we make. This is a hopeful, yet challenging concept.

Neuroscientist and Christian researcher **Dr. Caroline Leaf**[4] highlights that we have free will and choice. These are real spiritual and scientific concepts. Check out Deuteronomy 30:19:

> *"Today I have given you the choice between life and death, between blessings and curses. Now I call on heaven and earth to witness the choice you make. Oh, that you would choose life, so that you and your descendants might live!" (NLT).*

Dr. Caroline Leaf[5] has raised the bar in our awareness of the tremendous power and responsibility we have in our minds. One of her key points that we would do well to remember is that **we are not a victim of our biology.** Another point is that you are designed to be able to look beyond yourself and observe your own thinking and change it. Think about that concept. This is powerfully freeing.

What I am proposing is that **you will need to stop periodically and take an inventory of your thoughts and actions.** This will allow you to re-engage in new and different ways as you adopt a Biblical Sexual Ethic. You must choose it for yourself.

Are you listening more to Godly advice or to your peers and media? Find a consistent voice of hope, truth, grace, and forgiveness. A person who models a solid Biblical Sexual Ethic and hang onto them.

Where do we start? We will begin with a basic lesson on the Theology of Sex and Marriage and take a peek at some amazing findings in the neuroscientific world that should encourage you. We will conclude with a basic anatomy lesson. Enjoy the process!

Remember to Learn, Dream Big, and Stay in God's Word!

* * *

Working Questions – Now it is Your Turn:

Read **Romans 12:2**

"Do not conform to the pattern of this world, but be transformed by the renewing of your mind" (NIV).

What do you think about the most? Be honest!

____

____

How can you renew your mind?

Can you state in one or two sentences what you believe about each of these?

What do you believe about:

Homosexuality

Gender

Marriage

Dating / Courtship

Divorce

Relationships

Read **Galatians 2:20**

My old self has been crucified with Christ. It is no longer I who live, but Christ lives in me. So I live in this earthly body by trusting in the Son of God, who loved me and gave himself for me (NLT).

This passage teaches us that you can develop your spirit through choices you make in your mind and being led by the Holy Spirit — what are these?

Three Keys:

ONE: Learn, Learn, & Learn some more. Explain what this means to you. What are you going to maybe do different?

____

____

TWO: Dream Big. What do you want to do with your life? Who do you want to be? What do you want to accomplish? Who do you want to impact? How do you want to show up to our world – and change it for the better?

____

____

____

____

THREE: Search God's Word. My hope is these pages will encourage you to always turn to God's Word for insights, answers, and guidance.

A reminder: **1 Peter 3:15**
"... always be ready to give a defense ..." (NLT)

What does this mean to you?

____

____

Peter tells us to prepare to give a defense for our hope in the gospel. Do you find hope as a believer? If so, share what you find hopeful below. If not, honestly consider what you believe about Jesus, his death and resurrection, and the authority He claims over us.

____

____

Just as we are commanded to give a defense of our hope in Christ, we should be able to give a defense on what we believe about sexuality and gender if we claim that Scripture forms them. Locate the Scriptures that support the views you shared above.

____

____

What foundation are you laying surrounding the shaping and living out of your sexual identity, choices, and boundaries?

____

____

Do you have permission to say "NO" or to voice an opinion?

____

____

Do you know how to handle a situation where a friend, peer, or adult leader is asserting authority over you and you feel trapped?

____

____

What does it mean to be a man? What influences your understanding of the concept of masculinity? Is being a man a good thing or a bad thing?

____

____

What does it mean to be a woman? What influences your understanding of the concept of femininity? Is being a woman a blessing or a curse?

____

____

Are you learning to be kind and compassionate?

____

____

Can you handle confrontation, conflict, and your anger well?

____

____

Do you have a Biblical understanding of the danger of pornography and the power it has (or can have)?

____

____

What do you believe about God, sexuality, and sexual behaviors – how you were created, and what you were created for?

____

____

What would you like your future children to believe as adults about these?

____

____

Read **Proverbs 14:15**

Only simpletons believe everything they're told! The prudent carefully consider their steps (NLT).

Explain:

____

____

What steps do you need to take to ensure that you are wise and careful as a young man or woman that wants to honor God?

____

____

As you read the description of neuroplasticity of the brain and epigenetics, did you find it encouraging to learn that we can change what we think and that we have some control?

____

____

Where would you like to experience a change in your life?

____

____

Read **Deuteronomy 30:19**

"Today I have given you the choice between life and death, between blessings and curses. Now I call on heaven and earth to witness the choice you make. Oh, that you would choose life, so that you and your descendants might live!" (NLT)

You can choose life or death. The Lord sets both choices in front of you. What choices do you think lead to death? What choices lead to life?

____

| 4 |

We Are All Listening To and Following Someone - Micro-conversations

If we fast forward a few months and check back in with **Bill and Cara** from the end of Chapter Two, we find a family that has made a few changes. Everything on the surface seems the same. However, *micro-conversations* are now intentionally interspersed throughout their daily conversations. It has become normal to discuss sexuality, pornography, and the differences between men and women. An intentional ethic surrounding marriage is more than just modeled — it is openly and honestly discussed.

Bill and Cara are more confident than ever. They have resources. They continue to read, learn, and grow. They commit to staying ahead of their children and what they will see and hear at school. They are open about transgenderism and homosexuality. They have openly and honestly discussed gay marriage with care and sensitivity. Together, they are allowing their children to ask questions, disagree, debate, and feel. The culture being created in their home is one of safety, security, and grace. Another huge win is the building of a Biblical Sexual Ethic within their children.

I want this outcome for you as well. You are at a critical time of your life. You MUST decide who you will listen to and who you will follow. You are deciding on boundaries, key influencers, your ethics, and beginning to put the pieces together of who you will be as an adult. You may be in a time of crisis and you cannot wait to escape your family situation. I get that. It is a natural place to be. I want you to find success just as the family above did. I want this for you now and for your future self who will lead and influence your own family intentionally by going into the hard stuff early with your kids.

Without these *micro-conversations*, the ideas that you will believe in are left up to chance.

Allow this book to be YOUR *micro-conversations* – from me to you!

On Basic Human Sexuality

So I get to have some fun now. I get to teach you about a topic I love to dive into since it is SO personal and has such a profound impact on ALL of our lives. It is God's design of you as a sexual being.

What was He thinking? Why did He design you this way? What was His purpose?

This foundation leads to the potential of incredible stability – both today and in your future as life happens and you travel through each life stage.

You also need to be grounded in a Biblical interpretation of these findings and perspectives.

On What the Bible Says ... and Doesn't Say

Learn what the Bible says – and does not say – about the difficult choices you and your friends are facing today.

An important goal in our discussions will be to answer questions with Scripture when possible. It is equally important to be able to say, "I do not know", or "This is my opinion", when Scripture does not seem to have a clear answer.

I find 2 Timothy 1:7 to be encouraging on this topic. It reads:

> *"For God has not given us a spirit of fear and timidity, but of power, love, and self-discipline" (NLT).*

May you gain strength from this verse. Do not be afraid. Grab on to the power that He offers you. Love like Him. Live a disciplined life. It is in this discipline that we truly find the most freedom.

First Corinthians 2:16 defines our identity and power clearly:

> *"For, 'who can know the Lord's thoughts? Who knows enough to teach him?' But we understand these things, for we have the mind of Christ" (NLT).*

Really? Us? You? Me?
Yes! YOU!

We have the mind of Christ. So, let's dig in and use it!

On Choosing to Listen to Me – I am Honored to be a Voice

One last reminder why this is SO important. In my surveying of hundreds of Christian college students over the past fourteen years, I can see that **conversations with parents are what they lacked in most.**

I get to fill in that gap. I take this as an honor. It is not a replacement for these intimate and hard conversations. If you can have those – go there and do it! If not, this is a start.

I know a few things about you. You are probably a young person who wants (and needs) to hear from reputable sources. It saddens me to think about the number of students I have in my classes who have never had a safe place to talk, ask questions, and even just listen to sexual topics discussed in a safe, non-offensive manner. In my classes, I am careful and clear. I cut straight to it, which weirds out some, but they soon overcome that initial reaction. I ask hard questions. I present clear arguments and frameworks. I also realize that for many of my students, most of their programming is already in place, and to overcome the damage from their families, schools, movies, and pornography will be a steep hill for them (and me) to climb. In addition, most have already had experiences with sexual play and experimentation. I remain hopeful for them because I know how God can transform a life. **There is ALWAYS HOPE!** Our God is a redeemer.

For my college students, I personally would prefer that their parents had been willing to be the one to "go there" — not me, their university professor. But more often than not, this is not an option.

I am honored to be a safe person to talk to for many students. I am honored to spend this time with you here. I hope you will change your family tree by how you live. May you also pass this knowledge on to others. Many of my college students have made me SO PROUD as they have become teachers, speakers, pastors, and leaders who are changing the world by "going there." They are on the front lines, changing the lives God has given them to influence. It is a beautiful thing.

Proverbs 22:6 says,

> *"Train up a child in the way he should go: and when he is old, he will not depart from it" (NKJV).*

I am not your parent - but - I come at this as a father figure and pray this over you. May you not depart from it!

May you lead by example. May you fail and get back up with humility and continue on seeking to be the best version of yourself you can be for God's glory, not your own.

Our churches need you and others to "go there". Families need this. Our schools and society and everyone around you needs this intentionality.

These conversations - these ***micro-conversations*** - should be filled with grace, compassion, and care without minimizing the truth.

May you, at your age, now, today, be a leader that puts God at the center. Let's learn to do this together, in community. I'm with you. Now let's dive into **Sex Ed 101**.

* * *

Working Questions – Now it is Your Turn:

Do you believe we should follow and obey the Bible's instructions on sexuality today?

____

____

Read **2 Timothy 1:7**

For God has not given us a spirit of fear and timidity, but of power, love, and self-discipline (NLT).

How does a spirit of fear and timidity look different from a spirit of power, love, and self-discipline?

____

____

Read **2 Timothy 1:7** (see above) and **1 Corinthians 2:16**

For, "Who can know the Lord's thoughts? Who knows enough to teach him?" But we understand these things, for we have the mind of Christ (NLT).

These passages are great reminders of our identity. What does it mean to be full of power, love, and self-discipline? What does it mean to have the mind of Christ?

____

____

Read **Proverbs 22:6**

Train up a child in the way he should go, and when he is old, he will not depart from it (NKJV).

Do you know anyone raised by Christian parents and taught what was right, but who does not live as a Christian now? Is this you? What do you think is the reason behind this?

____

____

| 5 |

Sex - The Impact of MY BELIEFS

Abel is a 14-year-old young man. He recently attended a school outing and came back home and announced he had a girlfriend. Did his parents prepare him by discussing dating, boundaries, sexuality and age-appropriate behaviors? Were rules or limits set in place ahead of time to help him decide what to do regarding what is best for him at his age? Should he be left alone to figure this out?

Shea is a 13-year-old girl that asked her parents about homosexuality and marriage one evening at dinner. She wants to know what they would do if a "family member" were to come out.

Seth is an 8-year-old boy and **Gina** is a 10-year-old girl. They are both full of life and have carefree views of the world. In an instant, they both seem to have changed overnight. They stumbled onto a website with naked pictures. That site led to another site with videos of graphic sexual scenes of their favorite animated characters who now have additional odd sexual body parts and shapes. After only a five-minute exposure (that their parents don't know about), Seth and Gina are showing odd behaviors and attitude changes that seem unexplainable. What could this be? Is this normal? Can it be attributed to "just growing up?" Both Seth and Gina would rather die than share with their parents what they saw because of the weird feelings and shame they felt and continue to feel with each passing day. To make matters worse, they have found themselves drawn back to these sites multiple times, which only intensifies the fear of being found out and adding to the shame they feel.

What are your thoughts and feelings after reading these true stories? You've probably been there or know someone who has. You may have felt that same shame or fear or had similar questions.

For some of you reading this, you are picturing friends, their struggles, and the pieces of their stories you know. For others of you though, this is VERY personal. You have a ton of questions.

Let's start with foundational beliefs. **We need to know why we draw lines and set limits.** We need to have a framework — a theology — for dating, boundaries, sex, and marriage. We need to have a view of homosexuality that is both biblical and compassionate. We need to be proactive in drawing boundaries around pornography.

What do you need to know to begin?

The Importance of a Theology of Sex

I am sitting in a hammock at a camp deep in the Cascades, listening to a group of eleven to thirteen-year-old boys as they discuss girls, dating, marriage, and attraction. They are joking, laughing, arguing, and throwing things at each other when they feel embarrassed. They are revealing each other's secrets, being funny, being gross, calling each other names, and revealing who likes whom. These boys are from mostly Christian families and represent the range of schooling options.

The most revealing part is their ETHOS — their individual theologies and beliefs.

Where did each of these beliefs originate and how have they been nurtured? In their homes. Their families. Their schools. Their churches. By those people who are in their lives consistently.

The fact is that our theology matters. Your ETHOS matters.

The church has historically struggled to balance preserving innocence and preventing ignorance.

A lack of education is not innocence.

Being knowledgeable about your body's design does not rob you of innocence. It may even preserve it longer. It is easy to find documentaries, TV shows, movies, magazines, and podcasts that talk about sex — the birds and the bees — or focus on hot topics of the day. It is difficult though to find a resource that provides guidance as we sort out our Biblical Sexual Ethic. Most adults could not explain what they believe and why they believe it if I asked them to do so – let alone most teenagers.

In my experiences as a professor, counselor, and expert in the areas of gender and sexuality, I have found that the protestant evangelical church has not had a thoughtful, biblically sound apologetic on sexuality until recently.

In 2018, **Dr. Nancy Pearcey**[6] released a book entitled ***Love Thy Body*** (2018)[7]. Dr. Pearcey examines how the separation of the person — one with moral and legal standings — from the body, which is the physical being, has given rise to a host of problems.

Dr. Pearcey[8] argues that it is this separation of the person from the physical realities of the body that has given rise to the arguments for homosexuality, transgenderism, abortion, assisted suicide, euthanasia, and other troubling issues.

What you believe will shape your thinking as you grow and mature.

Prior to 2018, the best resource I had found was **Pope John Paul II's** *Theology of the Body.*[9] This work is available to the average reader through the work of **Christopher West.**[10] West highlights the importance of a theology of sex when he explains that:

> "The sexual embrace is the foundation of human life itself. The family — and, in turn, culture — spring from this embrace. In short, as sex goes, so go marriage and the family. As marriage and family go, so goes civilization. Such logic does not bode well for our culture. It is no exaggeration to say that the task of the twentieth century was to rid itself of the Christian sexual ethic ..." (p. 13).[11]

If we want to have an influence on our culture West says,

> "Christians must first find a way to demonstrate to the modern world that a biblical sexual ethic is not the cramped, prudish list of prohibitions it is often assumed to be. Rather, it is a liberating, redeeming path that fulfills the most noble aspirations of the human heart" (p. 14).[12]

If these thoughts are accurate — and I believe they are — then the study of sexuality, and God's design and purpose for it, is a worthy pursuit.[13]

Sex Idolized

You are constantly bombarded with sexually provocative and sexually explicit images. We live in a selfie world that influences what we do as we seek identity, attention, love, and affection. There is more pressure than ever before to engage in sexual behaviors in childhood. But engaging in almost any kind of sexual play is a recipe for disaster for anyone not in a long term committed relationship. There is also a tremendous impact on those who believe this pressure affirms or validates their sexual identity and/or prowess.

Many teenagers become sexual with experiences they didn't expect, and that they didn't truly want. Pressure from peers or adults leads many into activities which they may regret later on. How many teens attempt sexual intercourse because it is the cool thing to do?

How would you answer this question:

Is it enough to be in love with a person, or to feel you love a person, to begin a sexual relationship?

Statistics guesstimate that **seventy percent** of American teens have had sex. Many of them are terrified to think their parents will find out what they've done sexually and believe it will be the end of the relationship.

And yes, many parents **would** react negatively to this news. However, you need to know that after their shock wears off, parents do love their children more than you probably realize.

Why is there a disconnect?

Your parents know that you are not ready for sexual behaviors and the consequences that follow but recognize that you might think that you are an exception.

You could be a hopeless romantic prone to be over trusting. Your parents know that you need strict boundaries and limits to protect you from yourself.

If you have been harmed in a past relationship you need boundaries and a key person to work through this with before starting a new relationship. It is tempting to quickly seek someone else to fill a void.

We cannot eliminate sexuality. But how often do we act like it doesn't exist, either in action, in conversation, or by avoiding certain topics in conversation?

I want you to have such a thorough understanding of how God created you – your body, gender, and even personality – that you are not taken in by temptations and temporary pleasures.

Sex and sexuality are different at every age and need to be understood as a developing part of who you are. It is as much a part of us as breathing.

When you were first curious about sex did you go to dictionaries, encyclopedias or anatomy books? Probably not – that was your parent's or even grandparent's generation. You more than likely went straight to videos online. Today we live in a video world and this is gravely affecting our understanding of sex.

The problem with internet sources is that the answers to your questions are often factually wrong, deliberate lies, or guided by a sexual ethic that centers on the self and self-fulfillment primarily.

Sex and Worship

What kind of sex education have you had so far? Was it a one-time conversation from your parents that was more lecture than dialogue? Were your parents embarrassed? Has your sexual education been left to the school, the back of the bus, or your church? What were your first glimpses of nudity or pornography? If you want something different for yourself then you must do something different.

Does being told, "Just don't do it" work for you? It works for some, but not for most. This approach, as well as abstinence programs do not work. Why? This approach doesn't work because you need a reason to accept the worldview that says abstinence is the best option. Most of us receive the opposite message at home and from the media we consume via movies and music.

Do you see sex as a symbol of true love or as a tool or weapon to be wielded against others?

Do you need a reason that inspires you to believe that sex has a deeper meaning than "getting lucky?" (I promise that it IS worth waiting for).

You need a foundational ETHOS that you build on as you add information. For most of you reading this book, there have been zero conversations about sex at home. Some of you have only been exposed to locker room talk. You may be one that has already been victimized and knows more than we think. Research quoted in *The Society for Adolescent Medicine* and *PubMed* concludes that, "Abstinence-only programs threaten fundamental human rights to health, information, and life" (2006).[14]

I want you to be fully informed regarding the biological, emotional, and psychological effects of sexual behavior and choose abstinence because you have an understanding of God's design and you want His best for your life.

I often ask my students, "How do we worship God with our bodies? How do we worship Him with our sexuality? Is it even possible?"

How would you answer this question? What does worship look like? Can you imagine the words "sexuality" and "worship" in the same sentence? We will continue to unpack this as we move forward.

First Thessalonians 4:3–8 states:

> *"God's will is for you to be holy, so stay away from all sexual sin. Then each of you will control his own body and live in holiness and honor—not in lustful passion like the pagans who do not know God and His ways. Never harm or cheat a fellow believer in this matter by violating his wife, for the Lord avenges all such sins, as we have solemnly warned you before. God has called us to live holy lives, not impure lives. Therefore, anyone who refuses to live by these rules is not disobeying human teaching but is rejecting God, who gives His Holy Spirit to you" (NLT).*

What is God's plan for sex?

God intends for us to be celibate outside of marriage and celebrate within marriage.

What are we supposed to do with our sexual feelings and memories? For much of its history, the Church has fallen on the side of **repression** — don't talk about it, don't think about it, pretend like it doesn't exist. Sex is bad — a "necessary evil" to bring children into the world — but beyond that, don't do it! At one time, they even went so far as suggesting furniture skirts to cover the legs of chairs and couches so that men would not lust after their curves. Crazy! There have also been genital cuffs, chastity belts, castration, self-flagellation, burning, dunking oneself in icy water, and even gouging out eyes as a deterrent or punishment for sexual feelings.

In a reaction against repression, the pendulum has swung to the opposite side of the spectrum and you will find people suggesting that nothing is wrong in love and recommending books or counsel at odds with God's Word. They advise such things as using pornography as sex education for newlyweds or to spice up a marriage. **Many families defer their children's sexual education to the public schools and follow the secular culture's lead on what is appropriate sexually rather than what God has revealed to us.**

Both extremes are unacceptable.

Titus 2:1–8 says:

> *"As for you, Titus, promote the kind of living that reflects wholesome teaching. Teach the older men to be temperate, worthy of respect, self-controlled, and sound in faith, in love and in endurance. Likewise, teach the older women to be reverent in the way they live, not to be slanderers or addicted to much wine, but to teach what is good. Then they can urge the younger women to love their husbands and children, to be self-controlled and pure, to be busy at home, to be kind, and to be subject to their husbands, so that no one will malign the word of God. Similarly, encourage the young men to be self-controlled. In everything set them an example by doing what is good. In your teaching show integrity, seriousness, and soundness of speech that cannot be condemned, so that those who oppose you may be ashamed because they have nothing bad to say about us."*

Verses 11–14 say, *"For the grace of God has been revealed, bringing salvation to all people. And we are instructed to turn from godless living and sinful pleasures. We should live in this evil world with wisdom, righteousness, and devotion to God, while we look forward with hope to that wonderful day when the glory of our great God and Savior, Jesus Christ, will be revealed. He gave his life to free us from every kind of sin, to cleanse us, and to make us his very own people, totally committed to doing good deeds" (NLT).*

What does this passage require of you?

The way we worship and honor God with our bodies is through the **discipline of self-control**.

When you can say that you will respect and obey the boundaries that God established and will sacrifice a relationship or a behavior, you show to the world that you honor God above yourself.

My appeal to you is to enjoy **celebration with chastity**. What does this mean? It is feasting with self-control. I know this sounds weird. Desire is part of God's design of who you are and shows that you are meant to enjoy sex – with self-control and within boundaries. For too many young men and women, they dump all desire into the category of lust, so they believe that it's ALL bad. We need a strong sexual ethic to help us define these boundaries.

There's a world of difference between "having sex" and "making love." Satan is glorified, not God, when a sexual union comes out of lies, selfishness, lust, or disobedience. This can be experienced by both single and married people. Satan is the father of these lies. We reveal who or what we worship with our bodies.

Romans 12:1 reminds us to:

> *"Offer your bodies as a living sacrifice, holy and pleasing to God – this is your true and proper worship" (NIV).*

The truth is that our **sexuality and our spirituality are intimately tied together**. We glorify God when His name and Word are honored in a relationship. Making love expresses desire and commitment within the boundaries the Father has set for us. God uses marriage throughout Scripture as a picture of His relationship with us — His bride.

What does it mean to offer our bodies as living sacrifices?

First John 4:12b tells us that:

> *"If we love one another, God lives in us and His love is made complete in us" (NIV).*

We can find some beautiful scriptures regarding sexual love in the Song of Solomon.

Song of Solomon 5:16 reads:

> *"His mouth is sweetness itself; he is desirable in every way. Such, O women of Jerusalem, is my lover, my friend" (NLT).*

How can we dismiss desire as sin with a verse like this in the Bible? **We can't. He made you to desire your spouse and be desired by your spouse.** You are meant to enjoy the sexual relationship - within boundaries.

An example of these boundaries is set out in Proverbs 5:15,

> *"Drink water from your own well — share your love only with your wife" (NLT).*

Throughout Scripture, we see the protective boundary of marriage between a man and a woman as the proper place for a sexual relationship. There are no exceptions or exemptions.

As our culture careens wildly about redefining marriage, gender, and sexual behavior, we would do well to remember the warning in 1 Peter 5:8 to:

> *"Stay alert! Watch out for your great enemy, the devil. He prowls around like a roaring lion, looking for someone to devour" (NLT).*

Who is watching and seeking to destroy you?

Are you paying attention? Are you placing more value on God's Word or popular opinion?

What Does the Bible Say?

The Bible is NOT silent on sex and sexuality. Let us jump into the deep end on this one and read chapter seven of the Song of Solomon:

> ***Young Man****—"How beautiful are your sandaled feet, O queenly maiden. Your rounded thighs are like jewels, the work of a skilled craftsman. Your navel is perfectly formed like a goblet filled with mixed wine. Between your thighs lies a mound of wheat bordered with lilies. Your breasts are like two fawns, twin fawns of a gazelle. Your neck is as beautiful as an ivory tower. Your eyes are like the sparkling pools in Heshbon by the gate of Bath-rabbim. Your nose is as fine as the tower of Lebanon overlooking Damascus. Your head is as majestic as Mount Carmel, and the sheen of your hair radiates royalty. The king is held captive by its tresses. Oh, how beautiful you are! How pleasing, my love, how full of delights!"*

Solomon is undressing his wife. He is enjoying her. He is taking his bride in visually, sensually, and with his WORDS. Now come the best two verses in the Bible:

> ***"You are slender like a palm tree, and your breasts are like its clusters of fruit. I said, 'I will climb the palm tree and take hold of its fruit.' May your breasts be like grape clusters, and the fragrance of your breath like apples. May your kisses be as exciting as the best wine—"***

Wow! What a beautiful picture. This is sexuality expressed. This is enjoyment. This is THE BIBLE. Does this clash with what you have been taught about sex and your own sexuality? Let's keep reading this chapter as she replies to her lover.

> ***Young Woman***—*"Yes, wine that goes down smoothly for my lover, flowing gently over lips and teeth. I am my lover's, and he claims me as his own."*
>
> *"Come, my love, let us go out to the fields and spend the night among the wildflowers. Let us get up early and go to the vineyards to see if the grapevines have budded, if the blossoms have opened, and if the pomegranates have bloomed. There I will give you my love. There the mandrakes give off their fragrance, and the finest fruits are at our door, new delights as well as old, which I have saved for you, my lover" (NLT).*

Read **Song of Solomon** 7. Take notes on these verses. What stands out to you? Do you have questions? Thoughts? (Write your answers in the blanks at the end of the chapter)

These are powerful and beautiful words — not words we would use today to woo someone — but listen to their heart. We are meant to enjoy, to desire, to celebrate, to be captivated by, to revel, and to rest in our sexual selves. This is meant for us all, single or married. We were created with desire, but we were also given the responsibility to **steward** all things. This includes the powerful force of sexuality. The intertwining of our bodies in sex is a place of pleasure, yet it was specifically given parameters as well. God's design is perfect, as we will see soon, in our chemistry, our neurobiology, our hormones, and in God's design of our bodies and sexuality.

* * *

Working Questions - Now it is Your Turn:

Explain this Quote from Christopher West:
"The sexual embrace is the foundation of human life itself. The family — and, in turn, culture — spring from this embrace. In short, as sex goes, so go marriage and the family. As marriage and family go, so goes civilization. Such logic does not bode well for our culture. It is no exaggeration to say that the task of the twentieth century was to rid itself of the Christian sexual ethic …" (p. 13).

____

____

____

____

What does this second quote from Christopher West mean to you? “Christians must first find a way to demonstrate to the modern world that a biblical sexual ethic is not the cramped, prudish list of prohibitions it is often assumed to be. Rather, it is a liberating, redeeming path that fulfills the most noble aspirations of the human heart” (p. 14)

____

____

Is it enough to be in love with a person, or to feel you love a person, to begin a sexual relationship?

____

____

What kind of sex education have you had so far? Was it a one time conversation from your parents that was more lecture than dialogue? Were your parents embarrassed? Has your sexual education been left to the school, the back of the bus, or your church? What were your first glimpses of nudity or pornography?

____

____

First Thessalonians 4:3–8 states:

"God's will is for you to be holy, so stay away from all sexual sin. Then each of you will control his own body and live in holiness and honor—not in lustful passion like the pagans who do not know God and His ways. Never harm or cheat a fellow believer in this matter by violating his wife, for the Lord avenges all such sins, as we have solemnly warned you before. God has called us to live holy lives, not impure lives. Therefore, anyone who refuses to live by these rules is not disobeying human teaching but is rejecting God, who gives His Holy Spirit to you" (NLT).

What is God's plan for sex?

____

____

Titus 2:1–8 says:

"As for you, Titus, promote the kind of living that reflects wholesome teaching. Teach the older men to be temperate, worthy of respect, self-controlled, and sound in faith, in love and in endurance. Likewise, teach the older women to be reverent in the way they live, not to be slanderers or addicted to much wine, but to teach what is good. Then they can urge the younger women to love their husbands and children, to be self-controlled and pure, to be busy at home, to be kind, and to be subject to their husbands, so that no one will malign the word of God. Similarly, encourage the young men to be self-controlled. In everything set them an example by doing what is good. In your teaching show integrity, seriousness, and soundness of speech that cannot be condemned, so that those who oppose you may be ashamed because they have nothing bad to say about us."

Verses 11–14 say, "For the grace of God has been revealed, bringing salvation to all people. And we are instructed to turn from godless living and sinful pleasures. We should live in this evil world with wisdom, righteousness, and devotion to God, while we look forward with hope to that wonderful day when the glory of our great God and Savior, Jesus Christ, will be revealed. He gave his life to free us from every kind of sin, to cleanse us, and to make us his very own people, totally committed to doing good deeds" (NLT).

What does this passage require of you?

____

____

Ecclesiastes 7:16–8 says:

"Do not be over righteous, neither be over wise — why destroy yourself? Do not be over wicked, and do not be a fool — why die before your time? It is good to grasp the one and not let go of the other. The man who fears God will avoid all extremes" (NIV).

How would you explain this passage?

____

____

Romans 12:1 reminds us to:

"Offer your bodies as a living sacrifice, holy and pleasing to God – this is your true and proper worship" (NIV).

What does it mean to offer our bodies as living sacrifices?

____

____

First John 4:12b tells us that:

"If we love one another, God lives in us and His love is made complete in us" (NIV).

This passage says that the evidence that God lives in us is displayed by what action? How would you define "love"?

____

____

Song of Solomon 5:16 reads:

"His mouth is sweetness itself; he is desirable in every way. Such, O women of Jerusalem, is my lover, my friend" (NLT).

How can we dismiss desire as sin with a verse like this in the Bible?

____

____

An example of boundaries is set out in Proverbs 5:15,

"Drink water from your own well—share your love only with your wife" (NLT).

Explain these verses.

____

____

As our culture obsesses wildly about redefining marriage, gender, and sexual behavior, we would do well to remember the warning in 1 Peter 5:8 to:

"Stay alert! Watch out for your great enemy, the devil. He prowls around like a roaring lion, looking for someone to devour" (NLT).

Who is watching and seeking to destroy you?

____

____

How would you define the difference between "preserving innocence" and "preventing ignorance"?

____

____

Is it possible for a parent to do both – persevere innocence and prevent ignorance?

____

____

Is being "in love" all that is necessary to begin a sexual relationship?

____

____

Do you believe you ARE or ARE NOT ready for a sexual relationship?

____

____

What if you are a hopeless romantic? What do you feel you need in order to be successful?

____

____

Statistics guestimate that seventy percent of American teens have already had sex. What have your sexual experiences been? Have you shared these with your parents or another trusted adult?

____

____

How can we worship God with our bodies - specifically with our sexuality?

____

____

Define chastity.

____

____

Look back up at Song of Solomon Chapter 7 under the heading," What Does the Bible Say?" – What stands out to you? Do you have questions? Thoughts?

____

____

What do you think about love and sex?

____

____

____

____

What are the messages you receive from your parents, church, school, teachers, friends, media, etc?

____

____

____

What is meant by "bad touch"? What is acceptable? What is "sick", "disgusting", or "gross"?

____

____

What is "good touch"? What is beautiful and permissible?

____

____

Has trauma impacted you? If so, it most likely impacts your relationships, your view of yourself, and how you think and talk about sex and sexuality. Have you noticed any impacts in your own life?

____

____

| 6 |

Marriage - The Impact of MY BELIEFS

Have you thought through your beliefs, or theology, of marriage? What about sex within marriage? How is this topic dealt with in your church, community, and school? What about in your home? How do your parents deal with **"IT"?** There are many factors that influence the development of our ethics on marriage and sex within marriage. Some influences that have the most impact are:

- Our personal experiences (good and bad)
- Family history (historical and cultural tradition)
- Lack of conversation (the problem of silence)
- Biblical precedent (and/or interpretation)

What Is Marriage?

How much time have you spent thinking about this? Not much if you are like most people. What you believe will reveal itself in how you conduct your own marriage. My desire is for you to give this a lot of thought beforehand. I want your definition and understanding of marriage to be grounded in Scripture. Honestly, everyone has an opinion about marriage. Many of us also have dreams about what we want our marriage to look like. Where are these born?

Your ideas of what marriage should look like begin at home and extend from there. How your parents talk to one another (or not), how much time they spend together, how they spend their money, how they parent, and how they treat others. You have been observing their commitment to their church, friends, and those in need. You hear what they pray for, focus on, gripe about, and rage over. You observe their politics. You have been stocking up on more than the energy of your family - your stockpile also includes a culture full of opinions and thoughts on marriage equality, abortion, guns, and poverty. You have seen who they spend their time with as a family — and the diversity of those friends.

My greatest concern is that, if we are not careful, our personal experience growing up in our homes and the surrounding culture will end up shaping our beliefs about marriage more than the Word of God. Here are some key points for you to consider as you solidify your theology of marriage and sex in marriage.

God created marriage. He is the triune God, the God of love. He is three in one — the Father, the Son, and the Holy Spirit. In these, He is fully differentiated and fully intimate. The love and pleasure of their union spills over into creation in His design for marriage. Genesis 1:26 says,

"Let us make man in our image, in our likeness ..." (NIV).

We are created like Him. We were created to reflect His nature through our nature. How do we do this? Leviticus 20:7 says that we are to:

"Set yourselves apart to be holy, for I am the Lord Your God" (NLT).

What does this look like? We are called to love like Him — because He first loved us. We are called to forgive like Him — because we are forgiven. Is it at all surprising that we are also called to be ONE like Him? I think one of the most amazing gifts God has given us is the ability to be ONE through marriage.

God uses two key "institutions" to change the world.

The first, and the primary one we will focus on here, is **Marriage**.

The second is the **Church**.

We are created as sexual creatures to reflect distinctive differences — by design. These differences bring us together through our bodies in a way nothing else can. We are created to come together and experience true intimacy and sexual pleasure in marriage. An important aspect of our sexuality gets lost if we focus on ourselves, our pleasure, and personal fulfillment as the end goal of sex. Sex is more than two people having a good time together. It is also the means of bringing new life into the world.

The Importance of a Theology of Marriage - and Sex in Marriage

Did you know that God designed your sexuality to be fully expressed in intimacy with another person? The design is perfect. We are the ones that mess it all up. Sin destroys what God created. Sin corrupts. We MUST get this in the right order. If we don't, it can eat us alive inside, harm others, and create lifelong damage. This is why it is a beautiful thing that you are learning about this now as a teen or preteen. I hope God can use me to help you see the wisdom of choosing God's design and forsaking your immediate desires.

Did you know that most married couples struggle with their sex lives? It saddens me that, most likely, your picture of sex is what you have seen in movies, tv shows, and porn. **Sex is one of the most pervasive problems for married couples,** but it doesn't have to be.

So here is a prediction I have for you and your future: You most likely will struggle here as well. I know this seems impossible, but it is the truth. How? Couples really struggle with just talking about sex at all. It becomes something you just do – not a personal intimate part of their habits as a health couple. So many struggle with frequency, what to do, and what not to do (boundaries), and battles with their own view of themselves, their bodies, and liking themselves, yet alone giving and receiving pleasure. This is the reality. This is why communication becomes so important.

It is also a big deal outside of marriage, as it is practiced by singles — a place it was never meant to be experienced. If we step further back, we can see its impact on many lives through abuse, pornography, and the objectification of women which affects the whole of society, degrading and impacting marriages as well. I believe that if you, as a teen, learn to have healthy relationships with boundaries and save this stuff for later, you will exponentially increase your odds of a strong, healthy, and wonderful marriage. How we live as single men or women and the skills we learn in relationships directly impact how our marriages turn out.

Have you bought into the lie of the world that you should try to experience whatever you can, disregarding others and the impact this will have on both of your futures? One of the biggest mistruths about sex is that it is all about physical pleasure, and that sexual problems are a failure to give and receive pleasure accurately. This way of thinking stems from a variety of sources:

- One source is ignorance — a lack of education — on how the body's design works.
- Others are unskilled and just need to practice — within marriage and with one partner for life.
- For many, internal blocks create a wall that keeps them trapped. These can be sexual history, relational anxiety, or their upbringing.

What message did you learn about sex and sexuality in your home?

What message was taught by your church?

Have you had to deal with the impact of a bad relationship that crossed the lines?

Have you processed the hurt and loss from abuse you've endured?

Most marriages are impacted by these things. God invented our sexuality. It is not a mistake. It is perfect by design. It has a purpose. It also has boundaries.

You have to decide how you will live. No one else can do this for you.

If you live for yourself, focused on pleasure, you will be let down. A pleasure as temporary as sex never satisfies our soul.

If you live for God and by His design, you will see that sex within God's boundaries provides **protection**, **pleasure**, and a natural means of **procreation**.

I want you to think about the priority that these three "Ps" should have within the context of marriage, — specifically, as you think about sex in marriage.

We have the benefit today of gifted leaders that have paved the way for conversations about sexuality in ways previous generations did not. Conversations that are God honoring, respectful, careful, and not too graphic.

Leaders such as Clifford and Joyce Penner,[15] and Doug Rosenau[16] have opened the doors to these conversations in the Church and among Christians. Many couples that "have sex" have learned to "make love" and their relationships are thriving.

Their focus has been on these "**three Ps**". As our culture has grown bolder and louder, those inside the Church have listened to ungodly advice and two of these three words have been de-emphasized and the other has received heightened glorification. In my estimation, the message of today is that sex is all about your "**pleasure.**" But is it really? What's missing in this view?

I know this may sound weird to read about as a teen, but it is SO important that you know the purposes of sex. I promise this is critical and will directly impact how you make difficult choices when you're under pressure from peers or facing the temptation to do something you know you should hold off doing until you are married. Understanding what you believe can save your life – and your whole future.

Here is some food for thought on each of the "P's":

Protection:

Your sex life in marriage has an amazing effect on your body, your health, and your life. How? Regular sexual activity, with or without orgasm, improves your physical health. Regular orgasms amplify this effect in your body, decreasing the effects of depression, stress, anxiety, heart disease and other health complications. Your mental health is also seriously improved. Disease is contained because of a strengthening of your immune system. Sex in marriage is also a protection against temptation outside of your marriage. A routine — with some spice — with your husband or wife wards off the pull that pornography and potential affairs can have on you at your weakest moments.

Pleasure:

You are meant to find pleasure in life — through the food you eat, the things you set out to accomplish, and your body via sex. Sexual pleasure is a beautiful gift. Use it. Enjoy it. Give it. Receive it. Revel in it. Be thankful for God's gift of your spouse. Enjoy! Christians ought to have the best sex with their marriage partners. Christians should find deep pleasure in this part of God's design. **This is HOLY!** Pleasure is a beautiful gift from heaven. I hope you can find pleasure in your work and in your day-to-day lives, but there is something special about God's design in sex. Again — ENJOY (in marriage)!

Procreation:

What if this is God's main idea for sex? Yes, it is also about protection. Yes, it is also about pleasure. But what if the design served a grander purpose — that of bringing children into this world? A new life comes from the bringing together of the egg and the sperm. No other combination can do this. God's design for sex, marriage, and the family depends on this formula. **What if we held this "P" as the highest value? Let me take an even bolder stance — what if every time a male and female came together and had intercourse it was meant to produce a baby?** Praise God it doesn't every time! But what if this was the intent? If we elevated this "P" over the other two, would we have a different society? Would teenagers and young adults make different decisions with their sexual choices if they knew by choosing intercourse, they were saying they are ready for the potential baby, if God chose to allow it? How does this sound? Your theology matters. Your beliefs matter.

The Impact of Divorce, Single Parents, And the Blended Family

Jeff is a serious ten-year-old who is having trouble in school. He feels awkward in social situations and is showing signs of a learning disability. He could be diagnosed with ADD according to most of his teachers. He has a learning plan at school. He is anxious. He has become unusually silent lately. Why? He hasn't told anyone at school, but his parents just went through a divorce and he is now going back and forth between their homes. It has turned his life upside down. He is just a boy, but now he is at risk of viewing pornography, acting out sexually, and experimenting. Due to his parents' own troubles, they have given little thought to the *micro-conversations* they should have with Jeff about sex and sexuality.

Sean and Carrie are now step-siblings. They didn't even know each other a year ago. Sean is twelve, and Carrie is thirteen. They are now navigating adolescence together. They are battling hormones, desires, questions, parents, and step-parents. Their world just got more complicated.

If your parents are divorced, it is *very important* that you have micro- conversations with an adult that you can trust. The chances are high that you have two very different ethics at each parent's home. It may feel like betrayal on your part if you side with one which leaves you feeling torn. This makes it crucial that you develop your own personal ETHOS - your belief system that will guide you through this stage of life into adulthood. I am so sorry you are in this position, for whatever reason it happened. You still need your parents, even though they aren't perfect. Listen to both. Learn from both. But you must develop your OWN beliefs and your OWN ethic. Bless you in this process.

If you live with a single parent, more often than not you are living with your mom. It is vital that you team up with others to learn and grow. This may be a friend's parents, a youth pastor, an older cousin, or other family member. It doesn't matter which of these you choose, just pick the one who will guide you into a Biblical Sexual Ethic. Your church ought to be a safe place. Do not try to do it alone. You were designed to need two parents - a mom and a dad. When that is disrupted, it affects your development. You can make up for that in other relationships that feed good things into you. Your granddad could be one. Your coach. A youth leader. Be careful that you don't become resentful towards anyone. Lean into the opportunity to reach out to others and learn from their lives, and may they give you HOPE.

If you live in a blended family, the same advice applies. Be proactive. Build a team around you. Do this intentionally. Remember that these things are out of your control – but choosing to love your step-parent and step-siblings is a must. You must learn this. Why? This ability to choose to love when you don't want to will change your future and how you interact with the world in years to come.

Did you know that the rules of parenting for a single parent, divorced parent, or parent in a blended family differ from the approaches others might suggest or expect. Parenting is much more complicated. It is more complicated because it requires a different play book. So, it's possible that your parents are struggling. Give them grace. Be patient with them. And again, build YOUR community around you with great examples and influences that will help you to enter adulthood confidently.

* * *

Working Questions – Now it is Your turn:

How has marriage been defined in your church, community, or school?

____

____

What ideas do you have about marriage based on your family?

____

____

____

How have your parents dealt with "IT"?

____

____

What impact has the following had on your ETHOS as you develop a worldview on marriage and sex?

- Your personal experiences (good and bad)
- Family history (historical, cultural, tradition)
- A lack of conversation (the problem of silence)
- Biblical precedent (and/or interpretation)

____

____

Read **Genesis 1:26**

Then God said, "Let us make human beings in our image, to be like us. They will reign over the fish in the sea, the birds in the sky, the livestock, all the wild animals on the earth, and the small animals that scurry along the ground." (NLT)

What does it mean to be made in His "likeness?"

____

____

Read **Leviticus 20:7**

So set yourselves apart to be holy, for I am the Lord your God (NLT).

What does it mean to set yourself apart?

____

____

What are the two vehicles, or Key Institutions God has given us within which to live out being ONE?

____

____

____

What lessons have you learned about sex and your sexuality?

____

____

____

What lessons were you taught about sex from your church?

____

____

____

Have you had the experience of a bad relationship that crossed the lines? How do you think it has impacted you?

____

____

____

Have you processed the hurt and loss from abuse you endured? The effect of abuse can be felt years later.

____

____

What are the 3 “P’s”? How important do you think each of these are?

____

____

____

If you are living in a divorced family or have a blended family, write out some of your challenges.

____

____

____

What are some of the most difficult moments that need your attention and intention?

____

____

| 7 |

Love, Sex, & Neuroscience or - Forget the Flu Shot!

Now hang in there with me. You can think of this chapter as boring or as packed full of interesting information as you find out more about God's perfect design. I hope you can see the value as you read through these biology terms. Why do I think this is important? Because in all of its complexity, our brains point to an amazing Creator. Fascinating discoveries have recently emerged out of the fields of neuroscience and interpersonal neurobiology within your lifetime. The more I learn, the more I am in awe of God's perfect design in our bodies, masculine and feminine. There are no mistakes.

Why do you do the things you do in the way that you do them? Why do you obsess? Why do you get into ruts you cannot get out of? Why do you desire or feel certain things? What is love, really? How does the mind interact with the body regarding our sexuality? What is the impact of pornography? Why is it such a big deal? Why do some choose porn over a live human being?

Your Brain and Body on Sex

Did you know that there is one interesting cure and/or treatment for many of the physical and mental health issues many of us face? In his book, *The Brain in Love,* **Dr. Daniel Amen**[17] states that sex is an incredible healing force — a medicine. He says, "making love on a regular basis improve[s] mood, memory, and overall health." He continues to drive home this point with a study that found that regular sexual activity "decrease[s] the risk of heart attack and stroke by fifty percent." He concludes: "Hold the medicine, give me love."[18]

What does sex do to and for our bodies? It strengthens and lengthens our life expectancy. Sex positively impacts and renovates our immune system functioning. Sex can also be associated with more joy, a reduction in physical pain, and improved sexual and reproductive health.[19]

Researchers have correlated sexual activity with a decrease in the two leading causes of death in the United States — heart disease and cancer.[20] This should have you very excited right now and anticipating good times with your marriage partner in the future. I hope it does. Let us look at each of these benefits one by one.

When sex and sexuality are in the right place in a person's mind and body, the experience of sex helps to **reduce stress hormones**. This leads to a reduction of anxiety and a decrease in a person's violent tendencies and hostility.

One key finding makes me jump for joy as the science, once again, proves God's design. The research concluded that **the key to this positive effect of regular sexual activity was found in thoughtful sexual activity with a committed partner.**[21]

Matthew 19:5–6 describes the design in very simple terms:

> *"And he said, 'This explains why a man leaves his father and mother and is joined to his wife, and the two are united into one.' Since they are no longer two but one, let no one split apart what God has joined together" (NLT).*

Marriage IS the only context for sexual activity. One man and one woman only. For life. These are two sexually different people committed before God and community, until death.

Welcomed and safe physical touch increases our ***oxytocin***. ***Oxytocin*** is our bonding chemical, and when it is released, there is a boost in trust with each safe touch, as well as an anticipation of touch. This also lowers our ***cortisol*** levels, which impacts our body's inflammation properties. ***Cortisol*** is the stress hormone responsible for chronic stress and its effects. What a beautiful picture! **Sex equals closeness, oneness, less stress, and feeling bonded.** What more could we want? But there is more!

Sex within the above boundaries leads to **fewer sick days** and a boost to our immune system. We know orgasms alone increase infection fighting cells by twenty percent. Regular sexual activity also increases the antibody ***immunoglobulin A (IgA)*** that helps us fight colds and the flu. **Forget the flu shot!** I think we have a winner![22]

The impact of regular sexual activity with the same safe partner increases healthy hormone levels, impacts menstrual health, increases prostate health, improves our cardiovascular system, lowers cholesterol, promotes bone density, and aids to our skin's health. Our brain works better and cancer fighting properties are aided in their fight against disease.[23]

This is still not everything that sex can do for you! Other benefits to think about are: more restful sleep, pain relief, migraine relief, depression treatment, looking younger, improved sense of smell, weight loss, overall fitness, health and longevity, and happiness. These are only a few reasons we should put our sexuality and sex life in the right place — within a Biblical Sexual Ethic. Outside of this context, the results are NOT the same.[24]

So, you might be thinking, what does all of this have to do with me - a teenager? Are you tempting me? Are you baiting me? Not at all! I am painting the picture of what you can have if you make wise decisions today. The choices you make today impact your future. Many adults live with baggage, secrets, sexually transmitted diseases, and children they barely know. Let's change the possibility of that future for you. How? By choice!

Your Brain in Love

You might be tempted to skip this section, but if you read over it a few times, you'll see that it explains so much about what you do. **You do not act by accident.** You do not become pessimistic by happenstance. You do not suddenly become more violent, quiet, reactive, or fearful. **Chemical reactions in your brain are guiding you.**

The biggest question for me, as I try to wrap my mind around the complexity of how God made us, is which comes first, my biology or my choice?

Do I have free will? Do you?

Are we just the result of chemical reactions in our brain?

Do we have any say over these? Are we only biology?

Where is the soul? Who am I?

Can I really change? Is the ability to change limited?

Am I free? Can I ever experience true freedom?

Read through these descriptions of the brain and the function of each part. This synthesis of Dr. Amen's[25] work, among others, is meant to help you get a quick snapshot of the complexity of your brain — the most important sex organ in your body!

Falling in and out of love or lust is controlled by the ***limbic system***. Interestingly, ***dopamine (DA)*** acts like cocaine and lights up the brain, triggering feelings of pleasure, motivation, and reward. Whether it is sex, eating, taking risks, or drinking water, the neurochemical dopamine activates your reward circuitry. The "I've got to have it" neurotransmitter — or the craving brain — is *dopamine*. As more *dopamine* is released, the greater the reward. The greater the reward, the more addictive the feeling or experience can be.

Attraction occurs when the brainstem releases ***phenylethylamine (PEA)***. This speeds up the flow of information between nerve cells, working like a powerful drug. It's been found that the ***prefrontal cortex (PFC)***, which is not fully developed until age twenty-five, is involved in judgment, impulse control, organization, planning, forethought, and learning from mistakes.

Think about the reality that at twenty-five years old a young person's critical decision-making center has just finished growing. This is crucial information for understanding some of your choices. This should also indicate to parents that their children still need mentoring and guidance throughout the teen years as their *prefrontal cortex* is continuing to strengthen and develop.

So, the process of attraction and the role of *dopamine* for a man in the presence of a beautiful woman is that it causes the man's *limbic system,* which includes the *amygdala* and other brainstem structures that are in charge of emotion, to fire up while the *prefrontal cortex* totally checks out. This leaves his judgment area vacant. No forethought equals potentially erratic, unquestioned, and even emotional reactions. Think about how that works and the result it could have. What can we trust? Is this a setup?

The ***anterior cingulate gyrus (ACG)*** helps us feel settled, relaxed and flexible. It is the brain's major switching station or gear shifter. Healthy activity levels help us connect, give us cognitive flexibility, and make us more cooperative. When there is too much activity, ***serotonin*** levels lower and we become unable to shift. We get rigid, cognitively inflexible, over focused, anxious, and oppositional.

The ***deep limbic system (DLS)*** sets the emotional tone. When it is less active, we are more positive and have a more hopeful state of mind. When it is heated or overactive, negativity can take over. The *deep limbic system* controls sleep and appetite cycles. It is intimately involved in bonding and being socially connected.

The ***basal ganglia (BG)*** is involved in integrating feelings, thoughts, and movement. The *basal ganglia* set the body's idle, or anxiety, level. When it is overactive, we are anxious, fearful, and full of tension. Our feelings of pleasure and even ecstasy are guided by our *basal ganglia.*

The ***temporal lobes (TLs)*** are involved in memory and moods. These help with language, hearing, understanding, social cues, short-term memory, moving memories into long-term storage, along with the processing of music, tone of voice, and mood stability. When there is trouble in the *temporal lobes,* this can lead to both short- and long-term memory problems, reading difficulties, trouble finding the right words in conversations, trouble reading social cues, and sometimes a lack of spiritual sensitivity.

Johnny is a healthy fifteen-year-old male. He sees a beautiful girl and his ***dopamine*** increases while his ***amygdala*** revs up, which causes his ***prefrontal cortex*** to shut down. He really wants to talk with her, though. How does he make any good decisions at this point? If his ***anterior cingulate gyrus*** is running well, he can remain relaxed and flexible. If his ***deep limbic system*** is less active, he can be more positive about the outcome of his upcoming verbal exchange. If not, pessimism and doubt creep in. If his ***basal ganglia*** remains calm, he will not become overanxious or tense. Is that likely? If his ***temporal lobes*** malfunction, he will be at a loss for words and most likely become unable to respond to social cues.

Do you see how this can all go wrong?

Dopamine draws him in, but each of the other parts of his brain can work against him if they get out of balance. Some hormones and chemicals need more activity than others. The balance of our brain's functionality hinges on many factors. Has Johnny had a brain injury? If so, it will most likely have affected one of these key areas of the brain.

If you read any of Dr. Amen's[26] books, you will see these explained as having key roles in the specific impact on our mood, behavior, spirit, and sensitivity. We have NOT paid enough attention to this part in the past. If Johnny has a slight spike in activity in the ***basal ganglia***, he will become fearful and tense. See how this works? Imagine how complicated this gets for you and I.

I read about an experiment in which a researcher made the following offer to men and to women. The offer was to choose between $15.00 tomorrow or $75.00 in a few days. The person asking the men was a very attractive woman. They found that men stop thinking about long-term consequences once attraction chemicals kick in and they overwhelmingly chose the $15.00 over the $75.00.

What do you think the women did with the same offer from an attractive male counterpart?

Attraction had no effect on women's thinking process, and they waited for the $75.00.[27] Interesting. Yes, men and women are different!

Chemicals and Hormones

Speaking of attraction, fifty percent of the brain is dedicated to vision.[28] The *amygdala,* which controls emotion and motivation, is much more activated in men when viewing sexual material for thirty minutes.

The difference in the brain between love and lust is that **lust is fueled by *testosterone,*** and **love is fueled by *vasopressin* and *oxytocin.***

One is fleeting and unreliable.

The other is deeper, longer lasting, and has a bonding effect.

Love lights up the *caudate* and *ventral tegmental* areas of the brain.

The *ventral tegmental* area floods the *caudate* with *dopamine.*

The *caudate* then sends signals for more *dopamine.*

Sexual attraction impacts the *amygdala* and *hypothalamus* which controls drive.

So, what conclusion can we draw?

That feeling of love you experience may be more drive than emotion.

Love decreases brain levels of ***serotonin***, the neurotransmitter responsible for mood and flexibility.

Low *serotonin* means you can get stuck on ideas — even become obsessed.

Serotonin levels can be increased by exercise, carbohydrates, and thought distraction.

Men who have healthy activity in their *prefrontal cortex* have greater empathy, attention spans, and make better husbands.

If the ***prefrontal cortex*** is overactive, we can become obsessive, oppositional, and argumentative. When it is underactive, we can become impulsive, easily distracted, and bored.

Testosterone beefs up the hypothalamus—the area of the brain that is interested in sex—which is two times larger in men. Men with *high testosterone* levels are forty-three percent more likely to get divorced and thirty-eight percent more likely to have extramarital affairs. They are also fifty percent less likely to marry in the first place.[29]

Men with *lower testosterone* are more likely to get married and stay married, since low levels make men more cooperative.

The major chemicals involved in the primary phases of love are the following:

- Attraction—craving for sexual gratification: ***testosterone, estrogen, nitric oxide, pheromones.***
- Infatuation—intense, passionate love: ***epinephrine, norepinephrine (NE), dopamine, serotonin, phenylethylamine (PEA)***
- Commitment—connectedness, joy, stability, peace: ***oxytocin, vasopressin***
- Detachment—losing a love through breakups or death: deficiencies in ***serotonin and endorphins***

One model that I love to tell my students about is what I call **"Cocaine Brain."** I am referring to brain scans that reveal that the centers of the brain that light up when we are infatuated — in love — head over heels — are the same centers in the brain that light up if you were to take the drug cocaine. So, you are literally high when you are in love, or high on love! The takeaway — **DO NOT make any major decisions while "high"** — "cocaine brained."

What I will introduce next is a quick run through of the chemicals (hormones) at work in our bodies from a thirty-thousand-foot view, to lay a foundation for further understanding of the complexities of our bodies, brains, and sexuality. This is a fire hose, but it is worth it!

Testosterone:

Testosterone in men appears to make them more self-focused sexually. Lower testosterone in men reduces their sex drive, not necessarily sexual potency, which is the ability to achieve an erection. Testosterone is clinically effective for sex drive only in hypo-testosterone males.

Some women have found that testosterone treatment can move the dial slightly if they are hoping to increase their sexual desire. Women with higher levels of testosterone report less depression, experience more sexual gratification with their husbands, and show strength in forming good, healthy interpersonal relationships.

Masturbation without a partner does not increase testosterone levels, while intercourse with a partner does. Desire and response increase or decrease by complex chemical interactions including peptides, neurotransmitters, and hormones—not solely based on testosterone levels.

Estrogen:

Estrogen is both excitatory and inhibitory in women. It is solely inhibitory in men. Estrogen is primarily produced in female ovaries but is also found in both the male and female brains. When combined with a dose of testosterone, estrogen contributes to sexual desire and responsiveness in women. It promotes lubrication and vaginal health, while also facilitating the action of serotonin, opioids, prolactin, and oxytocin.

Nitric Oxide:

This chemical is released by the genitals when aroused, causing vasodilation, increased blood flow to the pelvic area for women — specifically the labia and clitoris—and increased blood flow to the penis for men. Medications known as PDE5 Inhibitors, such as Viagra, Cialis, and Levitra, work by helping stimulate the release of nitric oxide.

Pheromones:

These are chemicals that are "scent-signaling." Sweat glands secrete them primarily in the armpits. These are thought to influence how humans mate, bond, and take care of offspring. There is a direct connection between the olfactory bulb at the top of the nose and the hypothalamus in the brain — also known as the "erection center."

Driver pheromones affect the endocrine systems of others. An example of this is when women living in close proximity to other women find their menstrual cycles syncing up.

Epinephrine and Norepinephrine (NE):

These are produced in the adrenal glands, spinal cord, and brain, causing what we know as the "adrenaline rush." These facilitate both sexual arousal and orgasm. High levels are associated with anxiety, and low levels are associated with depression. Chronic stress, sedentary lifestyle, poor diet, and genetics can lead to low levels. The amino acid tyrosine can raise levels.

Dopamine:

This is one of the most important neurotransmitters in relation to our experience of pleasure, reinforcement, reward, movement, attraction, and other processes related to sexual desire, arousal, response, and satisfaction. Dopamine mediates pleasure, increases sex drive, and promotes orgasms. High levels of dopamine though can lead to psychosis. Low levels can lead to depression, Attention Deficit Hyperactivity Disorder (ADHD), excitement, and risk seeking behaviors.

Serotonin (5HT):

Serotonin is produced in the midbrain and brainstem. It is involved with mood regulation and emotional flexibility. It inhibits arousal and orgasm in both sexes. It decreases anxiety and aggressiveness. It is symbiotic with estrogen. Serotonin facilitates opioids and progesterone, which also mute sexual excitement. Low levels lead to depression, anxiety, Obsessive Compulsive Disorder (OCD), and what has been coined "new love." High levels are associated with lowered motivation.

Phenylethylamine (PEA):

PEA is the adrenaline-like substance that speeds up the flow of information between nerve cells and is triggered in the process of attraction to help us pay attention to feelings of love. It initiates a flood of chemicals into the brain along with norepinephrine (NE) and dopamine (DA) to create the feelings of euphoria and infatuation when we are attracted. This is also found in chocolate—which may explain a lot!

Oxytocin:

Oxytocin is a neuropeptide hormone that facilitates attraction and touch sensation. According to Dr. Amen, it is your brain's "love juice." Oxytocin levels increase following touch. Once a touching pattern is established, levels increase in anticipation of touching. It is involved in bonding, both as a cause and an effect. The coolest thing is that it spikes during orgasm—by five hundred percent for men. It plays a role in attraction, trust, touch, sex, orgasm, bonding, labor, parenting, and nursing—to name a few.

Oxytocin also has an amnesiac effect during sex and orgasm that blocks negative memories people have about each other for a period. This amnesiac effect also occurs during childbirth. Higher oxytocin levels are associated with increased feelings of trust and decreased stress levels.

Vasopressin:

Vasopressin is known as an antidiuretic hormone. It prevents water and salt depletion by stimulating thirst and inhibiting urination. It is a key thermoregulator. It limits "overheating" of brain areas involved in sexual activity. It is involved in regulating sexual persistence, assertiveness, dominance, and territorial markings. Men have higher levels. This hormone can make the difference between the stay-at-home family dad and the one-night-stand artist as vasopressin is shown to assist in the regulation of social pair bonding — sexual and social fidelity — in men.[30]

Why Do These Matter? — I fell in love with the word *"yada"* in my training as a sex therapist at the ***Institute for Sexual Wholeness (www.sexualwholeness.com)***.[31]

Yada is a primitive root and means – to know, to be known, to be or become known, to be revealed. **I love that we were created for that purpose — TO BE KNOWN!** We are known by God and we can be known by and know others.

Yada sex is fully sensuous, fully receiving, fully knowing, fully being known, becoming one in the quiet.

This is beautiful imagery. I personally zero in on the last one — ***becoming one in the quiet***. This is sexuality within the context of marriage, within the safety and security of someone that knows you, trusts you, and gives themselves to you and vice versa. What a beautiful picture. **You were meant *TO BE KNOWN!***

* * *

Working Questions – Now it is YOUR TURN:

Read **Matthew 19:5–6**

And he said, "'This explains why a man leaves his father and mother and is joined to his wife, and the two are united into one.' Since they are no longer two but one, let no one split apart what God has joined together." (NLT)

Explain the design for marriage based on this passage.

____

____

Oxytocin is our ______________ chemical. What else does it do?

____

____

Cortisol is what kind of hormone?

____

____

What is the antibody IgA?

____

____

The biggest question for me, as I try to wrap my mind around the complexity of how God made us, is which comes first, my biology or my choice?

Do I have free will? Do you? Are we just the result of chemical reactions in our brain? Do we have any say over these? Are we only biology? Where is the soul? Who am I? Can I really change? Is the ability to change limited? Am I free? Can I ever experience true freedom?

Do you have answers to these for yourself?

____

____

What is the main role of the Limbic System?

____

____

What is the role of dopamine (DA) in attraction, pleasure, and reward?

____

____

What is phenylethylamine (PEA)? What is its purpose?

____

____

The prefrontal cortex (PFC) is involved in what?

___

___

The anterior cingulate gyrus (ACG) — when healthy — helps us:

___

___

The deep limbic system (DLS) is intimately involved in our:

___

___

The basal ganglia (BG) is involved in integrating:

___

___

Temporal lobes (TLs) help with:

___

___

Does this section help you see the complexities and the beauty of God's perfect design in how we are created? What are some potential problems that can arise - both medically and emotionally?

____

____

What are the major chemicals and hormones involved in the primary phases of love?

____

____

Explain "Cocaine Brain":

____

____

What does the word YADA mean?

____

____

| 8 |

Basic Anatomy

I know this seems basic, but it is so important. I have found in my counseling practice and as a professor that many adults do not understand basic anatomy, let alone most teenagers. **We are a sexually explicit culture in our entertainment, yet overall, we are woefully misinformed and continue to pass on myths and lies as though they were facts.** We pride ourselves on not being a prude, yet we refer to a woman's vulva as "down there" or a man's penis as "his thing". We cannot talk about sex in a serious context at all without embarrassment, and most people wouldn't know if there was something wrong with their body since they haven't educated themselves. For example, many adults do not know what a clitoris is, where it is located on the body (female body that is), or its purpose.

Did you know that there is a current fad of shaving and shaping the pubic hair that covers the mons pubis (vulva)? (This is on women.) Is this healthy? Does appearance matter?

What about plastic surgery, boob jobs, lifts and tucks, and even labia reconstruction?

What is an erection?

Where does the egg meet the sperm?

When does life begin?

Is discussing your period embarrassing?

Do you understand the purpose and design of menstruation?

We should start with the basics.

First - **boys and girls are different.** Yes, I said it. We are different. Our bodies are uniquely and perfectly designed. What follows are the basics, followed by a brief description of the coming together of the man and woman, which is the primary way of bringing together the egg and the sperm. We are not earning our medical degrees here. We are learning to know ourselves, protect ourselves, educate ourselves, and live wisely. This knowledge will also help you ask good questions. It's okay to look something up - just be careful where you look it up. You need to have a foundation that you can expand upon as you mature.

Boys

Let us take a look at the unique design of boys:

Boys have a **penis** and a scrotum. The **testes**, also known as testicles, are inside the scrotum.

Please use these terms. Avoid using nicknames for private parts. Why is this important?

First, it demystifies them. **Second**, knowing the correct terms becomes critical when harm has occurred, and you need to have the words at your disposal to describe what happened. And yes, you, even as a teenager, can be mature and model a healthy vocabulary to others.

This modeling teaches others that their bodies are nothing to be ashamed of and introduces the concept of **dignity.** Dignity is that idea that we cover parts of our body out of respect for self and others, not out of prudish prohibitions.

Boys – you need to understand how your penis is designed — that it is not wood or bone. It rises and falls because of blood flow, and this is called an erection. There is nothing to be ashamed about here. (Stop your giggling – just kidding – giggle on).

You need to know what is normal for your testes (or testicles – or balls), — their sensitivity, and how sperm and testosterone are made. It is important to understand how sperm is made, stored, travels through the vas deferens to the penis, and is joined with a white milky substance from the prostate. This is called semen. Arousal by a fleeting thought, touch, or visual stimulation will lead – automatically – to an erection. This means your body works properly. **Truthfully guys, almost anything brings on arousal and we need to be careful not to make too big of a deal about it.** This is how you are made. An erection is not a signal that you need to go masturbate or do anything else. At your age, this could simply be caused by the wind blowing. Yes, it is that simple. (Insert laughs here – I know).

Boys need to understand that there are differences as well between individual males. Some have parts that are bigger, some smaller, and this **makes no difference** for their future marriage and sexual relationship. Circumcision is the removal of the foreskin and boys will see some penises with and some without in the locker room. Internally boys have very little to worry about in their bodies as they develop.

Stewardship is probably the most important concept for us ALL to learn. Learning how to manage your attractions, desires, passions, and lusts will be of utmost importance. **You always have a choice.** An erection does not trigger action. It is more like a suggestion, an automatic reaction, or a signal.

Choice is always present.

Girls

Girls' bodies are quite complicated. Their sexual system is an open system that requires extensive knowledge and self-care. I find that many women remain afraid of, or apathetic to, their own bodies, leading to difficulties with the sexual part of marriage.

Girls' external genitalia comprises their **vulva** (with many critical parts) and breasts. Their internal sexual organs include a vagina, uterus, fallopian tubes, and ovaries. It is critical to use the correct terms, so you know what is normal or abnormal for your body and giving yourself the vocabulary, you need to address problems. The pH balance of the internal organs is a critical part of a woman's sexual anatomy.

Girls must grasp the importance of self-care and the fragility of their sexual parts. Many girls find themselves as young women facing their first period, also known as their menstrual cycle, thinking they are dying. You need to be prepared for every stage that is coming with your body and development.

What is occurring with these changes? This is the way your body prepares each month to host a baby. If conception does not occur, the lining of the uterus that has built up is expelled in preparation for the next month. Each month, one of your two ovaries releases one egg, which travels down your fallopian tubes. Your understanding of this process and its complexity is a beautiful opportunity to wonder at the intricate design and intentionality of God.

The external genitalia include the **labia majora and minora** (which serve as a cover to the vaginal opening), the **clitoris** (which is the most sensitive part and made up of the same tissue as the penis in boys), and the hair that acts to protect the pH balance and cleanliness of the vagina. Understanding your design is critical so you can be prepared to take care of yourself, both physically and relationally. Knowledge is power.

Your breast development is another part of the journey that could include a lot of comparison and potential heartache if you let it. Be a good steward. It is critical to understand the purpose for your breasts. Part of your body's preparation for a baby is to prepare the nourishment to feed your baby. The mammary glands behind the nipple and throughout your breasts are part of your intricate design and serve a purpose. They are not a tool to wield and control others. They are also part of your beauty and design. Steward them well.

Ladies, it will be very important to learn about your body so that you can know if something is wrong. One of the ways to do this is with wellness checks. I know these can be difficult, but the repercussions of NOT catching a problem early could cost you your life. **This is not about scaring you; it is about preparing you to be wise, assertive, and smart.**

Coming Together

An example of the complexity of God's design is the process that begins after a sperm fertilizes an egg. Immediately, the cells begin to multiply, creating a person. Within weeks, a heartbeat is detectable. It is an amazing experience to see and hear this fast little heartbeat. I will never forget how life changing it was for me to hear my son's heartbeat. "Life! What an incredible miracle. We made that. Wow. God, You are amazing!"

As a baby forms, the tissues where the genitals form for girls and boys are the same. There is little evidence as to the gender of the baby – at first. Around ten weeks after conception, a hormone bath occurs, and these tissues form into the specifically male or female sexual organs.

The tissue that becomes the most sensitive part for the male is the glans of the penis (the tip). For the girl, this same tissue is the clitoris. The labia minora in the girl are the same tissue that forms into the shaft of the penis in the boy. The scrotum for the boy is the same tissue as the labia majora in the girl.

This is an amazing design — celebrate it!

The coming together of these parts in marriage through sexual intercourse is the process we call sex and is more specifically referred to as intercourse. This leads to orgasm for the man. This orgasm releases the semen that includes millions of sperm, all with the mission to find the egg and fertilize it. After the sperm swim their way up the fallopian tube and find the egg, they then battle to break into the egg. Once one swimmer makes it in, life begins while the egg continues down the fallopian tube. It then implants on the wall of the uterus and settles in for the next forty weeks. While this is happening, the cells of the new life continue to multiply.

This process is a miracle. **You are a miracle.** Know the truth about your bodies and your design.

Should I add here a few words on abortion? I think I will. Based on what you just read, does life begin at conception or at birth (their entrance into the breathing world)? Life begins at the first cell division after conception – as soon as the egg is fertilized with the sperm. We acknowledge this same reality in all other aspects of life, creation, and even living things like bacteria. So, we must start with life being at conception. What does this mean for abortion? This is murder. I know I may be stepping on some toes here but bear with me.

You were fearfully and wonderfully made. So was every other child at conception – and they had no choice in the matter. It is our duty to protect that life. It is crazy to me how many in our world are furious over the murder of a puppy or some animal – and so few seem to come to the rescue of a baby. I promise that there are hundreds and probably even thousands of families that would LOVE to adopt that baby that has been TERMINATED. May we grow in our compassion towards those defenseless babies and see that there are better options – other than murder.

* * *

Working Questions – Now it is YOUR TURN:

Describe the basic male anatomy.

___

___

Describe the basic female anatomy.

Describe the "coming together" of the anatomy of men and women.

What is your stance on abortion? How do you back it up with Scripture? Science? Be honest here.

| 9 |

Birth to Age 5 - Going Beyond "The Talk"

Picture these kids and teens in the stories below and answer this question - what would you do and/or say? What should they already know that would have prevented these or changed the outcome? What would you have wanted to know?

Your 12-year-old son or daughter informs you that they now have a girlfriend or boyfriend. What do you do? What advice do you give them?

Your 15-year-old son informs you he has a boyfriend. How do you react? Now what?

You caught your ten-year-old son in the closet with a neighbor girl playing, "Show me yours, and I'll show you mine."

Your daughter is a tomboy and loves all things boy and comes home from school one day and begins dropping hints about wanting to start hormone blockers and begin transitioning to male.

Your 17-year-old son just found out he has a child on the way. His girlfriend is pregnant. He had great plans for college and beyond. Now what? What do you encourage him to do? What's your advice?

Your 15-year-old daughter calls you urgently, requesting that you come pick her up. You race over to an odd part of town and find out she just had an abortion, and the guys ditched her there. How do you respond? What would you want her to know?

These kids and teens SHOULD have been prepared for these situations. It is the responsibility of a parent to prepare you. Statistically though, most parents do not. Some attempt to have "The Talk." This "Talk" usually comes too late and is almost always uncomfortable since the family Ethos is to avoid these conversations. **The critical thing missing from many of the above examples is a Biblical worldview that informed their choices, provided boundaries, and set expectations that prepared them for difficult decisions, temptations, and struggles.**

In my survey of hundreds of American teens, I found that most received no thorough sex education at home and only a few had **"The Talk."**

Someone will be your first teacher. Who was yours? Who will yours be? And what will be the values and worldview that they share?

Is this true for you? **Do your parents know the truth about all that you have experienced sexually with the same or opposite sex?** For most families, there is a discrepancy between what the children or teenagers are doing and what the parents think their kids are doing.

One of my goals is to help prepare you and go beyond any kind of content that could be considered a part of any "Talk." Wisdom matters. Your choices are so important - now and for your future.

A mother and her two daughters were talking honestly about sex, or at least that's what their mother thought. She had no idea that her daughters were not telling the whole truth. Her oldest had just lost her virginity to a guy she thought loved her, but now wanted nothing to do with her, and her heart was broken. The sad reality is that this parent had prepared herself for **"The Talk,"** but it was now arriving too late. Many parents find themselves in these same shoes, thinking that by having "the talk", they have prepared their kids, but finding out later that their children were already educated and experienced. Their kids had never shared with them what was going on inside their hearts and outside the house.

We can minimize the above scenarios through getting educated from the right sources and NOT relying on the wrong ones - truly ignoring their data and input.

I want to talk to you now as if YOU were the parent. I want to prepare YOU to have these, what I have been calling, *micro-conversations,* so you see how important your education and preparation is at age-appropriate stages. Most parents believe that I recommend addressing these topics at TOO young of an age. You decide. Do we prepare, empower, and educate to help them make wise decisions? Or do we wait until we think they're ready and play it safe? I would rather be too early than too late.

You MUST be ahead of the curve if you want to be influential.

Imagine a new parent arriving home with their baby, and regardless of whether it is their first or tenth child, they begin by

"raising their child in the way he should go" (Proverbs 22:6, NKJV).

It Begins at Birth

When should we begin to teach our children? At birth. All of our education begins at birth. This section is for you to see that in these first five years, a child is investigating the world and absorbing everything around them. These years are a critical foundation for all that is to come. What happens, and what does not happen, in these years matters. Healthy touch matters. **Vocabulary and ethic building occurs, even if very little language is yet present.**

During this stage of life, children are absorbing the ***"ENERGY"* of the home and environment**. As a counselor and marriage and family therapist, and after years of working with college-age students, I have seen that **an ETHOS is developed at a younger age than we probably think or want to believe.**

Even if the mind does not remember trauma, our bodies certainly do. Traumatic events impact our mental health, and our physical health for years to come. It is staggering when you realize how much of our mental and physical health crises today are symptoms of the abuse, neglect, abandonment, and trauma we experienced and observed in our early years, even before we were school aged.

That *"ENERGY"* we absorb from birth to five matters.

It Is Rarely Too Early (and too often too late)

Most parents do nothing to prepare their child for the way their body will change, or how they will need to **steward** their sexuality. During the first five years of a child's life, these topics are often avoided, ignored, and suppressed because it embarrasses the **parents**.

Were yours? Did your parents go there? You probably do not remember this stage of your own life. That is okay. That is why this stage is so important. I hope you will change this with your children one day. But that is way down the road.

Our families are constantly teaching and sending an unintentional, but very specific, message — that this stuff is bad. Sex is bad. Our bodies — especially "those" parts — are bad. Desire is bad. This is setting an unfortunate precedent of **silence** for you during your teen years. If you struggle with dating, gender, sexual identity, friendships, or anything else, it is often because of a lack of intentional teaching in our early years.

What I hear from most parents is **fear**. They think you are not old enough for these types of *micro-conversations,* but I would ask them to reconsider. There will be a first time you see porn. Someone will have an explicit conversation with you. **How would you prefer to address these topics for the first time?**

What I hear from college-age students — those I have spent over a decade surveying in my Human Sexuality course at a Christian university — is that their parents weren't willing to "go there" or that they waited until it was too late.

Most students I have gathered research from state that they wish their parents had been a safe place to go for those hard conversations.

So why didn't these conversations happen?

The students wanted these conversations, but they **expected the parent to act** as an adult and approach the subject themselves, and not put the responsibility on the child or teenager.

Too many parents tell me, **"I've told my kids they can come to me if they have questions."**

Would you go to your parents and start a hard conversation about porn, sex, sexting, or dating? I hope you will if they are a safe source for you. Most teens refuse to go to their parents with questions. Honestly, I wish your parents would come to you.

I am proud of you for reading this far and excited about the foundation you are laying for yourself. May you be a safe source for others as you grow, mature, make hard decisions, and face temptations.

Age-Appropriate Depth

Can you imagine talking with a 4-year-old about sexuality? Do you have a cousin or sibling that age that can help you picture the problem? Most parents would say, "I can't go there with my child. They are way too young. I want to preserve their innocence as long as I can." I would ask them to reconsider the word choice of "innocence". Children are NOT incurring guilt or losing their innocence by knowing the names of their body parts, how their body is designed, or how the reproductive system works.

Why is this so important? The seeds are planted from birth by someone. Remember, you are a future dad or mom, husband or wife, lover, leader, and adult! The actions of our parents impact us. Who else has shaped your sexual ethic? This is why this is so important.

We must use every possible incident as a teaching moment. When my daughter was four, she stood up in the bathtub, grabbed herself, and called out, "When am I going to get a penis?" This was a very reasonable question when you consider that she has two older brothers. It was a perfect teachable moment. It only took a few seconds to instruct her regarding gender, the observable differences between boys and girls, and that she was perfect just as she was.

Parents need hundreds of these moments to shape you. But the question remains - who else is speaking into the shaping of a child and young person's sexual ethic?

Another time, my daughter kept telling us that her bottom hurt, which is normal with little girls. It took my wife and I a while to realize she was calling the front — her vulva area — her "bottom," since she did not have another word for this part of her body.

This is why the terms we use matter as well. **When we use nicknames for body parts instead of using the appropriate term, we potentially create shame around that part of the body.**

It is not healthy to be an adult and be unable to say the words "penis", "vagina," or "breasts,". However, many can't say these words without embarrassment because of how they were brought up. I want you to be able to speak confidently and correctly.

It is also beneficial to know the **proper terminology** for your body when you must speak to a doctor or if you ever have to speak to someone about a traumatic event. I want you protected and prepared.

Using events in life helps prepare kids. I know you are a teen (or preteen), but the process continues with you at your age. Events in life are means we can use - from scenes in movies, people we see on the street, and even our own bodies. During the formative years of birth to five years old, parents can use nudity to foster *micro-conversations.* If a son or daughter walks in on their parents while they are dressing or taking a shower, try not to not freak out. Responding carefully and closing the door without a big scene is very important. While changing clothes after swimming, it is a good idea NOT to make a big deal as you share a changing room and they briefly see you naked. Can this go too far? Definitely. Absolutely. Children seeing their parents or siblings in various stages of undress needs to be coupled with dignity, which is appropriate covering. Healthy behavior is caught and taught.

A child at this age is unconsciously processing their gender and gender roles during this time. It is more about the energy in the home than anything else, but every conversation influences who you become.

This is the crucial stage of life where your foundation is being poured and your future is being shaped by understanding the choices you have. Society has a big need for men that are strong, yet gentle; and women that are tender with incredible strength.

Being Proactive

You are not 5 years old anymore. This stage is too late. But it is never too late to learn new habits, gain new knowledge, and equip yourself to make better decisions going forward.

When my sons were this age, they often played a motocross video game. I would watch their eyes as each round started, looking for a change. Before each race began, the screen showed a busty girl, baring her midriff, holding up a sign. I was watching for the day it clicked in their minds that she was interesting. The day I saw their eyes linger we entered new depths of conversations. This is being **PROACTIVE**. You are well beyond this stage, yet the same thing applies. It is about stewardship of your eyes, ears, and heart.

Another critical reason you must be **PROACTIVE** is for your protection. Protection is not shielding you from pain, problems, and avoiding choices. The biggest reason for learning about healthy sexuality and God's design is because abuse happens. Bad things happen. Prepare yourself so you will know what to do. If you have faithfully equipped yourself prior to a potentially harmful situation, you will be more likely to default to a fight-or-flight response, rather than freezing.

A mistake many families make that compounds abuse is preparing for "stranger danger" when this only covers about **9%** of the abuse that occurs, leaving us vulnerable to the other **91%**.[32] Unfortunately, harm, if it comes, will most likely come from a trusted family member, friend, or confidant that you would never suspect. Be prepared to yell "NO," kick, bite, and scream. It is so important to know what appropriate behavior is, and what behavior crosses the lines. Rehearsing scenarios can help strengthen this muscle we hope you will never need.

When our kids were younger, we had a lot of babysitters from the local Christian college that I worked at. After we returned home from a date night, we regularly asked them what they had done while the sitter was there — whether they had bathed them, changed their clothes, etc. We knew that the kids most likely would not tell us if something had happened, but we were looking for a change in how they answered — a subtle shift. How would we know, though? We would recognize this subtle shift because we knew what a normal response was, and the kids thought it was normal to be asked these questions.

I do not want you to remain "innocent." So many families I talk to are stuck HERE. None of us are innocent, and the real world demands intentional preparation. I am proud of you for reading this and making this a priority in your development.

Do you believe subconsciously — or consciously — that the sexual part of your body is dirty or bad, and that to understand how your body works and how to protect it is a sinful practice? I hope not.

It would be a great exercise for us all to look at our own beliefs about sexuality and determine why we avoid topics surrounding sexuality unless they are jokes and memes.

I want to urge you to consider that an understanding of sexuality and making wise choices from a Biblical Sexual Ethic will set you up for success and influence generations. The seed of this success began early — before you were of school age — when you were absorbing the **energy** and values of your home and world you lived in.

* * *

Working Questions – Now it is YOUR TURN:

Someone will be our first teacher. Who was yours? Who will yours be? And what will be the values and worldview that they share?

Do your parents know the truth about all that you have experienced sexually with the same or opposite sex?

Look for opportunities to have micro-conversations with your parents over the next few days about some or all of the following topics: nudity, boundaries, pornography, boyfriends/girlfriends, marriage, anatomy, and attraction. How could you bring up the topic?

Imagine a new parent arriving home with their baby, and regardless of whether it is their first or tenth child, they begin by

"raising their child in the way he should go" (Proverbs 22:6, NKJV).

What does this mean?

____

____

Someone will have an explicit conversation with you. Who do you think should be the first person to address these topics with you?

____

____

Would you go to your parents and start a hard conversation about porn, sex, sexting or dating?

____

____

| 10 |

Kinder to Elementary (6-10) - Going Beyond "The Talk"

Kinder to Elementary Age (6-10)

You might read this and be at the upper end of this age range. Good for you. This will be life changing. Dive in and **learn, learn, learn.**

What changed for you and others at around the age of 6 or 7? Awareness. New and more detailed questions. This is reality. It is important that we stay ahead of these. The sexual part of who we are is developing. Exposure to videos and even unhealthy experiences are a reality. Your preparation and a deepening of your understanding is even more important.

From about the ages of 6 or 7 through 10 or 11, you are absorbing the *"CULTURE"* of your home, and the world around you.

You have been absorbing the ***ENERGY*** of your home since birth, but somewhere around age of 6 or 7 a shift happens and with more maturity, experience, and understanding, your family's ***CULTURE*** becomes the focal point.

In the earlier stages of this age range, your vocabulary was growing by leaps and bounds. Your opinions and personalities are not only being formed, but already becoming more solidified.

A big question here is, would you rather be ready for what's coming or be blindsided? I want you to be ready. I want you to know how to face temptations and also have already wrestled with your beliefs and what you would do ahead of time. When this work is done ahead of time, your decisions are almost automatic in the face of struggles or temptations.

Do you remember when you were 8 years old? Imagine an eight-year-old full of life and energy, and his personality is being established. He is changing almost daily as his body prepares for puberty and his mind shifts its focus onto attractions and desires.

Can you believe it? The average age a child in America views pornography is!

Did you? Have you already? I hope not. But if so, hang in there and keep reading. I hope this transforms your heart, your life, and your future.

I know you are probably not surprised to hear that most of the parents I talk to believe and say that their child is the exception. I then talk to their children in college, and those parents were wrong. Their children were the norm — hiding behind shame, afraid of being exposed, living in fear, and living full of **desire gone mad** - another way to understand the word, "lust."[33]

Are you prepared to face your first exposure to a naked picture on a screen? What about a video (this is even more impactful and scarring)?

If you are a young lady, are you ready to see those images as you process where you are at in comparison? This can be a terrifying time.

Do you have safe people to talk to? You will turn somewhere for answers - will it be to a safe person, friends, porn, or even the internet via chatrooms and forums? If your parents are safe, I highly recommend approaching them first. I know, I know - it sounds scary - I also wish (as you probably do) that they would have the courage to come to you first. But, if they will not, you can still go to them. Take the risk. At minimum though - you have me via this book and through the online videos and resources I have provided for you to walk you through this life stage. You are NOT alone.

This Is the Most Crucial Age That Gets Missed

Have you ever wanted to ignore, delete, deny the existence of, or never address the truth that God made you as a sexual being? Did you know that you can already get a girl pregnant or become pregnant if you are a girl, right? The keyword we must remember is **stewardship.**

This is why you MUST be prepared. I would even dare say this is a responsibility you and I have towards everyone - to be good stewards of the power we have as sexual beings. This separates us from those living by a different ethic that is self-centered and reckless.

Between the ages of 6 to 10, most kids and preteens are looking for answers — and they are ready for those to be blunt and explicit (with very few exceptions). I have the honor of inviting you into some tough topics and areas you will need to wrestle with that are uncomfortable for most of us. This is about helping you form your belief system about sex, sexuality, gender, and your body.

This is NOT about making you more knowledgeable and self-aware so you can do things you shouldn't or gain more experiences. **This is about building your ETHOS so you can set up your own boundaries and live wisely.**

Our family's and churches preach silence. While the world is speaking loud and clear through movies, music, online videos, and social media about its beliefs on these things. They are not shying away. Why are we? Let's not be silent anymore. Let's be loud and clear about God's design for our lives.

There are key areas that should be explored during this formative stage. Remember, you will soon be a young man or young woman and what you believe will influence what you do.

Use the correct terms. Call a penis a penis. Call the vagina and vulva just that. It is very important that you have a clear understanding about masturbation.

In the Human Sexuality course that I teach at a university, I present a 3 hour "Theology of Masturbation" lecture. It is THAT important. Are you ready? Do you feel prepared for what you are about to feel, desire, and obsess about? I address each of these in the upcoming chapters.

This is the time in your life that questions abound, and learning will come from somewhere - and the source can truly be life changing. Who you learn about these things from, and the shaping of your ETHOS directs your current and upcoming steps?

We need to focus on a thorough understanding of anatomy during these years — as well as what is about to change in your body and in the body of the opposite gender.

Are you prepared to face the onslaught of sexual images that you probably have already noticed at the check-out stands, in entertainment, and from people you pass on the street? Do you feel shame surrounding your "covered" boy parts (genitals)? Remember that it is about dignity and modesty. These are not "dirty" words. God is the designer and the creator. He does NOT make mistakes.

This may seem premature, but it is crucial NOW to **establish a foundation regarding dating.** What are the guidelines and expectations of boyfriend/girlfriend relationships? Your parents probably have their views and opinions. Have they expressed these already? If they are safe people to talk to, ask them for their guidance. Making decisions now about the opposite sex and dating saves you from a ton of heartache and potential pain in your teen years.

Your knowledge of the real world and about abuse is imperative — knowing the real world we live in can save you. There is evil in the world, and not everyone has your best interest at heart. You have the right and power to say "NO," and to stand up for yourself. Be prepared to fight back.

Another big issue you might face if you are between the ages of six and ten is **learning to overcome disappointment and rejection.** It is so much better for you to face small hurts now and learn to cope than be overprotected from consequences and rendered incapable of facing bigger hurts later in life.

One of the biggest questions and areas of concern for many in this stage of life has now become that of **sexual identity.** Who am I attracted to? What do I do with these feelings? Is this right? Good? Okay? Biblical? Will I ever be loved or accepted or find that one person?

I know that it seems like it is too soon. It is not though when you consider the culture and time we live in.

You want this ETHOS in YOUR heart before you make decisions with your body.

I want you to have an ETHOS that is so settled and committed that it is a no-brainer when you have to make a decision.

There Is No Such Thing As "The Talk"

Have your parents given you "the talk" yet? This is a one-time lecture that gives you all the information you will need to transition from child to adult – all about the birds and the bees and answers to all your questions in one fell swoop.

In my work with young adults and teenagers I see a theme – and it is that most of their parents' report that they have had this conversation with their children, but their children (those I am surveying) say, "My parents never talked to me about sex."

Obviously, there is a disconnect here. One awkward evening will not open up the doors of conversation.

My recommendation is to begin at birth and have constant, continual *micro-conversations* so that our kids can say, "My parents were always talking to me about sex." This is a win. This book is my attempt to do that for you - plant seeds to prepare you well for your future.

I recommend parents go down this path often. Discuss marriage actively. Use stories you've heard, scenes in movies or TV shows, and occurrences around your own home to be introductions into teaching, training, and preparing their children to choose a Biblical Sexual Ethic for themselves.

Between the ages of six and ten, you are on a fact-finding mission about the world.

Boundaries become even more important at this developmental stage. I encourage you to **use the workbook that follows each chapter** and walk through each section and ask questions. Read Scripture passages aimed to encourage you, challenge you, and strengthen your resolve to live from a Biblical Sexual Ethic. No one can make you do this. It has to come from you. It is truly a work of God in your life.

One thing I know to be true is that it is more than likely true that you have seen pornography. I bet you are noticing gender differences, your body and its changes, others' bodies, and new desires. You are being told by culture and well-meaning friends and family that the expectation is to have a boyfriend or girlfriend. **This is saddening to me. I want to help reframe these. They are all areas that will still require you to decide - but let's shape how that plays out together.**

I want to set the stage for you by discussing dating, the opposite sex, and attraction ahead of time — preferably before you are even interested.

Do you already feel a pressure to date? Many feel that pressure even before the ages of thirteen or fourteen. I want something different for you — something better. I want to put you in the driver's seat. Don't let others tell you what you should or should not do, or experience. Again, be very careful who you listen to and whom you follow. This shapes everything for you and your future.

* * *

Working Questions – Now it is YOUR TURN:

Would you rather be ready for what's coming – or be blindsided?

____

____

Are you prepared to face your first exposure to a naked picture on a screen? What about a video?

____

____

If you have already seen these (and most likely you have), what happened inside of you? Body response? Emotional response? Questions? Was it confusing? Were you fearful? Or were you more afraid of getting caught?

____

____

____

What is "Desire gone mad"?

____

____

Explain the difference between "the talk" and micro- conversations.

Do you already feel a pressure to date?

| 11 |

Crucial Talking Points with your 6-10 Year Old

Crucial Talking Points (6-10 years old)

Have you been intentionally trained on how a young man should talk about women? About their clothing, their bodies, their beauty, their sexuality, their minds, their hearts, or their souls?

Do you have a Biblical Sexual Ethic on boundaries?

Who are your role models in terms of examples of how they treat their wife, mother, and other women?

As a young woman, do you understand boys - and the difference between a boy and a real man? Do you know much about the fragility of the male ego, their insecurities, their lusts, their desires, their boundaries, their bodies, their differences, their sexuality, their minds, their hearts, or their souls?

What have you learned at home about the roles of men and women?

Here are some critical talking points for us to use in the beginning. This is not exhaustive, but it is a start in the right direction. You are smarter than you realize, and I never want to minimize your intelligence.

Every child at this age is watching and absorbing their home's **energy** and **culture**. This forms the foundation for all that is to come in their future desires, compulsions, and obsessions.

Here we are laying the foundation for future learning and conversations. Others are also planting seeds along your developmental journey.

Topics for Developing Your ETHOS:

BOYFRIEND / GIRLFRIEND

Be intentional about developing a framework NOW regarding how to think about dating relationships - the do's and don'ts, expectations, limits, and standards.

What is the purpose of dating?

What does boyfriend / girlfriend mean? At what age would it be okay to use these words?

What are the differences between attraction, desire, and lust?

How can I manage these weird feelings?

Can you set limits and stick to them?

Do you feel prepared to question a culture that deems you broken or same-sex attracted if you do not lose your virginity in your teens?

Do you see dating as a fun activity best done in groups, and that there is NO NEED for singling out one individual to date until you have a job and your own money and car? Your parents should not be funding your dating life.

FYI - You do not need to date until you are mature enough to be responsible for someone else's heart and the baby that might be on the way when you date at a young age. This is too often the reality. Be prepared.

I want to inspire you with a desire for a marriage that will go the distance — a marriage filled with laughter and joy and also prepared to endure during the hard times.

When I was seven years old, my family was living in Costa Rica attending language school as we prepared as a family to be missionaries in South America. My mother went into emergency surgery and came out of surgery with a mastectomy (she had her breast removed). The doctors had discovered cancer, and it was war — for her life. I watched my father love my mother through radiation and chemotherapy. Watching my dad serve her through this was a tremendous example to me of what love should be. Over ten years later, when they went down the same road with a cancer battle again, his commitment and service continued to solidify the type of husband I wanted to be and this helped me to clarify what was truly important in a future wife.

MORE DESCRIPTIVE ANATOMY LESSON

You need to have a good grasp of basic anatomy.

You need to understand the human reproductive system, so you know the effects of bringing a penis and vagina together and when this is okay.

You need to know the "whys" and "why nots" of sexual activities before your hormones are raging and your decision making becomes further impaired.

Do you see beauty in your own body and the bodies of the opposite sex? Do you see how God created you, each unique and with purpose?

With this knowledge you can then become protectors and leaders of a healthy sexual ethic. As you live among peers that have a very different sexual ethic, I hope that you will treat others respectfully and show yourself to be a young person of honor.

It is important for both young ladies and young men to understand menstruation. Ladies especially need to know what to expect and what products are available to them. **Young men need to know that this is NOT something to tease a girl about and how to react when a female peer has a clothing issue during their period.**

It is critical to have the skills to know how to process visual stimulation that is arousing by normalizing it. Your thoughts and feelings should NEVER be your guide — this is usually unreliable data.

A key goal here is NOT just your actions, but your heart. If your heart is not changed, your behaviors will not last and will be more for show - for others - and not endure through times of testing.

THE "M" WORD

This is a real dilemma. My first word of advice is NOT to fuel shame.

Almost all boys — and even many girls — will engage in this behavior.

Be careful to refrain from pure judgment about this topic and to read on. We cover this subject in greater detail in chapter 20.

BOUNDARIES

At this age, it is so important to set your own boundaries. Being part of a family invites this continual activity. Conflicts between siblings and parents require the implementation of boundaries.

Do you see the setting of a boundary as an unloving act? Choosing these consciously puts you in control. When this activity is operating in the background of our minds — like an operating system — it is less helpful.

The goal is to bring this out into the open through dialogue with someone you can trust. The better you know your boundaries and the "why" behind them, the more assertive you can be at enforcing them and limit them from being crossed without your permission.

A key skill - to move your unconscious reactions to the forefront of their thoughts. It is amazing how this process can change everything in our decision-making routines.

Boundaries are a matter of self-care and an aid to prevent abuse.

Boundaries matter in all relationships: family, friends, dating, marriage, and even business. These will become a source of freedom, not constraint as others see them.

PORNOGRAPHY

I know it seems too early to address pornography, **but it is not.** When my middle son was seven years old, I took him with me to a presentation I did for a Young Life group of teen boys. The topic was porn. It was an incredible two hours full of honest and vulnerable discussion, which is not normal. It was a refreshing evening. As my son and I drove home, I asked him, "So, do you have questions about what we discussed?" His reply was, "I had NO IDEA what you guys were talking about." I probed more, since it is my job to be proactive, and saw that he was in a good place.

At age 10, he often attended classes I taught on the subject. We still discuss pornography at the dinner table, and it comes up almost every day in some form or fashion. It is a normal point of conversation.

In my family, my wife and I want to have talked about this so much that they have an almost automatic reaction when the door to porn opens so they can close it. The key is to continually verbally point things out. Keep things out of the operating system - the unconscious - and be sure intentional choice is the default. When faced with temptation, we want them to expose it and talk about it.

Do you see why pornography is damaging to your future selves? No one can protect you forever. There are great resources available like filters and trying to avoid all screens, but this only protects you if you are at home and on your monitored devices and networks. If you really want to "go there" plenty of options and temptations abound.

What will happen when a friend or cousin visits from school or church and has their own device? What about when you attend a sports or band camp — or church camp — and that door swings wide open? **The goal is that you know how to process the feelings and curiosity when temptation comes and can quickly respond with a "no thanks," and turn away from the screen.**

Pornography works. It sucks its consumer in because we are naturally and healthily drawn to nudity and beauty. This part is not a mistake - it is just not the means with God's design. **Create an ethic and ETHOS that is redemptive and not punitive.**

FYI - Remind yourself that each person in those videos and pictures has a story. They are real people, and most of them are being exploited and abused. For many of the "porn stars," this is a step up from the rough life they were brought up in, and they hope it will be a means of escape. This ought to be heartbreaking. I encourage you as you mature to learn more about the terrifying reality of human trafficking. I'd encourage you to get involved as a family in helping prevent and/or support efforts of organizations aimed at eradicating this gross exploitation of fellow humans from all walks of life.

Remember that the door to pornography, once opened, can rarely be shut permanently. I've often wondered why God chooses NOT to remove this temptation ten or twenty years down the road, and I believe that it serves as a reminder of our humanity and the need for a Savior. We cannot do this alone.

If you have opened this door — and the average age is between six and ten — tell someone and begin removing the power of temptation and ritual by talking about it to a safe person. You do not need shame unless you continue living and leaning into this temptation. Shame is meant to bring us to repentance. We cannot remain there for long and be okay. The voice of the enemy is already at work in your heart, telling you that you are dirty, broken, and irredeemable — that no one will look past this. That will need to be addressed separately. Prepare yourself for the REAL world that includes twists and distortions of God's best and God's perfect design that are lies from Satan, all about the here and now, and all about you. Run from these. Know how to recognize them and flee. May you NOT be deceived.

SEXUAL IDENTITY

This is probably not foreign to you. I am sure you know peers that have struggles with their sexual identity. Boys and girls ages six to ten are questioning their gender identity because they hear what others say about them and they believe what they hear. We must pay attention as these questions are processed internally and traumatic. You may not know that someone is struggling when they are dealing with it privately. This could also be your story. Stay tuned here.

I truly believe the goal is to paint a realistic picture of masculinity and femininity that does not tie activities with gender stereotypes to gender. **It is so important to understand that your biological sex isn't tied to the activities you enjoy or your personality traits.** The longer you and your friends linger on questions of identity, the more you will question everything. I promise. It gets stuck in the operating system - the unconscious - and the thoughts can become obsessive.

I personally know the battle of this one. I was an awkward preteen boy that loved pink and crocheting with my grandmother. I valued time with people and preferred long, deep conversations over watching sports. I still do. I loved music and played several instruments. This led to a lot of confusion as I was told that the things I enjoyed were for girls.

So many boys and girls battle with similar feelings and struggle as they clash with their values, morals, and beliefs. This causes even more distress.

Many today will tell you to claim a new identity — emphasizing whatever you feel.

Others will tell you to fight these feelings and suppress them.

For some children, preteens and teens, this confusion often centers on attraction to the same sex and they are wondering what they should do with these feelings. For others, it is a personality quirk. This may become a battle for some as they get older and wonder why they have never had a date or even wanted to go out with someone of the opposite sex. This is real.

Many, many, many preteens and teens will question their sexual identity. Most will settle it quietly and without worry or concern. Some will struggle. These emotions and thoughts will severely affect many, though.

May you take these out of your mind — out of the dark (your unconscious) — and process them out loud. You may not want to talk to your parents about this either, but if they are safe, I hope you will. Another option is to seek a trusted mentor and friend with a similar Biblical Sexual Ethic that is willing to listen, have these hard conversations, and offer guidance.

There are some great books available written for you on this subject to help you navigate these troubled waters. Do not do this alone. Seek counseling from a trusted, trained Christian counselor that works from a Biblical Sexual Ethic. Become knowledgeable by reading the work of those committed to a Biblical Sexual Ethic or attending conferences or lectures. I highly recommend resources from Godly examples such as **Mark Yarhouse,**[34] **Preston Sprinkle,**[35] and **Wesley Hill.**[36]

Remember that this is an honest and real struggle.

We need to be careful that we don't minimize your or your friends' questions and the draw of our attractions.

I have found that a powerful tactic is to lean into the feeling and follow its natural progression rather than trying to ignore it. This sounds counterintuitive. Exactly. Listen to that narrative and ask lots of "and then what" type questions to help yourself or your friend decide if this is truly a path you or they want to go down. Then talk through alternatives to just the initial gut path. This allows you and I to see that there are many paths, and it is not always a simple answer. It is complicated. Allow it to be complicated. Be patient with yourself and others.

If this is you, keep reading. If this is a friend of yours, keep reading. Remember that in all we do, **we are loving them with the long**

game in sight. We want to build bridges and continue in dialogue and influence. We may not see fruit today or in the next twenty years. This is a sobering reality. Love your friend - patiently.

I encourage you to always seek God's will for yourself by knowing His word. Separate fact from feelings and identify thoughts that are intrusive so you can consciously and intentionally decide for yourself. I know this sounds like we are talking about a twenty-year-old, but I have had conversations with parents whose children are between the ages of six to ten and are questioning themselves, and their attractions and desires at this tender age. It happens all too often. Go back to God's Word and His design for answers.

DIGNITY / MODESTY

What is your reaction to the word modesty? Do you get defensive? Do you have no opinion? This is a critical area that gets a lot of reactions from all sides. We are all learning about modesty and dignity every day from those we live with, what we watch, and how things are talked about and modeled.

Let me give you a weird example. We have an Alaskan Malamute that lives in our house. It is wild seeing this monstrous dog all over the house. He is huge. And the hair — it's everywhere! He has free rein in the house, but he never attempts to get on the furniture. The closest he ever gets is to raise a paw from a sitting position. Why? When he was a puppy, we always played with him on the floor. We sat on the floor. We never picked him up and allowed him on the bed or furniture. He is bigger now and could hurdle the length of the couch, but we trained him. **This is what I wish for you. Your future decision-**

making framework can be intentionally shaped. It is being embedded day in and day out from birth.

I want you to learn to honor others - and yourselves — this is dignity.

Modesty reflects the heart.

The impact of ALL your decisions affects you and others - including your clothing choices. This is where modesty comes in.

Young men - be respectful regardless of what a girl is wearing. Period!

Young ladies - it is important to think about what you wear and why you wear it when you are young.

Young men - you are fully responsible for your actions, thoughts, and eyes.

Young ladies - honor yourself and your brothers with your choice of clothing. This is dignity. This is not popular, but still important. Each family chooses how they define dignity and modesty to their children. Remember that dignity is covering out of care, not prudishness. This is countercultural.

ABUSE / TRAUMA

I SO hope you are not someone that has experienced abuse or trauma. Most families will deal with abuse and trauma in their lives. Abuse and trauma happens to all kinds of families and people. The best parents, even those that are aware and involved, will miss something.

Harm comes in all shapes and sizes, and that is why it is sometimes missed.

Can I give you a key? It is preparation to recognize, voice, and know what to do. You do this by having a voice. By gaining tools. The awareness that even trusted people may not always do good things is important. This is a hard concept to grasp. **I want to help you here by planting seeds.** It is important that you learn the skills to fight or flee, so you don't freeze when faced with danger. This is solidified through practice. Know what to do. Otherwise, trauma finds its way in more easily.

Be prepared to say, "NO."

Be prepared to have the awareness to see potential harm and flee.

Be prepared to stand up for yourself and others.

Fear is a terrifying emotion for most of us.

It is important to learn how to use that energy towards efforts of exposing and rescuing — not silence.

Can I tell you a secret? One reason many of our parents miss things is because of their own story. Be patient with them.

If you address your personal story, abuse and/or trauma, you will find yourself more intuitive and more aware of other's intentions. I find that many of us are reactive, undiscerning, and unknowingly contribute to the trauma of others because of our inability to listen, be patient, and not judge. **I encourage you as strongly as I can to seek help and healing for yourself so you can be fully available to others.**

These are weighty matters, but I already feel you are in a much better place than you were before. Now, what about when you are older than 11? What should be done then? Many families have a child older than 11, and they have never addressed the above topics.

* * *

Working Questions – Now it is YOUR TURN:

Do you have a Biblical Sexual Ethic on boundaries?

____

____

Who are your role models in terms of examples of how they treat their wife, mother, and other women?

____

____

As a young woman, do you understand boys - and the difference between boys and a real man? Do you know much about the fragility of the male ego, their insecurities, their lusts and desires, boundaries, bodies, differences, sexuality, minds, hearts, and souls?

____

____

What have you learned at home about the roles of men and women?

____

____

What is your ETHOS for dating and boyfriend/girlfriend relationships?

____

____

What is the purpose of dating?

____

____

Do you see the setting of a boundary as an unloving act?

____

____

How can you be careful and sensitive to the navigation of sexual identity, which can be a struggle for some?

____

____

What is your reaction to the word modesty? Do you get defensive? Do you have no opinion? What is dignity / modesty? Is it important?

____

____

| 12 |

Middle School to High School (11-17) - Going Beyond "The Talk"

Middle School to High School (11-17)

Do you want your independence? Now maybe? Absolutely YES? Even if you are thinking NO, you will want it soon enough. This is a normal thing to want. I have seen **independence** as a major priority to most preteen and teen boys and girls. This changes all relationships, choices, temptations, and more.

If you enter your teen years with complete freedom and zero boundaries, there is a tremendous risk to you, your future, and society at large. Entering the teen years without the freedom to expand, experiment, and grow, you will also suffer tremendous consequences which, ironically, are often the same as the young person who had no boundaries. That is why this is so important.

What did you as a baby and toddler need most? You needed complete care and oversight, which was exhausting for your parents. By the time you reach eleven years old, you can do most things for yourself and can be a great help to your family. Some preteens and teens embrace this independence and are ready to move out as soon as they can. I sure hope you are not the one that wants to linger in childhood and practically insists that you are incapable of meaningful work and will never leave home. This is not the goal.

Do you know what the key is for parents? It is changing the way they parent when a preteen enters this life stage. Many parents cannot recognize and adjust with their maturing child and their needs. What do you need? **You need more freedom and space to make choices, but remember, this is up to your parents, not me.**

I tell parents all the time that by the time their son or daughter reaches the age of ten to twelve, their job as a parent (as they know it) is over. You're welcome. This is a strong statement and a bit of an exaggeration, but if parents do not shift in their approach to their children by this age, in how they interact with them, guide them, and empower them, **rebellion is imminent.** Let's avoid that.

Adolescence does not have to be the nightmare many make it out to be. This stage of life is called the "**Age of Opportunity**" by **Paul David Tripp.**[37] Do you believe that? I hope so. This can be a great time in your life. It can be full of new adventures. It can even be a time of good relationships with your parents - and yes - even your siblings.

There are two key reasons adolescence can be so frustrating and NOT be an "age of opportunity":

First, parents parent their teenager like they did when they were a nine-year-old. Is that your parent?

Second, you are not prepared for this stage. In the pre-teen and teen years, you are seeing the fruits of the person you are. Let this be exciting. I hope it is.

That is what this book is all about - your preparation for your growth - and protection. It is never too late. **God is a God who is a redeemer.** Rest in this truth.

What we will look at next are key areas that are SO critical for your development. I hope this time in your life can be a great one for you. It can be a tough one for some (but it doesn't have to be).

Puberty, Dating, Gender, and Sexuality

Attention! What has your attention? What do you spend your time on? Focus. Down time. Wasting time. Compulsions. What takes your time away, whether intentionally or unintentionally? Many of the habits you put into place now will be carried with you into your adult life. Be aware of this.

How are you learning about what it means to be a man, woman, husband, wife, employee, friend, listener, steward, giver, and child of God? Who are your teachers of these roles and identities?

Your age now as a preteen or teen invites a whole new world of learning, testing, growing, and forward movement. Those things that demand, captivate, and/or grab our attention matter.

By the age of eleven, most of your programming and beliefs are already set in place in your heart. If you have been loaded down with too high of a demand, this sets you up for a fall. If you have had limitations placed on your experiences, exposure, and have too much free time, this sets you up to fail. Do you see the theme here? Either way, you face a struggle. I want to expect more from you! I want you to expect more from yourself.

Puberty has either arrived or will come soon. Are you prepared for those changes? I want you to enter this stage without fear and with anticipation. Are you ready to be a young man or woman that will steward your body, sexuality, and gender well? I hope so. I want you to be.

A key for your success will be the confidence you gain to become a leader among your peer group. It is natural at your age to pull away from your family. **This can be an amazing age of opportunity or a nightmare.** A lot of this will depend on your choices and your ethics.

This is KEY: Your dating standards, rules, and biblical sexual ethic MUST already be in place by your preteen years. It is so important that you know what you believe and what to expect - from yourself and from others. It is also important for you to work things out. This will be a critical foundation.

What kind of husband or wife do you desire to have one day? This sounds like a crazy question, but it is so important. Your picture of that person is being formed even today.

The media (movies, YouTube, and social media) will have a stronger influence on you than you probably realize. Does this scare you? It should. This is why this is so important. Ironically, this is the age that most parents are beginning these conversations ("The Talk") — and this is way too late.

Young men - your masculinity matters. You are a male. How you use, express, and live out your masculinity is as different and unique as you are. It is so important to be the man that God created you to be - especially when your masculinity is challenged by your peers or society.

Young women - your femininity matters. You are a female. How you use, express, and live out your femininity matters. You are unique. It is so important to have permission to feel in your own way, express yourself, find yourself, and become the woman that God created you to be.

A key to being the best YOU is **stewardship**. It is important to have clear guidance and boundaries when it comes to who you are, what you will and will not do, your gender, its expression, and knowing your limitations. It is also important to know that you are loved and cared for. Others will have potentially different ways they live out their masculinity or femininity. That is okay. The better you know yourself, the easier it will be to know who you are, as a male or female, and be able to say NO as needed.

You doing the intentional work now, at this stage of your life and development, can lead to an amazing time of growth and maturity. This sets you up for an incredible future.

This means that the teams you play on and how you are treated or mistreated, led, coached, and taught, all matter. The experiences you have at youth group, in school, and in other extracurricular activities matter. Signing up for activities because of peer pressure and expectations is not being intentional. Be careful with this temptation. Be intentional at who you look up to, listen to, and allow to invest in you. Some plant great seeds, others plant doubt, disgust, and despair.

Many families invest heavily into a sport to get a scholarship to college. I understand the parents' thoughts. However, many college students that I talk to share that there were other costs along the way. For many, locker room talks, and the stress of competition shaped their ideas of masculinity and femininity. This led them into eating disorders, promiscuous sexual behaviors, and a loss of other enjoyable activities.

Be intentional and thoughtful about why you are investing time in any activity and what the desired outcome truly is.

Social Media and Technology

I am often asked by parents, **"How do we handle social media and technology with our children?"** Do your parents keep up with technology? Most parents can't seem to keep up. This can quickly lead to a disconnect between you and your parents. This reality also leads to easily deceiving your parents and doing things that are unwise.

I have found that if I think of a smartphone (for example) as a tool and not as a toy, it helps me to put it in its rightful place. It is a TOOL.

Tools can be a great asset to our life. They can make our work quicker and more efficient. They can also cause a great deal of harm if we misuse them. I do not want to get into the weeds of which device is better or which filters will keep you safe. By the time this book is in your hands, that information will be outdated. The purpose and goal here is to give a gentle reminder and some pointers on the wisdom of boundaries. It is important to not play into the hands of marketers and peer pressure about what you must have and how you should use these tools.

Your parents felt like they had arrived at adulthood on a key day in their life - the day they got their driver's license.

Today, the new sign of being grown up is - wait for it - having a smartphone. And just like how a driver's license puts us behind the wheel of a powerful machine, the smartphone puts the world — the good and the bad — at our fingertips. Researchers are now reporting more and more ways that smartphones and other forms of technology are detrimental to our brains.

This is very important to know, remember, and heed. Online tools have minimum ages. Don't lie to get access. I'd even dare say that those ages are minimums, and it may be prudent to wait a few years before beginning to use many of them. Why? They are built to suck you in and take over. They are made to be like a slot machine that gives small doses of excitement with bells and whistles through likes, hearts, shares, and follows that hit the dopamine button and keep us coming back for more. They become an overwhelming temptation. Use wisdom here. I have found that many Christian families lie about their children's birth year to give them access to tools they are not ready to have. This is flat out damaging.

I want you, as a teenager, to have the ability, willpower, and wisdom to decide what you need access to — and when. Know "why" and "why not."

I have known many adolescents who were forbidden access and kept completely away from all forms of technology until they were 18. This does NOT play out well. I want you to learn **stewardship**. This empowers you to have boundaries in the future.

One way I have seen actual harm is in how friends at your age interact around topics they enjoy — video games, movies, smartphone games, and other forms of technology. I have found that when teens do not have the vocabulary or knowledge to engage with those around them, they often feel isolated, are made fun of, or ignored. On the flip side, though, many young people are harmed by bullying via text, a social media post, an email, a video that disappears, or, sometimes, all of the above. There is potential danger on both sides of this equation. **Be smart. Be aware. Be vigilant.** FYI - your independence is closer than you realize.

What you watch, whether while streaming a video or watching a movie, are key opportunities to have great *micro-conversations* with your parents or peers. Learn from these. Pay attention to how certain scenes make you feel inside. Is it wise to keep watching? Curiosity or intrigue are not enough reasons to continue. Is it wise? Use stories and things that happened between the characters as points of conversations to grow and ask hard questions. Technology is a great tool to continue to prepare and build yourself into the young adult God wants you to be. But boundaries are imperative. These will influence and shape your ETHOS. Your ETHOS leads you in how you make decisions, establish boundaries with movies and other content, and what you allow in through your eyes and ears. You have way more control and power here than most parents want to admit. Be a good **steward**.

Stewardship and Your Heart

Picture yourself as a young adult. You are all grown up. You are out on your own, or in college. What are the decisions you are now facing? What are the pressures and temptations you fight against?

The key word for success is "stewardship."

YOU are responsible. Every family is different and has a different set of rules. You are supposed to separate from your family and launch into the real world soon. When you do this is often dictated by your family. How you do this is up to you. Again, it is **stewardship**. No one else can manage your choices and the consequences. These are up to you.

Your responsibility has been increasing over the years. What I want to see for you is not just a bunch of good choices and good behaviors. These are great. But I want to see your heart transformed. Part of the evidence of this transformation is in your ETHOS - your belief system. This is played out in the recesses of your mind and heart, as you navigate big decisions, attractions, and temptations.

As you mature, your attractions naturally grow. Your sexuality, hormones, and feelings become a force to be reckoned with. Masturbation, pornography, and other forms of escape become even more enticing and alluring. Every decision you make impacts your future.

This book provides guardrails that keep you on the road. As you first start driving, you may hit the shoulder and come up against that guardrail. Over time, though, you can drive safely down the road, thankful that the guardrails were in place when you were learning but are not something you depend on daily to stay on the road. This day will come sooner for some than others, but we are all individuals and mature at our own pace.

What if you became a leader that helped others make wise decisions and overcome past choices and traumas?

What if you encouraged others to lead a life that honored the God of the Bible? This would be incredible. I set this dream before you. You can be a huge change agent in the lives of those around you. Everyone influences someone.

May you model redemptive speech in your conversations with others (even your parents). May you speak with compassion to others. May you steward your sexuality, treating others with respect. This will allow you to stand out in the crowd and provide an opportunity to share with others about a God who loves them and designed them with a purpose.

* * *

Working Questions – Now it is YOUR TURN:

What is the "Age of Opportunity?"

____

____

How do you spend your free time?

____

____

How would you describe the husband or wife that you want to be one day?

____

____

How would you describe the husband or wife that you want to marry one day?

____

____

What is important to you (in the future) in the raising of a son and his masculinity?

____

____

What is important to you (in the future) in the raising of a daughter and her femininity?

____

____

How can you model discipline, wisdom, and integrity in your interactions through social media?

____

____

What boundaries do you think ought to be in place to help you be wise with social media and technology?

____

____

Define stewardship.

____

____

Do you want to be a leader that helps others make wise decisions and overcome past choices and traumas? How can you encourage others to lead a life that honors the God of the Bible?

____

____

| 13 |

You Were Created as Male OR Female - Questions About Gender

Questions About Gender

Do you think there was ever a time that it was easy to deal with questions about sexuality and gender? I don't think those days ever existed. You may remember a time when the church and even the culture were not forgiving, gracious, or understanding with someone that was fighting internal battles over their gender and attractions. These are real fights. Today, these battles are still fought internally, but those fighting are encouraged to go public with their battle or give up on the battle altogether. In modern society, men and women are encouraged to surrender to whatever feeling is strongest at the moment and claim that as an identity.

I feel like I have a responsibility to you and your future self to address the critical issues of gender, homosexuality, and same-sex attraction from a biblical perspective with grace and compassion. **This chapter is a steppingstone for you in developing your own ETHOS based on biblical truth, scientific evidence, and grace.**

It is so important to have a theology and framework — and an understanding — of the beauty and intricacies of maleness and femaleness, masculinity and femininity, and gender.

Is it a simple binary belief (male or female) with only these two options?

Or is it filled with the intricacy, differences, and beauty with which God created every one of us — in His image?

What are your theological, personal and familial attitudes, conversations, and even jokes surrounding homosexuality and same-sex attraction?

Most of your sexual ethic is established when you are young through your observations of the world around you and personal experience.

Today, gender questions are an important part of growing up.

Establishing an understanding of masculinity and femininity and how God designed each of you as unique, separate individuals with purpose and intentionality is a critical foundation.

Gender Questions

I am not surprised by the gender questions that are filling the airwaves today. When your parents were growing up, some of these same questions were being asked. Even then, it was common for many to be bucking traditional gender roles. Women were working outside the home and men were helping around the house. Others were asking why they should look or act a certain way or enjoy certain things simply because they were a boy or a girl. Boys grew their hair long and pierced their ears. Girls cut their hair and joined the football team. This is normal.

The big difference today is that we hear about it more vocally than ever before. It is all too common for pre-teens and teenagers to wrestle with who they are when they don't fit the stereotypes. How does this play out? What is the outcome? **Statistically, most will not give this issue much thought if we leave them to themselves.** (This means they are not forced by family or culture to decide NOW who they are.) Extreme rhetoric - even violence - surrounds today's questions about gender. This is the world today, so how do we engage in conversations that allow us to be confident and secure in who God created each of us to be? Let's start with what Scripture says about who you are - how He created you:

Genesis 1:27 says:

> *"So God created human beings in his own image. In the image of God he created them; male and female he created them" (NLT).*

The follow up to the creation of two genders is the bringing together of the two in Genesis 2:18:

> *"Then the Lord God said, 'It is not good for the man to be alone. I will make a helper who is just right for him'" (NLT).*

Verse 23 says:

> *"'At last!' the man exclaimed. 'This is bone of my bone, and flesh from my flesh! She will be called 'woman,' because she was taken from "man"''" (NLT).*

Next came the creation of the place these two were united as one. Verse 24 says:

"This explains why a man leaves his father and mother and is joined to his wife, and the two are united into one" (NLT).

Verse 25 takes it one step further:

"Now the man and his wife were both naked, but they felt no shame" (NLT).

Boy-Man-Masculinity

First off, I want to state clearly that the idea of two genders — and **only two genders** — is not a mistake. It is by God's design. What you believe about gender will shape how you live and how you influence others. The vast majority are clearly male or female at birth.

A few people are born with ambiguous genitalia and this creates a lot of difficulty and confusion for themselves and their parents in knowing who they are. The percentage of people may be small, but it is a real struggle for those families and should not be discounted. These families need incredible support and biblical counsel. The decisions they have to make are never simple.

Everyone else is clearly born either male or female and our gender is determined in the womb by hormones. How our gender plays out individually is a different story. How you personally relate to your masculinity or femininity matters. But even more important is how we relate to the image of who we think we are supposed to be.

My personal development was filled with angst, confusion, frustration, and questions — with little to no answers. This led to disturbing beliefs and hatred towards myself. This is not uncommon. No one knew that I was struggling — I told no one.

I learned from this experience that the key players who influence our beliefs are the main people in our lives - our parents, grandparents, teachers, coaches, and mentors. We need them to step up and engage in these conversations with us. The truth is that most of us will resort to silence if we are struggling.

I challenge you to find safe people to talk to about your thoughts, feelings, and struggles. You need to be given permission to verbalize and process your own ideas, questions, feelings, frustrations, and any opposition.

You need to know that it is okay to process out loud ideas you have heard elsewhere. You need safe places and people in your life that you can trust. If you do not consider your parents or other key people in your life safe, you will need to find help somewhere else. I hope that you will find this in a healthy faith community, with a Christian counselor, or even a trusted friend. **Please don't try to navigate these questions and struggles alone. This is your future. Be proactive in asking healthy people (and growing people) in your life the right questions. I hope this chapter will help you do just that.**

So, who should influence you and your view and understanding of the concept of gender? Who is actually influencing you? Please be intentional at seeking out wise advice and input. Everyone has an opinion. Too many people are quick to give and force their opinion on all of us. Be aware! If you believe the Bible to be the inerrant Word of God, be sure what you are learning is founded in God's Word. Media and culture speak into how to think about gender through every movie and tv show. Be wary of the ethics promoted there. YOU decide whom you listen to and trust in shaping your beliefs.

Engage these key people in challenging conversations that help you prune and develop a healthy self-awareness, identity, and biblical sexual ethic.

I am listening to music on YouTube right now as I write, and a video has popped up as an advertisement stating we need to ditch the definition of masculinity and "**#EvolveTheDefinition.**"[38]

I agree up to a point. Why is this so complicated? It seems like it should be obvious, but for many, it is not clear.

So, what is the problem? The way we define 'male,' 'men,' and 'masculine' needs a framework. The definition of 'woman,' 'female,' and 'femininity' needs some boundaries. This is a critical point. Our family culture, church culture, and national culture drive the framework and boundaries that we live in. If we watch the average sitcom or T.V. drama that tries to define masculinity, we will see one of two extremes portrayed. Sitcoms usually portray men as weak, submissive, powerless, and foolish. Dramas tend to portray men as violent, angry, sexually aggressive, and selfish.

Ladies, do you want to marry a man like the ones portrayed on these shows?

Gentlemen, I SO hope you do not desire to be either of these types of men.

In his book *Boys Adrift* (2007), **Dr. Leonard Sax**[39] states that five factors are driving the growing epidemic of unmotivated boys and underachieving young men.

FIRST: **changes in our school systems** over the years have hindered boys' ability to learn as they fail to acknowledge that they have different needs than girls.

SECOND: **excessive video game play**.

THIRD: **ADHD medications.**

FOURTH: **endocrine disruptors** — hormones in beef, plastics, and the like are impacting us and our physical and sexual development. Boys are being hormonally feminized, and girls are developing and starting their periods at a younger age, which Sax then connects to their failure to launch into adulthood.

FIFTH: **a loss of positive role models.**

So, what are the **solutions and a framework for masculinity**?

Some solutions presented by Dr. Sax[40] are:
First, to **challenge the traditional K–12 educational system.** It does not promote growth and health in boys. If they can, I would encourage your parents to be involved in your school and be a change agent there. You are also a powerful change agent in your school. Be proactive and tactful at challenging your school. Let's raise the standard, not lower it.

Second, you need **opportunities to engage in the real world** so that there is a decrease in the need for the fake world of video games. This is the heart of the problem with video games. It is not the games in themselves, but the replacement of real-world interactions. Go outside. Get involved in serving in your church, school, or community. Pick up a hobby. Learn a new skill that could be of value for the rest of your life. Learn how engines work; do yard work for a neighbor; build something; create something; practice an instrument. These are all valuable, worthy pursuits.

Third, it is important to **educate yourself about the medications for ADHD and their long-term effects.** Check out **Dr. Daniel**

Amen's book *Healing ADD*[41] in which he discusses seven types of ADD. There is not one simple diagnosis with one treatment that works for everyone. He also provides suggestions for alternatives to try prior to medication. Become the expert on your body and what you need. You need to know when you need a break, better nutrition, water, etc. This is not about being needy or high maintenance. This is about being smart. These are not demands. This is using wisdom.

Fourth, research and **be aware of environmental estrogens** and the impact of these on your growth and development.

Finally, and most importantly, you need to **be sure you have positive role models**. You need strong, consistent examples of what it means to be a man, and what masculinity looks like.

The advertisement I mentioned seeing on YouTube, stating that we need to redefine masculinity and "#EvolveTheDefinition,"[42] raises some questions.

For many, when they think of masculinity, their experience leads them to associate it with negative stereotypes of foolishness or aggression. And it is right to challenge these stereotypes and their damaging expressions.

What have you been taught about masculinity in your home?

What do you see as important in understanding what it means to be masculine?

Is it okay for a boy to learn that taking care of others before himself is an honorable thing to do, or is this sexist and gender stereotyping?

Dr. Philip Zimbardo, a well-known psychologist and researcher, has written a book called *The Demise of Guys* (2012)[43] and has an excellent TED talk on the subject as well.

The **three factors** he identified for the demise of guys are:

- pornography
- excessive video game play
- absent fathers

The research above from Sax and Zimbardo gives us an amazing roadmap. Let's keep developing this.

The first thing we need to do is understand the power of pornography — its allure and its danger. This is NOT a one-time conversation with a friend, parent, or mentor. It is too dangerous to only discuss a few times. Your ETHOS is continually growing and developing. What I want to say to you is that it is important to find someone that loves you and cares about you and your health and wellbeing to help you prepare for this porn-filled world. Unfortunately, the pattern I have seen over the years, as I sit with hundreds of families, is that most do not have these conversations. They are afraid and so they leave it to culture, the media, and even pornography to teach you. This breaks my heart. **BE AWARE! Pornography steals, kills, and destroys.**

Limit your video game play and seek out real-world engagement. Go outside. Learn valuable skills.

I recommend that teens should be employed as soon as they are legally able. You may or may not have a good example of a healthy work ethic. This is invaluable, though. You were designed to work. You were meant to produce. I hope you enjoy the work you put your hands to. Work is a blessing. I had a dad that always modeled LOVING what he did every single day of my life. This set the bar high. I SO appreciate this today, since I have always found joy in what I do, from Wal-mart to McDonald's, from driving a limo to waiting tables at Red Lobster. I loved my job at Hollywood Video and as a janitor at a church. Now I get to teach, speak, counsel, write, and coach families on a Biblical Sexual Ethic, how to overcome trauma, and how to build strong healthy families. I LOVE what I do.

I want to encourage the dreams, passions, and interests that help you see outside of yourself and into the lives of others. Video games are often a selfish escape used to avoid relationships with others. They aren't always an escape from reality, but it is important that you think through why you play and how long you play.

Your ETHOS of time management, relationship engagement, and investment in others is invaluable.

Did you know that your dad (or any close adult male) is a critical role model in your life, whether they are good or bad? They are an example of how to talk to and treat a wife.

If you live in a single parent home, it is imperative that you **intentionally seek healthy male role models to spend time with.**

So much of your future depends on having a healthy, biblically sound understanding of masculinity. It is NOT aggressive but can be assertive when it needs to be. It is NEVER domineering, but is a servant leader with a voice, vision, passion, and insight.

What else would you add to a definition of masculinity?

I want to challenge you to spend some time in prayer and studying Scripture for yourself to see the characteristics of a man that is praised by God as presented in the Bible.

I have high hopes for you and the kind of man you will be. I have high standards. I hope you will make these your own as well. May this also be true in your view of femininity. God's design and gift in creating women is magnificent. So is His design for marriage - the bringing together of the two.

Girl–Woman–Femininity

How would you define femininity and womanhood?

Would your definition include their bodies, personalities, actions, or character?

Which should it be? Do you think of cooking and cleaning, pornography, empowerment, boss babes, or something else?

Your definition matters.

My goal here is to expose the way you think about womanhood and femininity. Much of what occurs today in conversations about femininity is reactionary and not well thought out. A lot of what is said and taught is abusive and offensive. I am saddened as a father and husband by the narrowing definition of identity centered on the female as just a body. The church's definition has not been much better when it limits women with a strict definition linked solely to their roles as a wife, mother, and homemaker.

How do we counteract this message as young men and women who will marry one day?

Girls quickly compare themselves to others and wonder, "Am I good enough, pretty enough, smart enough, tough enough...?"

Girls are at risk just as much as the boys. You have so much against you, but the most powerful forces at work are the battles in your own mind. **Nancy Leigh DeMoss** writes in *Lies Women Believe* (2001)[44] that listening to the lying serpent leads you down a slippery slope of disobedience. The truth is that what you believe matters. Who you listen to matters. This is critical as you grow and develop into the woman God wants you to be.

Who is speaking into your life, showing you your value, identity, courage, and strength?

Your ETHOS, or belief system, is in the process of developing every day. Is it being developed from a place of truth or lies? What lies do you already believe about yourself, your mind, your body, your identity, and your skills? Are you aware of any lies you might have been taught surrounding your view of God, yourself, sin, marriage, children, or your emotions? I want your foundational beliefs about yourself and your body to be based on TRUTH and not the lies you may be tempted to believe.

This is only the tip of the iceberg. **Dr. Daniel Amen** discusses the uniqueness of women in his book *Unleash the Power of the Female Brain* (2013).[45] Men and women are vastly different, and this is a good thing. As we discover more about neurobiology — a fascinating field of study — the complexity and brilliance of God's design of the sexes becomes apparent. Women have assets in their minds that men do not possess. They also have liabilities. I want to encourage you to understand yourself — your unique intuition, your ability to empathize and collaborate, and the power of self-control.

Ladies, your endocrine system is incredibly complex. The food you eat, your exposure to toxins, and the fluctuating hormones in your body will affect your mood and outlook on life. If you are not careful, it is easy to find yourself battling addictions, anxiety, and the comparison trap. These are deadly to optimal health.

Your social connectedness is a powerful tool that God uses in your life — and it can be both an asset and a liability. You were uniquely knit in your mother's womb. Are you more impulsive, or more compulsive, or maybe even both? Do you lean more towards sadness or anxiety, or are both temptations for you? I want to see you prepared to know yourself and equipped with tools you will need to succeed in life and mature into adulthood.

In his book, *Why Gender Matters* (2005), **Dr. Leonard Sax**[46] shows that boys and girls are different. The better we understand these differences, the more free we are to be ourselves. This is taught, modeled, and lived out in our homes. He shares an example that when asked to draw a picture, **girls typically draw nouns** (people, places, or things) and **boys typically draw verbs** (actions, states, or occurrences).

Your own personal development and understanding of your uniqueness will empower you to be the best YOU that you can be. Embrace your differences. Embrace your OWN uniqueness, skills, and strengths.

What you probably need most from the adults in your life are strong influences in your earlier years — birth to ten — but then **the freedom to wrestle with ideas as you get older.**

Preteen or teen, picture this: **Your parents have approximately ten years to speak into your life as your primary influence.** After that, life changes drastically. And this is probably where you are at. Your attention and focus and your primary influences naturally switch to your peers and other sources around age 10. Now you are more vulnerable than ever, and many of the adults in your life are (and were) unwilling to engage in the hard conversations. They honestly are afraid. Many adults are dealing with their own struggles. This is not an excuse; it is just the reality. Many want to wait until you are 12 or even 14 to begin these conversations - and more often than not, this is too late.

By the time you are in your pre-teen years, you are much more interested in what your peers and the media say than what your primary caregivers say. So, I am proud of you for reading this book. This separation from your parents is a natural process. It is not because of bad parenting or misguided desires. You are supposed to grow up and separate from your family. **This is God's design.** And so is your gender, your uniqueness, your quirkiness, and the possibility of marriage. These are God's inventions.

What do you think is beautiful? Over the years, what your parents or primary caregivers have voiced as **beautiful** drastically influences what you will see as **beautiful**.

When someone close to you complains about their body or their spouse's body, your opinions are being shaped and formed.

What these key people say and do affects what you see as negative, unwanted, or unacceptable. The discussions you have driving around town influence them as well.

Have you ever said a verbal comment that sounds offensive — even downright mean — and are immediately chastised for it, but you remember hearing your parents say the same thing? You grew up as a sponge. This is why **Going BEYOND "THE TALK" before puberty** matters more than almost any of the other conversations you could take part in during your teen years.

Are you prepared to be the woman God wants you to be?

The truth regarding gender is that it is NOT as simple as "boy" or "girl."

That aspect is almost always clear and determined by biology. As the young child in Kindergarten Cop told us, "Boys have a penis. Girls have a vagina." Both genders come with their own limitations, despite what the world tells you. And you will have your own unique limitations. We can live within these and find freedom, or we can fight them our entire life and live a frustrated and angry existence.

Now What?

Last night, I was sitting outside with my twelve-year-old son after an eight-mile bicycle ride through Salem, Oregon. We discussed girls, dating, and marriage, but our conversation also dove into peer pressure, the fear of walking into a room and not knowing where to sit, and the stress of others' opinions about us. All of this was initiated by him, not me. I followed where the topics went.

How did this happen? A million *micro-conversations* have been the theme of our home and created a foundation — an ETHOS — that gave him the confidence to be vulnerable.

I tell my children, even before puberty, that they are **their own person**, **make their own decisions**, and are **fully responsible for those decisions.** This matters as you will increasingly bear the weight of more difficult decisions and their consequences.

If my child forgets to take something to school or camp, and I come bail them out, what are they learning? Are they learning responsibility, or that others will cover for them? It is SO important to let small mistakes shape them, so they can avoid the larger ones down the road. I want this for you!

I hope your teenage years are NOT full of conflict. They do not have to be. I want YOU to be trustworthy and use wisdom as you make choices regarding your sexuality, dating, and relationship boundaries.

Take Action: I want you to prepare a list of the character qualities and skills you would love to see in your own children (a long time from now) when they leave your home. List ideas for how to prepare them to meet these goals.

It is SO important to ask hard questions. Who you are as a male or female is perfect and unique. May you discover who God wants you to be - His best design for you. He does NOT make mistakes. Know what you believe about yourself: who you are, who you will be, and also boundaries in dating and relationships in general. If you decide on these early, you will avoid a lot of heartache and difficult in-the-moment decisions.

* * *

Working Questions – Now it is YOUR TURN:

Now let's dive into a really difficult topic, which many teens are trying to understand.

What are some questions you and your friends have regarding homosexuality, same-sex attraction, and gender?

____

____

____

____

What is your theology and understanding of the beauty and intricacy of gender, male and female, masculinity and femininity? Is it a simple binary belief and or is there more to it?

____

____

Define masculinity.

____

____

Define femininity.

____

____

What have you been taught about masculinity in your home?

____

____

What have you been taught about femininity in your home?

____

____

How can you be respectful of others' bodies and privacy?

____

____

How can you have respect for your own body and not expose it or use it as a tool or weapon?

____

____

How can you use your masculinity or femininity to serve others? Brainstorm some ideas here.

____

____

God created us as two distinct genders. Why do you think God did this (**Genesis 1:27**)?

So God created human beings in his own image. In the image of God he created them; male and female he created them (NLT).

____

____

Read **Genesis 2:18–25**

Then the Lord God said, "It is not good for the man to be alone. I will make a helper who is just right for him." So the Lord God formed from the ground all the wild animals and all the birds of the sky. He brought them to the man to see what he would call them, and the man chose a name for each one. He gave names to all the livestock, all the birds of the sky, and all the wild animals. But still there was no helper just right for him.

So the Lord God caused the man to fall into a deep sleep. While the man slept, the Lord God took out one of the man's ribs and closed up the opening. Then the Lord God made a woman from the rib, and he brought her to the man.

"At last!" the man exclaimed.
"This one is bone from my bone, and flesh from my flesh!

She will be called 'woman,'
because she was taken from 'man.'"

This explains why a man leaves his father and mother and is joined to his wife, and the two are united into one.

Now the man and his wife were both naked, but they felt no shame (NLT).

This passage takes gender further and explains how it fits into His design for marriage and children. Brainstorm your own ideas as to "why."

____

____

____

____

Dr. Leonard Sax outlined 5 factors that are driving a growing epidemic of unmotivated boys and underachieving young men – what are they? Why is this important? What can we do to change this tide?

____

____

____

____

____

What are the 3 factors that Dr. Zimbardo has identified for the "demise of guys"?

____

____

____

What has become the leading cause of girls committing suicide or straying from what they were taught in their homes? (Hint: it is not the same as with boys...)

____

____

I challenge you as you study Scripture to take note of the qualities God praises in men and women. I think you will notice it is different from what we normally encourage and praise.

| 14 |

What Does it Mean to Be Transgender?

Do you have a friend that has transitioned, or that wants to transition? Are you filled with questions about your gender and "who you REALLY are?" This may be a completely foreign idea to you. That is okay. Let's go there.

What does "transgender" mean? It means that someone feels that they don't fit the gender they were born into (biological male or biologically female). For example, if your friend is a biological male, they may feel like they have little to nothing in common with other guys, yet they feel like they have tons of connections with girls in their life. **Their internal dialogue and the lens through which they see the world seems to follow more of a script of the opposite sex or gender.** This is a complex issue, but I hope this helps you see what is going on internally. They are then told and/or taught that if they change their body, they will find their true self.

Did you know that the statistics of transgender people in the United States are between 0.3% and 0.78% - so about 0.6%?

What is gender dysphoria? Gender dysphoria is the conflict a person feels because of a mismatch between their gender identity and their sex assigned at birth. This is more of a psychological term used for diagnosis and billing purposes for insurance companies.

What is gender identity? This is important to consider. You have a gender identity, and so do I. We are pretty much all on a spectrum of some more feminine and some more masculine characteristics. Mine, personally, is more female – more feminine in so many ways that my brain and approach to life is wired. This does not make me less of a male. Many believe that it does though. I used to think it did as well. This is the impact of culture and society. We definitely need to reconsider the ways we have socially categorized people, professions, talents, skills – and masculine and feminine traits.

What is social transition? This is presenting oneself either part time or all the time as their identified gender - in public. This might include packing, which is using a penile prosthesis to give a masculine genital contour. Some use tucking, which is placing the testes in between their legs, held in place with tight undergarments. Women may use binding, which is a tight chest garment to flatten their breasts. Some use breast, hip, or rear end prostheses, which are inserted into clothing or a bra to augment sizes and shapes.

What is coming out? This is the sharing of one's internal world with family, friends, and the world.

Based on these feelings of incongruence, many choose to identify themselves as trans and begin taking steps towards becoming the other gender. You might be wondering how they go about changing. This is done by taking medications, specifically hormones and hormone blockers, that stop their body from either going through puberty and developing into an adult man or woman or halting those processes.

A biological female that takes these hormones will not develop breasts, or they will stop developing. They will grow hair everywhere, and within one year become sterile, which means they cannot have children. Aggression will increase. Their muscle mass will increase, their voice will lower, and their clitoris will be enlarged. They become more masculine.

A biological male that takes these hormones will get softer skin, grow breasts (at least small ones), and have their penis either stop growing or shrink. They will also become **sterile within one year** as their testicles cease to create sperm. Their testosterone levels will drop and make them more emotional, less aggressive, and more sensitive. There will be a redistribution of body fat and a decrease in muscle mass and strength.

Surgeries can follow this treatment. Surgeries continue this process by giving a biological male breasts and taking their penis and turning it inside out to create a space to accommodate a penis for sexual pleasure. A biological female will have her breasts removed for her upper surgery and have skin taken from elsewhere on her body to create a penis-like appendage above her vulva.

On the physical side, there are risks associated when surgery is chosen, which is why few go down this road. For a man that is transitioning to female, there is tissue death of the skin from the penis and scrotum as they are sewn together to create the vagina and vulva. There is a narrowing of the urethra that can block the flow of urine and lead to kidney damage. Fistulas, or abnormal connections, between the bladder or bowels and the vagina can occur as well. For a female transitioning to a male, they can also have narrowing, blockages, or fistulas in the urinary tract. Another possible result can be tissue death of the newly made penis.

These invasive surgeries and hormones have not been tested on minors, and they have consequences we do not know about yet. They are performed by professionals who are perfecting what they do each year. This is supposed to be a life altering process. It is meant for the man or woman who feels trapped in the wrong body and wants to be in another. This is what transgender means.

So, now back to my initial question, - do you have a friend that has transitioned or is transitioning? This is the stage in which a person is, in a sense, in between two genders. It is important to understand what you can do and how you can love them. Being in this place is overwhelming.

For most of us, it is "above our paygrade" and we feel ill-equipped to know what to do to help them. This goes for you and all the adults in their life. So, they may feel completely alone. This needs to change. **You may well be the only friend they will listen to – IF you are tactful and careful and honest and bold in how you ask questions, walk alongside them, and are a friend to them. Telling a friend what they want to hear is not helpful – and is often quite harmful – or being a true friend.**

What I want to do here is help you navigate those friendships by giving you information on the issue and how to care for someone in the midst of this struggle.

If you are going through this, I also want to walk alongside you and provide you some food for thought. You have free will to choose. No one can make your decisions for you. Many can try, many can persuade, but, in the end, the decision is yours. I want to make sure you are as informed as you can be.

Let's look at what is going on in a young man or woman's heart from a couple of different angles.

You Are Fearfully and Wonderfully Made

In a recent YouTube video I saw, **Dr. Sean McDowell**[47] from Biola University explains that: Each of us have a worldview - a belief that answers these three questions:

1. What is Creation?
2. What is the Fall?
3. What is Redemption (how do you fix it)?

Many of you reading this are familiar with a Christian, evangelical, or conservative view of gender, sexuality, and marriage which is what I am focusing on in this book. **Just because you are familiar with something, does not mean it is actually your worldview. What do YOU believe? What is YOUR Ethos? This is critical.**

A beautiful part of Christian belief is that God created us to be in relationship WITH HIM! He, God, is active in and through our lives. He cares about every intimate detail.

Genesis 1:27 says, "So God created mankind in his own image, in the image of God he created them; male and female he created them" (NIV).

You were created IN HIS IMAGE! Male, and Female. This is God's design. Perfect. Not a mistake. Gender was not an idea created by humans; it is a part of God's design from the beginning.

> In Psalms 139:13-18 we read, *"You made all the delicate, inner parts of my body and knit me together in my mother's womb. Thank you for making me so wonderfully complex! Your workmanship is marvelous – how well I know it. You watched me as I was being formed in utter seclusion, as I was woven together in the dark of the womb. You saw me before I was born. Every day of my life was recorded in your book. Every moment was laid out before a single day had passed. How precious are your thoughts about me, O God. They cannot be numbered! I can't even count them; they outnumber the grains of sand! And when I wake up, you are still with me!" (NLT).*

This is perfection. This is beauty. You were created perfectly. Those with deformities, or parts of our body we would like to change – you are perfect. Those with speech troubles, with height challenges, that dislike their straight or curly hair – you are perfect. He delights in YOU! He saw what your life would be like BEFORE your first day!

However, **this beauty was marred by the Fall when sin entered the world.** What is sin? It is you and I going against our Creator creating an eternal separation. The Fall brought a corruption of all of creation, including our sexuality and the experience of our gendered selves. Now, instead of seeing beauty in diversity, humans create standards of beauty by which we measure each other. We define masculinity and femininity in ways that box people in and make them feel like they don't belong.

A common question that always comes up now is "**What about intersex?**" What do they do? Who are they? How do they answer these questions? First, I would say that this is very, very difficult - for a select few. For most though, it is discovered later and does not have to be the trauma that the medical community often makes it out to be (but it tends to be). Intersex can be at the chromosome level, making it harder to detect early on, or at the genital – so more physically evident. Some people require surgery. For some it is much more of a challenging experience – often quite confusing and overwhelming. It is like an assault to my identity.

The number of intersex people in the United States, putting all the different types together, are 0.05% to 1.7%. **It is more common than it is discussed in our culture.** It is very private as well. Gaining a basic understanding can be eye-opening towards the compassion and care that ought to characterize ALL Christians.

For those of whom it is obvious at birth, it seems like no matter what gender the parents or doctors choose, they struggle with who they are.

The reality of the physical condition of intersex men and women is a reminder that **we live in a broken, fallen world.** No one should have to deal with that. In the same way, Downs Syndrome, autism, missing limbs, birth defects, and genetic predispositions are other painful reminders of the fall.

The question I have for us, and for these men and women, is **what would happen if we focused elsewhere?** What if we spent the same amount of energy serving and loving others? It is too easy for any of us to get so wrapped up in our own story that we lose sight of others. I believe this is one of the biggest dangers in our gender questions and struggles.

This is why the belief in Redemption and Restoration is critical to Christians. **Yes, we look forward to Christ's second coming, but we also have peace and comfort from knowing that His presence**

is with us now and He has suffered too. We are not alone in the universe.

God created us for a monogamous, male / female relational reality. When we submit to Jesus' claims of who He is and that His creation is meant to reflect His Kingdom, we can see that God is good, even in the midst of chaos, brokenness, fear, and anxiety. We MUST learn to lean on Him and trust Him. Marriage is the picture God chose to use in Scripture to compare and contrast relationships of us and Him and male and female. This is beautifully redeeming – NOW! In the present. Not only when we are done here and in Heaven. Now!

Our hope is found in believing that Jesus is who He claims to be and that He made a way for us to be reconciled to God – NOW! We then accept the gift of salvation which He freely offers to us as a form of grace. **This is the Christian story. This is the Kingdom Present. We are NOT just waiting for Heaven. We are living today experiencing life and His gifts and blessings – even in the midst of pain and suffering.**

The honest truth is that we do NOT truly experience the fullness of emotion without pain and suffering. This can be tough to grasp.

An Alternate Worldview

In the transgender worldview (those advocating and promoting such radical body changes to fix this incongruence), we are NOT made in the image of God. We are not defined at birth or created in the womb as gendered beings – male or female. There is no fixed essence of what it means to be human. Gender and sex have no meaning.

The problem of sin and the Fall in the transgender worldview is that gender identities are oppressive and bring suffering.

In **Ann Travers**' book *The Trans Generation*[48] she said,

> "My general argument in the book is that trans kids are incredibly vulnerable because of the way in which gender identities are imposed on children in general, with particularly negative consequences for trans kids."[49]

What is redemption in the transgender worldview? According to this worldview, a person may be saved by having the freedom to define their own sex and gender identities. Ultimately, it is getting rid of gender as a category altogether.

The question you have to answer is which of these worldviews is true?

How Do We Love

A quote from **Dr. Preston Sprinkle's** new book *Embodied: Transgender Identities, The Church, and What the Bible Has to Say,*[50] he states that

> "our interpretations of sex and sexed bodies might be socially constructed, but sex itself is not socially constructed."

The truth is that sex and gender at one point in history (recent history) were pretty much synonymous. That is not the case anymore. A widely agreed upon definition of **GENDER** is:

"The psychological, social and cultural aspects of being male or female."

This definition according to Dr. Sprinkle[51] is broken into two overlapping parts: gender identity, and gender role.

Gender Identity is about the psychological, while Gender Role is about social and cultural frameworks.

Gender roles are all about what we are or are not supposed to do as a male or female. This is about actions, behaviors, and they are tightly tied to what is typical or expected in a given society. These can also fall under the word stereotypes.

Gender identity is a more complex aspect of who we are. Some define this as "one's internal sense of self as male, female, both, or neither." Dr. Sprinkle states that this term has an elusive meaning in popular discourse. He sees four questions that are important to consider.[52]

First, does gender identity exist? Think about this bold statement – is a body of a woman essential to being a woman? Or can one truly experience being a woman outside the body of one? These become tough questions. Sheila Jeffreys, a feminist quoted in Preston Sprinkle's book says that "the idea of 'gender identity' disappears biology."[53] That is an important, and bold statement.

Second, how many gender identities are there? Facebook allows for over 70 to choose from. This is so complex today. We cannot assume we understand what another person even means by the term "gender" today.

Third, how do you determine a person's gender identity? Is it self-identified? Or is it predetermined and thus if my gender identity is not matching my biological sex, then I have a disorder? See how complex this gets?

Fourth, is gender identity malleable? Changeable? What if I told you that absolutely yes it is. You grow and change and adapt all throughout your life.

As we see here, gender identity, a part of **GENDER**, is quite complex. Some see it us even made up. Those in distress and questioning who they are see it quite differently. Dr. Sprinkle[54] later in his book states that "the best way to smash exaggerated stereotypes is to get to know actual trans people and become a good listener and friend." Listen! Stop talking. Be in relationship.

I want to go back to the imagery of Creation, the Fall, and Redemption. Your sexuality and the goodness of your physical self as a gendered person brings with it differing aspects of your sexuality. **Dr. Mark Yarhouse** describes these in his book *Understanding Gender Dysphoria.*[55] The different aspects of your sexuality are GENDER sexuality, EROTIC sexuality, and GENITAL sexuality.

Gender sexuality – some say this is more of a socially constructed term. As seen above it is quite complicated.

Erotic sexuality – this is about arousal. Sexual desire and being sensitive to sexual stimulation defines the erotic side of sexuality.

Genital sexuality – this is your biology – how you were physically made – your plumbing.

Dr. Yarhouse presents three contrasting frameworks or lenses we can use to better understand the experience of gender dysphoria, or that of being transgender, plus one additional one I will conclude with.

The first is the "Disability Framework." This view sees gender incongruence as part of the fallen world and as a disability that is non-moral and which should be addressed with compassion.

The second is the "Diversity Framework." This one has two forms. The strong form involves the deconstructing of sex and gender as a whole. The softer version sees the transgender experience as reflecting an identity and culture that must be celebrated as an expression of diversity.

The third is the "Integrity Framework." This framework is the one that many Christians and conservatives might gravitate towards. It sees gender dysphoria as confusing the sacredness of maleness and femaleness and it sees specific ways of resolving this dysphoria as violations of the integrity of how you were designed and created.[56]

Dr. Yarhouse says that in the integrity framework, same-sex sexual behavior is seen as sin in part because it does not "merge or join two persons into an integrated sexual whole." The "essential maleness and essential femaleness is not brought together as intended from creation. When extended to the discussion of transsexuality and cross-gender identification, the theological concerns rest in the denial of the integrity of one's own sex and an overt attempt at marring the sacred image of maleness and femaleness formed by God."[57]

You might like this explanation. You might be uncomfortable with this. That is okay. Keep reading.

Our People - An Integrated Lens

A very important point I want to reiterate is that people of faith - Christians - who are navigating gender identity issues or anything else like this are "OUR PEOPLE," as **Dr. Mark Yarhouse** says, and is an important reminder that we are on the same team.

A fourth framework that might be much more helpful for you is **the "Integrated Lens."**[58] This is much more caring and compassionate. This approach avoids speaking past one another. It is about relationships and navigating them together. This approach leaves room for each individual's own way of thinking, feeling, and seeing the world. It refrains from immediate judgment. A great part of this framework is that it allows for a person to pull the best they can from the other three frameworks.

The "Integrated Lens," as **Dr. Yarhouse** calls it, is distinctively Christian, and does these three things:

- It preserves the integrity of sex differences. It gives pause when considering the most invasive procedures. It seeks wisdom and maturity in light of a Christian view of sex and gender.
- There is a compassionate management of gender dysphoria. There is room for empathy and compassion.
- There is an emphasis on meaning-making, identity, and community. It is so important to identify meaning-making structures that inform identity. This approach allows us to locate them within a broader community of support, a kinship network that affirms the person's worth and insists on navigating this terrain together.[59]

This is very different from the ways many in the Church and Christian community have handled a child or young person coming out as transgender. The truth is that a person of any age that is experiencing this is overwhelmed. Let's look at this from the perspective of the young person who is struggling. They are experiencing gender incongruence. What does this mean to them? **Each person will have a dif-**

ferent story. Listen to them. Be a safe place for them to talk - no matter what they say- or find them a safe person to talk to. These influences are critical and life altering. This is where the message being received by online research can have a deleterious effect because it can further increase the dysphoria and struggle. What storyline are they hearing from the Church, from parents, or from friends? If this is negative, angry, and hateful, I can guarantee I know how this will play out. They will reject the church as a whole. Be careful. Be a source of friendship, safety, security, and friendship. If this is you, be very careful who you let in to influence your heart.

My Greatest Concern

It is so important to be careful regarding where we get information, advice, and mentoring. This is why I wrote this book. Remember that everything I say and write here must pass through the filter of Scripture – God's Word. That is the ultimate authority for everything – who we are, who we were created to be, how we are to live, etc.

I worry that if you google help, or talk to an affirming therapist, or even some medical professionals, they will push you quickly to "Do it. It is the right thing to do. You'll find yourself. You will finally be yourself. You will discover true joy and happiness." YIKES! No! This is not necessarily true.

Let me explain the research and realities we have found so far. **Did you know that if a person who is struggling with their gender identity remains in this struggle through puberty and into adolescence with no drastic interventions, like hormones and surgeries, 75% of them resolve themselves to be okay with their gender from birth?** Some reports even state 90+%. Some will continue to struggle whether or not they transition.

Our current culture is exacerbating (making worse) a problem that will work itself out for most people given time and maturity. Some men enjoy sports, hunting, and value physical strength, while others are more artsy, musical, and creative. Some women love pink, baking, and beautiful things. Others are much more comfortable in camo and on a four-wheeler, horseback, or a Harley. However, by urging and forcing young people to settle on an identity, they are taking advantage of their youth and inexperience.

One thing we must remember is that none of us are guaranteed an easy life. If we are not careful, an easy life becomes the goal. If we are not careful, this becomes an IDOL. If we are not careful, we become obsessed with trying to give everything a meaning. This is a debilitating place to be stuck. It seems easier to form quick, simple answers to complex struggles and problems. Please don't. Please don't guide others to these. I love this quote from **Melinda Selmys,** quoted in Dr. Mark Yarhouse's work.

> "... suffering in Christianity is not only not meaningless, it is ultimately one of the most powerful media for the transmission of meaning. We can stand in adoration between the cross, and kneel and kiss the wood that bore the body of our Saviour, because this is the means by which the ugly, meaningless atheistic suffering of the world (the problem of evil) was transmuted into the living water, the blood of Christ, the wellspring of Creation. The great paradox here is that the Tree of Death and Suffering is the Tree of Life. This central paradox in Christianity allows us to love our own brokenness precisely because it is through that brokenness that we image the broken body of our God -- and the highest expression of divine love. That God in some sense wills it to be so seems evident in Gethsemane: Christ prays "Not my will, but thine be done," and when God's will is done it involves the scourge and the nails. It's also always struck me as particularly fitting and beautiful that when Christ is resurrected His body is not returned to a state of perfection, as the body of Adam in Eden, but rather it still bears the marks

> of His suffering and death—and indeed that it is precisely through these marks that He is known by Thomas." – **Melinda Selmys** [60]

I love the language Dr. Yarhouse uses when he says that we should be "**navigating terrain**"[61] with others as we facilitate a walk with Christ and a place for them to explore meaning and purpose. We want them to be able to explore. Questions are SO important. Do not shut down questions. Invite them.

I hope this gives you a grasp of the experiences of those struggling with gender dysphoria and wrestling with whether or not they are transgender.

* * *

Working Questions – Now it is YOUR TURN:

What is gender dysphoria?

____

____

What is gender identity?

____

____

Read the first two chapters of Genesis. What questions do you have?

Genesis 1:27 says, "So God created mankind in his own image, in the image of God he created them; male and female he created them."

____

____

____

In Psalms 139:13-18 we read, *"You made all the delicate, inner parts of my body and knit me together in my mother's womb. Thank you for making me so wonderfully complex! Your workmanship is marvelous – how well I know it. You watched me as I was being formed in utter seclusion, as I was woven together in the dark of the womb. You saw me before I was born. Every day of my life was recorded in your book. Every moment was laid out before a single day had passed. How precious are your thoughts about me, O God. They cannot be numbered! I can't even count them; they outnumber the grains of sand! And when I wake up, you are still with me!" (NLT).*

What is a key takeaway from this passage?

____

____

____

____

Explain the 4 Frameworks from Yarhouse:

____

____

____

____

How can you apply what you have learned in this chapter as you walk alongside a friend that is struggling with their gender identity?

____

____

What questions do you have?

Write them down here and then email them to me at questions@healinglives.com. I would love to walk alongside you throughout this process.

____

____

| 15 |

Questions About Homosexuality

A distraught young Christian woman came into my office needing advice and direction. She was in a lesbian relationship and felt conflicted about it. She thought that since I was also a Christian that I would condemn her for her behavior and act very parental.

I surprised her though by asking her to tell me more.

I began by asking her explicitly how the physical parts of her relationship were going. She looked confused.

I asked her if she felt safe with this person. She said yes. I asked her if touch was wonderful. She said, "Yes."

I asked her if being close was intoxicating. She said, "Oh yes!" She was confused about where I was going with this, since it was the opposite direction of where she had expected me to go.

I then asked her why she was here — why did she feel guilt and shame? She declared it was because she knew that her behavior was wrong despite her feelings.

I asked her again why she had come to me for help. She knew that a lesbian relationship was not God's designed place for this kind of sexual expression. She was stuck.

The reality is that touch from a person we consider safe can invigorate and feel good as the dopamine release increases. However, the same touch by another person can raise anxiety, fear, and an adrenal fight or flight response.

God designed our sexuality with **purpose**. As most things of value, our sexuality is meant to be **stewarded.** There are **consequences** to its misuse and abuse. This young woman knew what she needed to do. **She knew her heart's desire.**

Another question she had was, **"Who am I?"** – she felt conflicting definitions as a Christian and a lesbian. For many people they define themselves by their gender and sexual preferences. When asked who they are, this is THE defining characteristic of their life. As evidence of our need to be known by "my" definition of myself, Facebook has added over 73 options for gender. However, as a Christian, she knew that this behavior was not God's design and desire for her.

We are ALL looking for similar things — to be known, to be loved, to be accepted, to belong, and to be somebody. This young woman had tremendous wounds from her family of origin. Her wounds from men were heartbreaking.

I helped this young woman in my office understand that what she felt was normal.

I helped her see that her desire for love, intimacy, and security were good, God-given, and beautiful.

I helped her see that touch is amazing, especially when received from someone safe.

I also helped her see she had value and an ability to choose for herself. **She did not have to be driven by whatever made her feel good at the moment**, but she could be guided by a Biblical Sexual Ethic.

If she had had an ETHOS grounded in Scripture from a young age, it would have been much easier for her to resist the temporary high of attraction.

She was able to redefine herself with an identity in Christ, and not be defined by her sexuality or attractions. Today, she is single and a faithful servant in ministry.

How We Got Here

Approximately fourteen years ago after working as a Counselor in private practice and in churches I entered the academic world as a Professor. I was now working with more college-age students than I had previously, and I saw that most of them believed that "love" — feelings and emotions — trumped truth — both God's revealed truth and biology.

In years past, the Church reacted to sexual choices that were outside of God's design with criticism and anger, not **redemption** and **compassion**. A lot has changed over the years. Unfortunately, the Church's growth in compassion and understanding was not balanced by discipling believers as they taught the Truth of Scripture. Young adults now increasingly believe that everyone should make up their own mind as to what makes them happy and embrace it — whatever it is.

As a Result, the sexual ethic of Christians is the weakest it has been in recent history as the call to love our neighbor has NOT been accompanied by teaching on healthy sexuality in our homes and churches.

I want to equip you so you can address these complicated issues with **compassion**, **biblical truth**, and a **servant's heart**. I hope that you will be a young man or woman that knows that **the gospel is for everyone** — just as they are.

The power of the gospel is that it transforms.

We were never meant to stay where we were when Christ saved us.

We are meant to be challenged, do hard things, and give up idols (and even some relationships we may desire) for the sake of the gospel.

We must die to ourselves to live. This is critical. This is compelling. Thank God for grace!

A quote commonly attributed to Dietrich Bonhoeffer says,

> **"The ultimate test of a moral society is the kind of world that it leaves to its children."**

There have always been men and women who are same sex attracted and others who are asexual. We have always had men and women that questioned their sexuality. The difference is that today we do everything in a much more public manner. There is also a movement to classify the words of anyone that speaks out against the behaviors of the LGBTQ+ (Lesbian, Gay, Bisexual, Transgender, Queer/Questioning+) community as hate speech. I want to equip you to understand today's reality, so you can live and lead from a Biblical Sexual Ethic. I want your responses to be Christ-honoring, humble, compassionate, and always Biblical.

In recent years, bullying has been highlighted — rightly so — as a problem among children and teenagers, but with a bent towards protecting LGBTQ students.

I want you to think about this. Is this wrong? NO!

No one should be bullied. However, there is a twist. While it may have started with protecting and normalizing LGBTQ students, it has morphed into embracing and encouraging these behaviors. This is a critical shift.

Many churches have been pushed into a corner to avoid the label of "hate group", and they have defaulted to embracing and affirming sexual behaviors that Scripture warns against. There is no middle ground left.

How did we get here? There have been strategic shifts in our culture and the language used. In the 1990s, the idea was pushed that we are "born this way." But only a few weeks after gay marriage was legalized in the United States in 2015, the shift in the conversation was to gender fluidity.

That is where we are now — you choose. **"YOU do YOU!"** This statement is very dangerous. You aren't, in fact, "born this way." Letting a child born today decide if they want to be a boy or girl is a dangerous proposition. We are told that it is more loving to let them choose. Who are we to tell them? This is a terrifying stance with grave consequences. We know just from basic developmental theory that most of a child's decisions need shaping, instruction, direction, and influence. These are critical for their future. **It seems like children today are being used as experiments and sound research has gone out the window.** I hope you will NOT decide to live like this.

LGBTQ+ beliefs, also known as Queer theology, is where theologians eloquently attempt to reconcile Scripture with their lives and behaviors. Interestingly, it includes true statements – but always coupled with very misleading assumptions. Here as some examples:

- God made you in His image — your identity matters.
- You should embrace what you feel, since God does not make mistakes.
- Your desires are from God and of God, so they must be good and acted upon.

In Queer Theology, everything is about you — not God or His Son. There is no discipleship or dying to self. Marriage is mocked, and families are divided.

I fear for you, whether you are a Christian or not. You have a battle before you to reclaim a view of masculinity and femininity as God designed.

A biblical view of masculinity and femininity has both sexes honoring and complementing the other, supporting the other. Each person embraces their complete self — faults and all — for the glory of God. Our sexual selves are also perfectly made and designed. We need to be careful with how we interpret our desires, attractions, and feelings. This is incomplete data. May you be very careful to not make decisions based on these alone.

Real People We Love

Your ETHOS — what you believe and live out — matters.

How you discuss and live out gender matters.

In my marriage, one of us is very sensitive, emotional, processes everything they are thinking out loud, and even cries with most commercials. The other one of us is quiet, introspective, analytical, skeptical, and an internal processor that does not like to share emotions.

Which one am I? Which one is my wife?

If you were to read only this chapter of this book, you would likely fall into the stereotypes trap and quickly assume that the first one is my wife. You, having read this far, have heard my story and should know enough about me to know which one I am. I cry every time at the end of the movie "Cars." I am the "girl" in my marriage. Or, should we perhaps challenge our assumptions about gender and recognize that both men and women represent the full spectrum of human behavior, thought, and emotion. I am the emotional one. I am the external and verbal processor. I cry at almost every movie. But I can also fix almost anything in a house or car and have a healthy male sex drive. We have a lot of work to do to expand — maybe better said, to deepen — these definitions, not rewrite them.

The truth is that most men are not "manning up" and showing themselves to be someone of character, leadership, and tenderness. They don't have a strong work ethic and they don't use their strength to protect others. Women are being used, abused, and discounted just as often today as they were in the past. We have serious inequities. Our actions reveal what we believe as healthy, normal, good, right, and Biblical. **So many of the things we wrestle with do**

not have chapter and verse answers in Scripture, which leads to more questions.

We are all looking for something. We all want to be desired, to be known, to have worth, or to accomplish something. Somewhere along the way, though, a key part of who we are, our sexuality, gets messed with in the process. **Without a guiding principle as to why you should or should not do something, decisions become arbitrary.**

We have to start with laying a foundation. I must reiterate again that in God's perfect design, you were born as either male or female. This is not radical. It is deciding to place my starting point in biological facts that I ascribe to God as His prerogative as the Creator. You and I had no say in the matter when the hormone bath in-utero made us male or female. This is a foundation.

What is your foundation for creating a Biblical Sexual Ethic of Homosexuality?

For many, the foundation is tradition. We love or hate the things we do because that is the way our family has always done them. **We hold views that are entrenched in tradition — not the Bible.** Or, on the other side of the spectrum, we become so frustrated with our family that we decide to do everything opposite to their values and beliefs to assert our independence.

So, what will your foundation be? It is truly up to you. Your answer will dictate so much of your life and health for the rest of your years.

Homosexuality is a reality today just as it has been throughout all of time. This is not a new thing. Some societies have embraced it while others demonized it.

The reality, as you know in your heart, is that **we are not talking about an issue — we are talking about people.** We are talking about hurting people, who are just like you and I. You and I are desiring and deeply yearning for something.

Some say that we should never deny people anything that makes them happy. That argument falls to pieces, though, when we insert anything else that may potentially be harmful in the place of homosexual sex – i.e., driving without a seat belt, drinking a lot drugs, etc.

The majority of the LGBTQ+ conversations center around the individual and their feelings. However, **I would dare to say that the gospel commands us to die to ourselves and our families and live for Christ.** Am I willing to sign up for that? Are you? This requires us to choose things we might not want to choose for the sake of a greater call on our lives. This requires sacrifice, loneliness, and suffering. Ironically, in our talk of self-denial, we are getting closer to the example of the life of Christ.

God has a perfect design for sex and intercourse and that is in a heterosexual marriage. Understanding this is critical. Living this out is imperative. It is so important to know what you believe and why. In turn, I want you to be able to lead others towards good things, and not condemn them. We ought to be full of love, grace, compassion, care — even worry — and then reach out a helping hand and be patient for God to do His work in the lives of those we are serving, in His time, and in His manner. We are just called to be faithful. Your theology matters. Your beliefs about homosexuality matter.

So now a big question - **What does the Bible say about homosexuality – and the place He designed us to express our sexuality?**

There are five key passages that specifically mention homosexuality. Personally, what I have found is that these Scripture passages are quickly twisted and manipulated to mean different things than a traditional evangelical ethic. I have found that I personally do NOT use these passages for any debate or argument.

The few passages specifically referencing homosexuality are:

- Leviticus 18:22 and 20:13 clearly condemn homosexuality.
- Romans 1:26–27 prohibits same-sex behavior.
- 1 Corinthians 6:9–10 and 1 Timothy 1:9–10 mention same-sex sexual behavior.

What I personally choose to do is to stick to a Biblical Sexual Ethic in a more general sense. Scripture clearly limits sexual relationships to one single place — between a man and a woman within a committed marriage.

There is no other place for genital sexual expression. This confirms a sexual ethic that answers questions about homosexuality. Genital sexual experiences are never permissible with the same sex.

Know What God's Word Says!

You are now a preteen or teenager. It is imperative that you know what you believe, have a defense, and stand up for what you believe.

There are a lot of competing voices today. It is critical that you build a solid foundation. This does not give you license to be a bully towards others who believe differently from you. However, you also need to be wise and not become a pushover, falling for any message that kind of sounds good - or even kind of feels right.

You are meant to pull away from your parents and caregivers in your teenage years. This is by design. I want you to be proud of who you are, what you stand for, and the ETHOS you are choosing to live by. **I hope that your home is a safe place. Even more importantly, I hope that YOU are - in how you present yourself and live in relationship to others.**

Are you getting excited about YOUR potential? I hope so. It ought to be scary as well. You are a powerful influencer. How? **Our society NEEDS you to develop your ETHOS young, so that you are living it by the time you are preteen or teen. You can do this.**

So now the most important foundation: A Biblical Sexual Ethic on Homosexuality and God's design for the place for sexual expression rests in Scriptures such as these:

Naked and Unashamed — Genesis 2:24–25:

"This explains why a man leaves his father and mother and is joined to his wife, and the two are united into one. Now the man and his wife were both naked, but they felt no shame" (NLT).

Her Breasts — Proverbs 5:19:

"She is a loving deer, a graceful doe. Let her breasts satisfy you always. May you always be captivated by her love" (NLT).

Lust = Adultery — Matthew 5:28:

"But I say, anyone who even looks at a woman with lust has already committed adultery with her in his heart" (NLT).

Become One Flesh — Matthew 19:4-6:

"Haven't you read," he replied, "that at the beginning the Creator 'made them male and female,' and said, 'For this reason a man will leave his father and mother and be united to his wife, and the two will become one flesh'? So they are no longer two, but one flesh. Therefore what God has joined together, let no one separate." (NIV).

Remain Single — Better to Marry than to Burn — 1 Corinthians 7:8–9:

"Now to the unmarried and the widows I say: It is good for them to stay unmarried, as I do. But if they cannot control themselves, they should marry, for it is better to marry than to burn with passion" (NIV).

Sexual Immorality — Matthew 15:19:

"For from the heart come evil thoughts, murder, adultery, all sexual immorality, theft, lying, and slander" (NLT).

Acts 15:19–20:

"It is my judgment, therefore, that we should not make it difficult for the Gentiles who are turning to God. Instead we should write to them, telling them to abstain from food polluted by idols, from sexual immorality..." (NIV).

1 Corinthians 6:18–20:

"Run from sexual sin! No other sin so clearly affects the body as this one does. For sexual immorality is a sin against your own body. Don't you realize that your body is the temple of the Holy Spirit, who lives in you and was given to you by God? You do not belong to yourself, for God bought you with a high price. So you must honor God with your body" (NLT).

1 Corinthians 7:2–7:

"But since sexual immorality is occurring, each man should have sexual relations with his own wife, and each woman with her own husband. The husband should fulfill his marital duty to his wife, and likewise the wife to her husband. The wife does not have authority over her own body but yields it to her husband. In the same way, the husband does not have authority over his own body but yields it to his wife. Do not deprive each other except perhaps by mutual consent and for a time, so that you may devote yourselves to prayer. Then come together again so that Satan will not tempt you because of your lack of self-control. I say this as a concession, not as a command. I wish that all of you were as I am. But each of you has your own gift from God; one has this gift, another has that" (NIV).

Galatians 5:19–21:

"When you follow the desires of your sinful nature, the results are very clear: sexual immorality, impurity, lustful pleasures, idolatry, sorcery, hostility, quarreling, jealousy, outbursts of anger, selfish ambition, dissension, division, envy, drunkenness, wild parties, and other sins like these. Let me tell you again, as I have before, that anyone living that sort of life will not inherit the Kingdom of God" (NLT).

Colossians 3:5:

"So put to death the sinful, earthly things lurking within you. Have nothing to do with sexual immorality, impurity, lust, and evil desires. Don't be greedy, for a greedy person is an idolater, worshiping the things of this world" (NLT).

1 Thessalonians 4:3–5:

"God's will is for you to be holy, so stay away from all sexual sin. Then each of you will control his own body and live in holiness and honor—not in lustful passion like the pagans who do not know God and his ways" (NLT).

Hebrews 13:4:

"Give honor to marriage, and remain faithful to one another in marriage. God will surely judge people who are immoral and those who commit adultery" (NLT).

* * *

Working Questions – Now it is YOUR TURN:

Why is it important that you have a Biblical understanding of homosexuality?

____

____

Write out some talking points you would use to discuss homosexuality from a biblical perspective.

____

____

____

____

Write down some questions you have and email those to me at *questions@healinglives.com*

____

____

____

____

"The ultimate test of a moral society is the kind of world that it leaves to its children."

What is your takeaway from this quote?

____

____

What is your foundation for creating a Biblical Sexual Ethic of Homosexuality – the Bible or personal experience (yours or others)?

____

____

So now a big question - What does the Bible say about homosexuality – and the place He designed us to express our sexuality?

The passages on homosexuality are:

Leviticus 18:22

"Do not practice homosexuality, having sex with another man as with a woman. It is a detestable sin (NLT).

Leviticus 20:13

"If a man practices homosexuality, having sex with another man as with a woman, both men have committed a detestable act. They must both be put to death, for they are guilty of a capital offense (NLT).

These two verses clearly condemn homosexuality. What are your reactions to these passages? Questions?

Romans 1:26–27

That is why God abandoned them to their shameful desires. Even the women turned against the natural way to have sex and instead indulged in sex with each other. And the men, instead of having normal sexual relations with women, burned with lust for each other. Men did shameful things with other men, and as a result of this sin, they suffered within themselves the penalty they deserved (NLT).

These verses prohibit same-sex behavior. What is your reaction to this passage?

____

____

____

1 Corinthians 6:9–10

Don't you realize that those who do wrong will not inherit the Kingdom of God? Don't fool yourselves. Those who indulge in sexual sin, or who worship idols, or commit adultery, or are male prostitutes, or practice homosexuality, or are thieves, or greedy people, or drunkards, or are abusive, or cheat people—none of these will inherit the Kingdom of God (NLT).

____

____

____

1 Timothy 1:9–10

For the law was not intended for people who do what is right. It is for people who are lawless and rebellious, who are ungodly and sinful, who consider nothing sacred and defile what is holy, who kill their father or mother or commit other murders. The law is for people who are sexually immoral, or who practice homosexuality, or are slave traders, liars, promise breakers, or who do anything else that contradicts the wholesome teaching (NLT).

These verses mention same-sex sexual behavior. What is your reaction?

Note here that other sins are listed in some of these lists above. How are you doing in obeying God's Word and staying away from these other sins? None of us are perfect – so which one(s) is your nemesis?

Go back through the list of other Scriptures that refer to a Biblical Sexual Ethic on human sexuality in general. What are some takeaways that could and/or should influence your beliefs?

| 16 |

Questions About Same-Sex Attraction

Jeff is 17, and he feels that he isn't a sexual being. He is active with school, is succeeding at work, and has friends, but he has never had a girlfriend and wonders if something is wrong. He has always felt attracted to guys, but this has not been a sexual thing either.

Phil is 15 and has no interest in dating girls. He is attracted to men that give him attention and value. He is a Christian and confused about what he should do with these feelings. Everyone around him seems to say his feelings are wrong. Should he be in a same-sex relationship and eventually get married? Deny his feelings? Embrace them? Be disgusted by them?

Janice has always dreamed of being married and a big wedding. Now, at 17, she finds herself very interested in the girls in her life and completely turned off by all the boys her age. What does this mean?

Pam is an attractive athlete. She is a confident leader with a strong personality. She never dreamed of being attracted to girls. She is now 21 and not interested in marriage like her friends. She had a brief sexual experience with an older woman a few years earlier, and she is very confused about her feelings today. "Am I gay? Am I broken? Am I okay? Is this okay?" She feels lost.

Same-sex attraction was not talked about much in years past. Today, it is a topic of conversation everywhere. Is it normal? Some research points out that over twenty-five percent of adolescents will struggle with their sexual identity during their teenage years. This struggle, for most, will end by claiming a heterosexual identity.

This struggle is a normal part of growing up. **Dr. Mark Yarhouse,**[62] a Christian researcher, added a framework to the discussion years ago through his scholarship and teaching. Many people that identify themselves as gay are probably more accurately placed in the space of being same-sex attracted. But, what does this mean? It means that they are attracted to the same-sex, but they are not claiming a gay identity. Though "same-sex attracted" and "gay identity" may sound synonymous, they are not.

By adding this distinction, it **creates a space for individuals to wrestle** and admit to a struggle without having to claim an identity. This has led many people — particularly young people — into a more complete understanding of themselves, the appropriate amount of weight they need to put on their feelings and attractions, and the complexity of who they are. This is a space they desperately need.

You may be in the midst of this struggle. You may have a close friend in this place. I want to give you a word of caution regarding your friends: **be careful about how you love and encourage them in this process.**

They probably already know your thoughts, opinions, and judgments regarding homosexuality. **They need space, questions, care, touch, and friendship.** You will hopefully still have permission to dialogue with them — at least somewhat — so take what you can at this stage.

Prayerfully walk with them, offering friendship through their struggles and questions.

On the other side of this equation, be careful that you do not equate loving them with accepting their behavior. What does this mean? It means you can love them and also disagree with what they are doing. This is important. The current cultural rhetoric tells us we MUST embrace ALL of them in order to love them, or it is a rejection of the whole person. This is nonsense. **Be a leader** - and lead them towards a Biblical Worldview that promotes health and growth, but also reinterpreting of the power and strength of one's desires and attractions. I promise it is worth the tension and stress, even if it is hard.

If you are the one questioning and struggling, please find people that can help you. Who you choose to listen to and follow is life altering. A counselor, a parent, a mentor, or a teacher can change your life forever — for better or worse. This is why the worldview and the truth they believe matters. The choice you make regarding whom you let influence you during your teen and young adult years is of utmost importance. It is life and death to your future on many fronts.

There are some great resources for you already available to you today. I would highly encourage you to read the thoughtful books written by **Dr. Mark Yarhouse**[63] and **Dr. Preston Sprinkle**[64] for a compassionate Christian viewpoint.

Identity struggles are real. The strength of attractions can be overwhelming. I could take the time here to describe the research and findings on the various aspects of the debate on same-sex attraction, but I prefer to focus on **YOUR** heart.

Did you know that every parent does some harm to their children? Yes, even yours. For some of you this is not surprising since there might be a lot of pain here. I am so, so sorry. This is not how it should be. Every parent has spoken harshly at times and caused harm or been too soft when they needed to be strong, and they unintentionally caused harm. This is a reality of the fallen world we live in, but it is not God's perfect design.

Dr. Dan Allender[65] describes a **hunger** that grows in all of us as we mature and prepare to leave our father and mother. Why? **God never meant for your family to be all of the things to you. It is part of the design for you to leave, grow up, be your best self, and separate from your parents.** This doesn't mean you leave and never speak to them again, although there is a time and a place for this when there has been serious harm.

Most parents seem unwilling to embrace this reality and make adolescence a more difficult life stage than it should be. You DO NOT have to strive for perfection. When you fail, you can model seeking forgiveness and restoring the relationship – with friends as well as with family members. When your parents fail, you have an opportunity to practice forgiveness. You will go through a lot of wrestling and struggles because of who your parents are and what they have been through. Some parents blame themselves for their children's choices for the rest of their lives. That extreme isn't right either though. You have free will, and yes, your parents also share the responsibility in raising you and shaping you - both what they did intentionally and with all the things they missed. It is sad to say, but some parents are completely unaware or unable to admit they had any negative impact on their children's development. Again, I say that I am SO sorry. This is not how it was meant to be.

Do you and your family spend a lot of time out with other people in social settings? One child may thrive in this environment and enjoy the social setting, while another child may shrink back in the face of crowds and learn to loathe social situations.

Is your family active or sedentary? This impacts your life and development.

Do you eat a healthy, balanced diet, or do you eat poorly? How your family related to food, food prep, and mealtimes impacts your growth and development.

Were your parents openly affectionate in front of you? This has a huge impact on your sense of security — even if you acted like it was gross.

The energy and culture of your home has a tremendous impact on your physical development, spiritual formation, and sense of security.

A Theology (A Belief System)

So, let's address a question I hear often.

Is attraction to the same sex a sin?

Let's start by unpacking 'attraction'. I believe we have such a distorted view of attraction that it confuses a lot of our life choices. It is critical we have 'attraction' in the right place no matter who we are attracted to.

Do you have control of your attractions?

Can you see someone and control whether you think they are "good-looking" or not?

Do you have the ability to NOT be aroused by someone that you find attractive?

Is arousal sin?

Some people place 'attraction' under the umbrella of self-control. I actually disagree, though. Picture this: The men and women I know that have learned the art and skill of "controlling" their attractions, or "managing" their attractions and arousal face different challenges and difficulties. Picture a young man or woman that has done this beautifully, and essentially turned themselves off. They marry one day and cannot "turn on" what they successfully conquered, controlled, and "turned off." **This is not stewardship.**

It breaks my heart that we would likely parade this young man or woman around as the picture of the perfect young "self-controlled" Christian. I would say emphatically — NO! They are not being human. **That is NOT stewardship.**

It is more like a denial or a dismissal of a part of God's perfect design, stating it is flawed and bad — maybe even evil. No, No, NO! **Stewardship is the key.** You and I have feelings, attractions, and experience arousal that we must learn to value correctly.

The data we receive in our brains based on attraction, feelings, desires, and arousal is ALL subjective. **How are you stewarding your sexual attractions?** Think about what happens when this data is a large chunk of someone's identity, and it is telling them something different from everyone else around them. This is a confusing space. **This is the space where that person (or you) needs accurate data, support, and God's Word the most.**

They (or you) need a place to ask questions, to feel, to hurt, and even to grieve. An important aspect of having feelings, desires, attractions and urges that you say "NO" to, is that **the next step is often experiencing GRIEF**.

You will have chosen to die to yourself, which is unpopular today, and that can leave you lonely.

What would motivate someone to give up something they want? It is in seeing a bigger picture and a greater reward. This is why our **theology matters – our beliefs**.

So, **is attraction to the same sex sin?** I do not think so.

Attraction is part of the **data** being processed that leads someone to make a decision.

Will this define me? Should I act on this feeling? What do I do? Who am I? Am I gay? What does God want from me? What is His best for me? Who do I follow? **The TRUTH is: I ALWAYS have a choice!**

This is why we need the 'space' to process, hurt, ask questions, and grieve.

Your beliefs about attractions should inform all of your other relationships.

Think about it this way: if I lined up five hundred men and five hundred women and had you decide who stays and who goes based on **attraction**, you could eliminate many from the line easily – if not most. If we took this a step further, and you had a lengthy conversation with each person, you could eliminate more, both male and female.

I honestly think that many of us would eliminate the person who would be our best friend or the best match for us in marriage in the first or second evaluation. So, what am I saying?

I am saying that **attraction is a bad measuring stick.**

Beware of how much weight you place on feelings and attraction — no matter what stage of life you are in.

I could go into a lot of the biology behind attraction and same-sex attraction, but I don't believe that will be helpful at this point. The purpose of this section is for you to learn skills and gain some perspective to help you navigate your attractions so that you live guided by an ETHOS that is not based solely on what you feel.

What Do I Say or Do?

Have you ever made an impulsive purchase that you regretted later? Have you ever realized you have blanked out for an entire class and you know that you took notes, but you cannot consciously remember anything the teacher said? These are examples of how easily we act without thinking. Are we thinking at all during these moments? Yes, we are, but our operating system is running in the background, in our subconscious. If it is so outside of our awareness, did we really think it through? Nope. Not at all.

The goal is to move our decision making to the forefront, to the **prefrontal cortex**, so that there can be an honest evaluation and appraisal of the decision that needs to be made. It is important for everyone to learn to bring wisdom to our decision-making process.

Has your family ever discussed the impact of a big purchase "as a family?" This can be an important lesson to learn.

Do your parents act impulsively? If so, don't be surprised if you struggle with impulsive decision making yourself.

I want you to learn and remember that by moving things out of your subconscious and into the decision-making center — the **prefrontal cortex** — you are gaining a leg up on everyone that does not learn this skill. Others will continue to base their decisions on emotions and impulses, which honestly, cannot be trusted.

Sin loves the **operating system of the subconscious**. It can sit there and work in the background, corroding the system, and it can go completely unnoticed. It is important to see that you have control. I want you to be a young man or woman that helps others expose sin and darkness. It is critical to do so tactfully so you preserve future relationships.

So, what should you do if a friend expresses they have attractions towards the same sex?

The answer is simple: Listen. Be patient. Challenge them to think deeper. Have conversations that help shape their worldview, but do not demand that they conform, or feel something they do not feel.

The more that these feelings and attractions are processed verbally and not in the subconscious operating system, the better. This could be with you, a caring Christian counselor, a mentor, or a teacher. Usually, most teens DO NOT talk to these adults, but they will discuss their thoughts with their peers - possibly with YOU! This is why it is important that you know what to do - and what NOT to do.

Do these feelings ever change? Actually, yes, they do. They can. And YES, they will definitely morph over time. They are never static. This is why LOVE is hard - it takes choice and intention and investment.

Remember "**the space**"[66] of same-sex attraction that I was talking about earlier? This is what I want you to create. Once an identity is settled on, and once they (or you) have engaged in sexual activity with the same sex, further movement becomes much more difficult. The process of identity formation is a critical process we all go through. It matters who we say we are and how we define ourselves. This goes for all areas and parts of ourselves.

If you tell yourself that you're just a lazy bum, don't be surprised at how this plays out down the road.

If you tell yourself you are not smart and that you can't learn, you'll find your limiting beliefs are becoming true in your life. **So, take every thought captive.** Scrutinize it and decide whether it is capital "T" Truth. Do this consciously, intentionally, and with the knowledge that it will be a battle. Do not settle for being guided by feelings or attractions. Don't let a desire become your identity.

Care and Compassion – A Biblical Response

Moms and dads often ask me how they can love their child without accepting or supporting their behavior or lifestyle. This is a heart wrenching place to be in as a leader or parent.

There is a setup in the system today that allows only two options going forward, as I have mentioned before:

- You must either accept me as I am, asking nothing of me;
- or, you hate me.

It is selfish and limiting to view the world, relationships, and reality this way. So many people, young and old, make one decision that changes their lives forever and also has a huge impact on those that love them, but they demand that everyone else remain silent and accept it or be labeled a hater. This is unacceptable and unattainable - but it is also our current reality.

What you believe about love matters. Some people's definition of love means that others cannot use their own discernment, make judgments, or question anything they do. This person will seldom see growth or maturity.

Other people have a definition of love that allows others to use their own discernment, challenge them, and disagree. This person will experience growth and enjoy their relationships. I hope this is you. If not, I hope this is who you want to become.

Which of these is biblical? I would have to say the latter one. **God loves us so much that He does NOT let us stay as we are, but he expects growth, maturity, and sacrifice so that we become more and more like Christ every day over a lifetime.** The first definition of love demands its own way and is looking out for itself— not others.

So, what do care and compassion look like?

It is being gentle, yet still pushing. It is having compassion, but not lowering or altering your standards.

When you were five years old, the bar was pretty low. At fifteen, it got higher. At twenty-five, it will rise even higher. When you were a new believer, God adopted you with NO requirements. **Years later, though, you are being shaped and challenged, and there is an expectation that your life will bear more fruit than in your early days as a new believer.**

Expect more out of others. Expect more out of them, though, **with care and compassion** — not an iron fist or demands.

Think of it this way: **You are playing the long game.** They may not be willing to listen to you today, so remain in their life, listen, be compassionate, and show genuine care for them.

Playing the long game is staying "in relationship" so that when their life falls apart — and everyone's does — you are there and have been there as a constant reminder of God's love and faithfulness.

Remember that loving anyone is **ALL** about the long game. God is at work. You are only a small instrument. **He** changes people. Nagging, sarcasm, and anger are not tools that He uses.

Be consistent in your love for them. Wait expectantly for an opening to enter a new level of relationship where they may listen to you for the first time. Be present, even if it is uncomfortable. Choose your battles wisely, ruled by God's love for them, and with care and compassion. What does compassion look like?

Compassion is a heart breaking for someone you deeply love. It is patience. It is endurance. It is the long game.

If this is YOU, finding a person who is doing the above is imperative. Who you listen to will greatly shape who you become. You can reach out to key people to influence you. I hope you will. But this can also go any way you desire. Who you choose to listen to shapes everything for you. Are they grounding everything they say and ask you to do on God's Word? This is the test. There are a lot of false prophets and teachers out there. Beware!

* * *

Working Questions – Now it is YOUR TURN:

Same-sex attraction might seem like a foreign concept to you. Think about these questions in relation to yourself:

Do you have control over whom you are attracted to? Can you see someone and control whether you think they are "good-looking" or not? Do you have the ability NOT to be aroused by someone that you find attractive? Is arousal towards someone of the same sex sin?

____

____

____

A critical part of attraction is learning to die to some feelings for a specific reason. What are some reasons we deny ourselves things, feelings, attractions, and passions? Why would we ever deny ourselves?

Based on this reading, what will you do when a friend expresses they have attractions towards the same-sex?

What is care and compassion?

| 17 |

What is Polyamory?

I wish I could leave this out of a book like this, but I cannot. This is a growing reality that is becoming more and more acceptable in our society. What is polyamory? These relationships can be structured in many different ways.

The simple definition is **3 or more people**. Terms like "open couples," "vees," "triads," "quads," or even "moresomes" involve 3 or more people that share a life together and some sort of sexual relationship with one or more of the partners.

These families vary in how they look but tend to be very strict on openness and honesty as they work out the rules and roles of this experimental relationship. It is not a relationship between 3 or more people with no rules. All relationships have parameters, boundaries, and expectations. These are obviously less prescribed in the polyamorous relationship and require work.

Question – Could you explain why a polyamorous relationship is against God's Word? What are the biblical arguments for and against such a relationship? Does the Bible explicitly make

a case for a heterosexual, monogamous marital relationship, excluding all other alternatives?

I want to begin this explanation on poly relationships by looking at the white paper written by **Dr. Branson Parler,**[67] a Professor at Kuyper College and a Writer / Advisor at the Center for Faith, Sexuality, & Gender headed up by Dr. Preston Sprinkle.

Dr. Branson Parler[68] gives us a great look at what the Bible includes that is pro-polyamory. I know that sounds weird. But this is important. The Old Testament has plenty of examples of polygamy – ranging from Abraham, Jacob, Gideon, Saul, David, and Solomon. How can David – known as a "man after God's own heart" (1 Samuel 13:14) – be in a non-monogamous relationship and be called that by God Himself? Are men and women in the Bible meant to be examples for us – are their lives and choices prescriptive? The Bible is descriptive more than it is prescriptive. This means the Bible is less about telling you the how to's of everything, and more about painting an overall picture.

Did you know that Old Testament allowed for polygamy? It did. Deuteronomy 21:15-17 helps us see the world at the time – what to do if you have two wives and you leave them both? The law accounted for this, so does this mean they are permissible?

Could it be that polygamous relationships are bad because they are patriarchal? What does that mean? Patriarchy means men are over women. Could this be true? Are women only for baby making? It is true that the Bible is written in a time where culture was extremely patriarchal. But this is not the teaching of Scripture. We will get to that in a minute.

Have you ever heard that the trinity is polygamous? That one blew my mind. Then I paused and realized there is a truth to that. But are they "in bed together" figuratively speaking, or are there fully separate, and more like a family? The language used, as Dr. Parler[69] points out, is more of the **father and son tone.**

Could you picture God's Word expressing a sexual or polyamorous relationship with each and every one of us? How does that sit with you? Is the sexual more strong and more important than friendship? Which supersedes? Does this get messy here? What if it is more along the lines of Christ and the Church (which includes us all)? **This picture is much more along the lines of monogamy.**

One last thing to consider regarding a pro polyamory from Scripture – it is all about love. Is it? Really? **Does a sexual ethic mean anything goes if it is consensual?** I sure hope not. What does sex mean? Is it also up to each individual – or is there a grander design?

A bonus – are polyamorous people born this way? Or is it a choice? Is there a poly orientation? Let's say that it is true – people can be born this way – what does that mean to a Biblical Sexual Ethic? What does that mean to my own personal choices? What if I feel that way?

Monogamy

So, what does the Bible really say about monogamy? Dr. Parler[70] notes that the Bible was written in a world where exclusive monogamy was NOT the norm. **Did you know that sexual exclusivity (monogamy – one man with one woman for life) has NOT been the norm throughout the majority of civilization.**

Genesis 1 and 2 clearly unfolds creation highlighting a creation of a woman for a man – one to one. This is not polygamous (multiple wives for a husband), nor polyamorous. It is singular. Another important highlight in the creation story is that Adam and Eve are to be faithful to one another, and permanent – for life. This is sacrificial. This is also placing the sexual union between the two as exclusive. There is a clear definition. I challenge you to investigate this and take notes at the end of this chapter.

In Matthew 19, Jesus is tested about marriage. Dr. Parler[71] emphasizes that Jesus highlights here **three characteristics of marriage.**

First, marriage is between a man and a woman. He quotes Genesis 1:27. Sexual differences are critical in terms of God's original intent and design.

Second, marriage is for life.

And **third**, marriage is monogamous. Matthew 19:5-6 clearly establishes the parameters of "two."

Discussions throughout Scripture about divorce continue to back up the design of one man with one woman for life. **Two. Sexually different.** This is the only design and purpose. **The emphasis here is a man leaving his family and clinging to, cleaving to his bride.** Adding another man or woman creates a divide. This creates an imbalance and a built-in competition and jealousy factor that cannot be managed, just ignored. It is a setup.

Ephesians 5:25-32 teaches us that love is self-giving. It is also singular. Christ had the same mission –
"to love the church and give Himself for her."

I would even dare say that you and I CANNOT show this devotion and singular focus to more than one person – at this level, and in this way. We are designed to "forsake all others." Another beautiful statement and perspective that Dr. Parler states is that "a husband and wife who live out this calling will make the Gospel more believable as their singular devotion becomes a sign and symbol of Christ's love for us."[72]

Thoughts? **How do you respond to a peer that is proud to be bisexual?** Or to be poly? Keep wrestling.

* * *

Working Questions – Now it is YOUR TURN:

What would you say to a friend that is in a polyamorous relationship or considering one?

____

____

Matthew 19 *(the whole chapter)*

What is Mathew teaching about here?

What is your takeaway from these verses regarding marriage?

Do you see the clear parameter of 2 sexually different people qualifying for a biblical marriage relationship?

____

____

Genesis 1:27

"So God created human beings in his own image. In the image of God he created them; male and female he created them."

Who's idea was it for 2 genders - and for these two to come together to create the world?

____

____

Matthew 19:5-6

And he said, "'This explains why a man leaves his father and mother and is joined to his wife, and the two are united into one.' Since they are no longer two but one, let no one split apart what God has joined together."

What is your takeaway from these specific verses from Matthew 19?

____

____

Ephesians 5:25-32

For husbands, this means love your wives, just as Christ loved the church. He gave up his life for her to make her holy and clean, washed by the cleansing of God's word. He did this to present her to himself as a glorious church without a spot or wrinkle or any other blemish. Instead, she will be holy and without fault. In the same way, husbands ought to love their wives as they love their own bodies. For a man who loves his wife actually shows love for himself. No one hates his own body but feeds and cares for it, just as Christ cares for the church. And we are members of his body. As the Scriptures say, "A man leaves his father and mother and is joined to his wife, and the two are united into one." This is a great mystery, but it is an illustration of the way Christ and the church are one.

What does these verses say regarding marriage and one man and one woman and the purpose of marriage?

____

____

| 18 |

Porn and Intimacy

The amount of pornography present in today's culture is overwhelming. It is rare to not have seen nudity in some form or fashion by your early teen years (if not sooner). It is normal to see a lot of pornography and for it to consume many teens. I hope this is NOT you, but if it is, there is hope for renewal.

You are a target. If an advertiser can hook you now, then they will have a customer for life. This is true for all products — from phone and computer apps to pornography and the food industry. Some industries sell products and services that are morally and ethically neutral. Others are predators, preying on you, your naivete and your unquenchable curiosity.

Pornography is a powerful drug that has entered nearly every life and home in some way. There is no place for it in a Biblical Sexual Ethic. It steals. It distorts. It harms relationships and destroys families. It rewires the brain.

Mark 7:20–23 reminds us of what we are dealing with inside:

> *"And then he added, 'It is what comes from inside that defiles you. For from within, out of a person's heart, come evil thoughts, sexual immorality, theft, murder, adultery, greed, wickedness, deceit, lustful desires, envy, slander, pride, and foolishness. All these vile things come from within; they are what defile you'" (NLT).*

You and I both have the potential to be unwise and make poor choices. This passage of Scripture hits hard. **We are sin bent**, but we have **choice** as well!

These desires and our bent towards these things is truly normal, but is this what YOU want for yourself? Or do you want a better story for your future?

Pornography

Sara, age 10, slams the computer closed as her mom enters the room and runs off. Her mother opens the laptop and the browser to find pictures of naked people. What should she do? Her next move matters tremendously.

Jeff easily found a way around his parents' internet filters and goes to his drug of choice multiple times a day. He is only 13 years old, but he has spent hours on devices that his parents didn't know could access pornography. He doesn't own a cell phone, laptop, or tablet. He uses his iPod touch, his old Gameboy, and the browser in his video game system. He knows how to hide his tracks, and his parents have no idea of his secret life.

Pam is 11 and has discovered that she gets a good feeling when she looks at videos on her smartphone. Her parents gave her the phone to keep her safe when she walks home from school alone every day. She spends hours each day watching pornography and scrolling through images from the time she arrives home from school until her parents return home from work.

Pornography is nearly inescapable.

I often wondered when my own kids were younger **who will show pornography to my kids first?** Someone will. I know it.

Let me sum up everything in one sentence:

While you are young, you must establish what is NOT okay regarding nudity, images, and video. This is a powerful force that can change your life forever.

I want to say that parents need to prepare you. But, as I have seen in my research, most families do not. You will have to be intentional here. If you don't prepare yourself ahead of time, someone will be able to sway you more easily. It only takes one view to be sucked in. Even though most report that their first-time viewing pornography elicited a "gross" response, it pulls at our natural curiosity and draws you back in for more.

How can you limit the attraction and draw of this powerful drug? It is a drug – at least in the way it reacts and works in your brain.

TALK ABOUT IT! Be honest regarding its impact on YOUR heart and relationships. Develop an understanding that it distorts love, intimacy, and it steals peace. Move your habits out of your unconscious and into your conscious. You always have a choice.

Pornography rewires the brain for **novelty**. It makes the ability to settle down with one spouse and find satisfaction with just one person nearly impossible. Today's pornography is more shocking, abusive, and disturbing than ever before. It lacks true intimacy, and it draws the viewer in by the skin, bodies, and freedom that many imagine.

True freedom in sex is not what we see in pornography. Pornography is bondage. It is never enough. Sex becomes a drug, and it NEVER truly satisfies. No one person will ever be enough. As screens have become a larger part of our lifestyle, virtual reality has become a new form of pornography. No human being can measure up to an avatar. Marriages fail. True intimacy always loses.

Here is a wild truth for some. Many of the women that film porn videos view this work as a step up from where they were before, and my heart breaks for them. Doing porn, dancing naked on stage for money, prostituting, and offering escorting services are places where many of them find value, respect, and even feel the power of being worshiped. They may love the attention and power, yet they are still being exploited. We cannot deny that part either. Many remain in this line of work because it gives them a sense of satisfaction and a sense of control. This ought to be eye-opening.

Nudity ROCKS! Nudity has a place and a context biblically. **It is reserved for marriage between one man and one woman**. Outside of that protective relationship, nudity decreases in value, erodes, and is never enough. Ironically, our culture sees the latter as freedom. It isn't though. **It is bondage**.

Freedom is not having to worry about sexually transmitted infections and diseases.

Freedom is giving and receiving love that honors, serves, gives, and respects.

Freedom is sexual satisfaction and enjoyment without pressure, demand, exchange of money, or performance. Ironically, freedom is found in marriage. Monogamy.

This is so amazing. **The only place that naturally creates life is the sexual relationship between a man and a woman.** Sex is more than a game for fun, for self, for pleasure, or for release. It should always remain in the context and protection of a marriage relationship. I hope you will want to raise the bar to require just that — relationship. Commitment. Boundaries.

What should Sara's mom do now, after catching her ten-year-old viewing explicit content online?

This is the time for a ***micro-conversation***. This is NOT the time for a lecture. This is NOT the time to yell at her and make her feel shame. Sara probably already feels shame inside, even though she does not know how to express it. A parent's job is to help her process what she has seen and to let go of the shame trapped inside her young body and be free. Shame takes a deeper root and sets its talons in her heart and soul the longer she holds it inside. She needs comfort. Help her have a safe space to process, feel, and ask questions — even explicit ones. The truth is that whatever "innocence" she had before, it is gone now. Treat her with care, but also as if she is older than she may be. **She is now stewarding a heavier load in her head and heart.**

Help her carry it. How? Help by moving her thoughts and habits out of the subconscious into the prefrontal cortex. And talk about it.

Help her evaluate it.

Help her decide and say out loud what is best and what is harmful. This is not something you can do for her, but you can walk her towards a decision and let her make it. You are the guide, while your child is the main character. Be a great guide.

How Porn Has Intensified – and it Corrupts

The prevalence of pornography is mind blowing to many adults today. For many preteens and teens, the first time they viewed pornography they are viewing videos of graphic, gross, and abusive scenes that most of us would consider horrifying – at least at first. **After no time at all we become more desensitized.**

Think about this: if this is your first exposure, where do you go from here?

Pornography has gone to places most of us cannot imagine. If you go online and search for any beloved cartoon and add the word porn to it, you will find that someone has taken those animated characters and turned them into sexual fiends. I recently learned about My Little Pony porn. Each pony has huge breasts *and* a penis. Think about that. This is not normal and quite confusing – and arousing, nonetheless.

Another new form of pornography involves men who have undergone hormone replacement to grow breasts and now possess both sexes' sexual parts. It shows these men engaging in sexual play with other men like them. Think about the implications of this on you and your peers. It is confusing and seriously damages your future relationships and sexual ethic.

It ought to terrify you to know the perverse extremes of nudity and sexual activity that are available online, just a few clicks away, on a device most of us carry in our pockets. With all that is out there, it is tempting to say that it isn't a big deal if you see a naked picture of a man or woman as God created them. However, Scripture states there should not be:

"even a hint of sexual immorality" (Ephesians 5:3, NIV).

Can it be said that there is "not even a hint" of immorality in your own life?

The impact of sexual images on our hearts and minds is immeasurable. Of all things, graphic videos portraying sex between multiple people is nothing short of abusive and animalistic. This is an unacceptable image. **Sex is about relationship.** This is God's design for sexual intimacy — reserved and preserved for the marriage relationship between one man and one woman. There is NO other place.

The nudity of past years in magazine spreads, calendars, and posters had a huge impact on society, drawing men and women into a space they never should have entered into. Naked pictures impact you to a small degree. This is nothing though when compared to what you may see on video. This changes everything.

Imagine the impact these easily accessible video clips portraying abuse and "anything goes" will have.

Imagine the even graver impact it will have on you if you see these things and never verbally process what you have seen with someone.

There is hope if you can move it from the subconscious to the conscious — to the prefrontal cortex. How do you do this? **By asking hard questions and being willing to listen.** This is a dark subject with a tremendous impact on your future.

Impossible Intimacy - Challenged And Redefined

Consider the impact of these video clips on your understanding and framework for what is healthy between a man and woman in marriage. This assumes that a Biblical Sexual Ethic is important to you. I hope it is being taught in your home. If not, then you are in the right place. God's design for marriage and intimacy is simple, well defined, and safe.

Imagine how your intimacy in the future with a real person will be affected after a few years of viewing pornography. This is hard to imagine, I know. It is very important to think about, though.

Imagine the impact that the constant downloading of video clips into your brain over the course of years will have on your ability to settle down and marry.

How will pornography influence your view of how you should treat your "love" and/or how they should treat YOU? This is HUGE!

This is why it is SO important that YOU develop a clear picture, understanding, and theology of marriage and intimacy. It is important that you know how to recognize healthy touch so you can discern abuse in all of its forms. **This requires that you read and keep studying and grounding your beliefs in God's Word and good research - not emotion.**

I am so glad that you will now be able to further strengthen your ETHOS. **I have the honor of helping you and your family in equipping you, so you are growing up:**

> *"in the way they should go" (Proverbs 22:6 NKJV)* - **the way YOU should go**.

Thank you for trusting me.

Sex Over Relationship

A final aspect to consider is where pornography puts **sex** compared to **relationship**.

Sex trumps relationship in porn.

Relationships require time, patience, managing differences, having conversations, and compromise.

Sex requires almost nothing. A lonely future awaits you if you buy into the belief that **sex** is "no big deal." If you have ever watched video clips of porn or XXX movies, then you know that there is always something important missing in each encounter, despite the drama and cinematic wizardry. It is all "doing" and void of intimacy and **relationship**. This is a million miles away from God's design. It is not about the bigger orgasm, longer foreplay, or the experience of ecstasy.

God means for sex between a husband and wife to do three things — yes, the 3 P's — provide **Pleasure**, **Protection**, and **Procreation**.

Scripture is clear about our hearts, our minds, our eyes, and our bodies. Here are a few samples from God's Word:

Job 31:1

"I made a covenant with my eyes not to look with lust at a young woman" (NLT).

Explain how you can live out what Job did. What are some practical ideas? (Answer in spaces at end of the chapter)

Proverbs 5:15–23

"Drink water from your own well — share your love only with your wife.

Why spill the water of your springs in the streets, having sex with just anyone? You should reserve it for yourselves. Never share it with strangers.

Let your wife be a fountain of blessing for you. Rejoice in the wife of your youth. She is a loving deer, a graceful doe. Let her breasts satisfy you always. May you always be captivated by her love. Why be captivated, my son, by an immoral woman, or fondle the breasts of a promiscuous woman?

For the Lord sees clearly what a man does, examining every path he takes. An evil man is held captive by his own sins; they are ropes that catch and hold him. He will die for lack of self-control; he will be lost because of his great foolishness." (NLT).

How would you explain this passage? Are you living by this truth?

Proverbs 6:32

"But the man who commits adultery is an utter fool, for he destroys himself" (NLT).

Explain how this destroys him (or her).

Matthew 5:27–28

"You have heard the commandment that says, 'You must not commit adultery.' But I say, anyone who even looks at a woman with lust has already committed adultery with her in his heart'" (NLT).

This seems impossible. What are we supposed to learn from this passage?

Matthew 6:22–23

"Your eye is like a lamp that provides light for your body. When your eye is healthy, your whole body is filled with light. But when your eye

is unhealthy, your whole body is filled with darkness. And if the light you think you have is actually darkness, how deep that darkness is!" (NLT).

What does this passage teach?

Romans 13:13–14

"Because we belong to the day, we must live decent lives for all to see. Don't participate in the darkness of wild parties and drunkenness, or in sexual promiscuity and immoral living, or in quarreling and jealousy. Instead, clothe yourself with the presence of the Lord Jesus Christ. And don't let yourself think about ways to indulge your evil desires" (NLT).

How can this help you in leading well?

1 Corinthians 6:18–20

"Run from sexual sin! No other sin so clearly affects the body as this one does. For sexual immorality is a sin against your own body. Don't you realize that your body is the temple of the Holy Spirit, who lives in you and was given to you by God? You do not belong to yourself, for God bought you with a high price. So you must honor God with your body" (NLT).

Explain what the Lord tells us to do in this passage.

Colossians 3:5

"So put to death the sinful, earthly things lurking within you. Have nothing to do with sexual immorality, impurity, lust, and evil desires. Don't be greedy, for a greedy person is an idolater, worshiping the things of this world" (NLT).

How do we "put to death" these things?

1 Thessalonians 4:3–8

"God's will is for you to be holy, so stay away from all sexual sin. Then each of you will control his own body and live in holiness and honor—not in lustful passion like the pagans who do not know God and his ways. Never harm or cheat a fellow believer in this matter by violating his wife, for the Lord avenges all such sins, as we have solemnly warned you before. God has called us to live holy lives, not impure lives. Therefore, anyone who refuses to live by these rules is not disobeying human teaching but is rejecting God, who gives his Holy Spirit to you" (NLT).

What does this passage remind us to do and be?

Hebrews 13:4

"Give honor to marriage, and remain faithful to one another in marriage. God will surely judge people who are immoral and those who commit adultery" (NLT).

Write out this passage in your own words as a reminder for yourself.

* * *

Working Questions – Now it is YOUR TURN:

Mark 7:20–23 reminds us of what we are dealing with inside:

"And then he added, 'It is what comes from inside that defiles you. For from within, out of a person's heart, come evil thoughts, sexual immorality, theft, murder, adultery, greed, wickedness, deceit, lustful desires, envy, slander,

pride, and foolishness. All these vile things come from within; they are what defile you'" (NLT).

What is your takeaway?

____

____

Scripture states there should not be:

"even a hint of sexual immorality" (Ephesians 5:3, NIV).

Can it be said that there is "not even a hint" of immorality in your own life?

____

____

Scripture is clear about our hearts, our minds, our eyes, and our bodies. Here are a few samples from God's Word:

Job 31:1

"I made a covenant with my eyes not to look with lust at a young woman" (NLT).

Explain how you can live out what Job did here. What are some practical ideas?

____

____

Proverbs 5:15–23

"Drink water from your own well — share your love only with your wife. Why spill the water of your springs in the streets, having sex with just anyone? You should reserve it for yourselves. Never share it with strangers.

Let your wife be a fountain of blessing for you. Rejoice in the wife of your youth. She is a loving deer, a graceful doe. Let her breasts satisfy you always. May you always be captivated by her love. Why be captivated, my son, by an immoral woman, or fondle the breasts of a promiscuous woman?

For the Lord sees clearly what a man does, examining every path he takes. An evil man is held captive by his own sins; they are ropes that catch and hold him. He will die for lack of self-control; he will be lost because of his great foolishness." (NLT).

How would you explain this passage? Are you living by this truth?

____

____

Proverbs 6:32

"But the man who commits adultery is an utter fool, for he destroys himself" (NLT).

Explain how this destroys him (or her).

____

____

Matthew 5:27–28

"You have heard the commandment that says, 'You must not commit adultery.' But I say, anyone who even looks at a woman with lust has already committed adultery with her in his heart'" (NLT).

This seems impossible. What are we supposed to learn from this passage?

____

____

Matthew 6:22–23

"Your eye is like a lamp that provides light for your body. When your eye is healthy, your whole body is filled with light. But when your eye is unhealthy, your whole body is filled with darkness. And if the light you think you have is actually darkness, how deep that darkness is!" (NLT).

Explain what this passage teaches.

____

____

Romans 13:13–14

"Because we belong to the day, we must live decent lives for all to see. Don't participate in the darkness of wild parties and drunkenness, or in sexual promiscuity and immoral living, or in quarreling and jealousy. Instead, clothe yourself with the presence of the Lord Jesus Christ. And don't let yourself think about ways to indulge your evil desires" (NLT).

How can this help you in your leading of others?

____

____

1 Corinthians 6:18–20

"Run from sexual sin! No other sin so clearly affects the body as this one does. For sexual immorality is a sin against your own body. Don't you realize that your body is the temple of the Holy Spirit, who lives in you and was given to you by God? You do not belong to yourself, for God bought you with a high price. So you must honor God with your body" (NLT).

Explain what the Lord tells us to do in this passage.

____

____

Colossians 3:5

"So put to death the sinful, earthly things lurking within you. Have nothing to do with sexual immorality, impurity, lust, and evil desires. Don't be greedy, for a greedy person is an idolater, worshiping the things of this world" (NLT).

How do we "put to death" these things?

____

____

1 Thessalonians 4:3–8

"God's will is for you to be holy, so stay away from all sexual sin. Then each of you will control his own body and live in holiness and honor—not in lustful passion like the pagans who do not know God and his ways. Never harm or cheat a fellow believer in this matter by violating his wife, for the Lord avenges all such sins, as we have solemnly warned you before. God has called us to live holy lives, not impure lives. Therefore, anyone who refuses to live by these rules is not disobeying human teaching but is rejecting God, who gives his Holy Spirit to you" (NLT).

What does this passage remind us to do and be?

____

____

Hebrews 13:4

"Give honor to marriage, and remain faithful to one another in marriage. God will surely judge people who are immoral and those who commit adultery" (NLT).

Write out this passage in your own words as a reminder for yourself.

____

____

Can your parents protect you 100% from pornography?

____

What are some negative effects of viewing pornography?

____

____

What is your reaction to the bizarre and troubling types of pornography available such as My Little Pony porn? (I do not advise you to look this up.)

____

____

Have you been exposed to pornography? If so, tell your parents. If not, have you had micro-conversations with them about what you should do if you see it?

____

____

What does “intimacy” mean?

____

____

What does “sex over relationship” mean?

____

____

What boundaries should you put in place regarding intimacy, pornography, relationships, and community?

____

____

| 19 |

Dating - Reimagined

"Single, never married" is a status on the rise for adults. "Newly single" (divorced) has also hit more than its fair share of adults that never thought they would be single again. When you get married later in life, there is a high probability that you will find yourself single as an adult. So here is the problem: **You are still a sexual being, and it is imperative that you develop the skills that will allow you to build healthy relationships and steward your sexuality well as an unmarried adult.**

I want you to think through the following and commit to doing things differently from those around you – those outside of the Church, and those in the Church. I believe that most single adults are setting themselves up to fail with each decision they make. I don't want you to be in their shoes. I also believe that most teenagers and even preteens are doing the same.

So, what's your plan? Do you have one? Do you have an approach for healthy dating and relationship building that you plan to use to protect your heart?

Did you know that a PLAN can protect you from your worst enemy – YOURSELF?

It is true. YOU make your own choices. Live like your friends and your results may vary. Live intentionally, thinking through your decisions with the long view in mind, and you will live from wisdom.

I want to help you build a strong, healthy framework for dating. This is a lifesaving tool that is critical in being able to avoid the pain that most go through as young adults.

An arena of tremendous controversy in human sexuality is masturbation — the "M" word. (We will dive deeper into this in the next chapter). What does the medical field say? What does culture say? What does the Church say? What should you do? Is it okay? Is it neutral? Does it cause blindness?

I want to prepare you to use wisdom and knowledge in your favor – to make wise, conscious choices.

As our culture learns more about trauma, we realize that its presence has a serious impact on the whole person. It is important that you avoid experiencing serious trauma, but also that you have the skills to **address past trauma as it has a high rate of resurrection, haunting its victims.**

One of trauma's tools is **shame**. Shame is a destroyer of our soul, our motivation, and any vision we might have for a bright future. It cripples us in many areas of our life, robbing us of confidence and forward momentum.

Forgiveness, for many, is a hard concept to accept, let alone give freely, yet it holds the key to the freedom we desire. To move beyond trauma and its grip, you will need to be able to express both **sorrow** and **gratitude** as we discussed earlier.

For those of you that have been through deeply scarring events, have you wept for the loss you endured because of the trauma?

Have you been able to orient your heart towards **gratitude** for the other blessings in your life?

Gratitude cannot coexist with **shame**. The peace found in joy is not found through penance. Penance is the "acting out" of a payment that has no end. You cannot find resolution this way.

Equipping yourself with skills that will minimize the impact of potentially traumatic life events is a start.

Developing **resilience** that helps you rise above difficulties, disappointments, and pain is a critical life skill. I want you to find this freedom to live and lead well. Keep reading.

Imagine that you are sixteen and dating a sixteen-year-old peer.

Are you ready?

Are you prepared to steward this kind of responsibility?

What is dating?

What is this word from the past called **courtship**?

I want to share a practical framework to guide you towards a Biblical Sexual Ethic in your relationships with others.

Learning What True Sexual Freedom Looks Like

You are a sexual being. You have been from birth. As you grow, the level of **stewardship** required is proportional to your physical and hormonal maturity. This does not come with a switch! It takes conscious decision making and forethought.

Most teenagers and young adults base their decisions on convenience and impulse.

I want you to develop forethought and strength of character before you face temptation in a relationship that invites sexual gratification.

Regardless of whether you are 12 or 15 years old, you need guidance on **stewarding** these awkward feelings and attractions.

Who is teaching you how to navigate these things? Is it left up to your school? Friends? The media? Your church? Continue working through this and I hope you will feel empowered to use wisdom in the stewardship of who you are, of your choices, of your sexuality, and in dating.

Be intentional at working through the questions at the end of the chapter. They are meant to help you think through these things before you have to act on them.

Imagine that you are a 16-year-old young lady and a senior invited you to the prom. What you do with this invitation and at this event will be determined by how you planned for these moments.

My ideal is that your parents are using ***micro-conversations*** to prepare you to have a plan and the confidence to execute that plan. I am not offering an opinion on whether you should go to the prom. That is up to you and the convictions of your family. I am saying that if you choose to accept the invitation, it is imperative that you already have a Biblical Sexual Ethic setting the boundaries you live by and equipping you to defend these without apology.

I know, for some of you, your parents have not planted those seeds. That is okay. You can team up with me and let me help you strengthen your resolve and exercise that muscle of choice so that you are living from a Biblical Sexual Ethic, using wisdom and forethought.

If you are older than 16, it is much more difficult for me, or anyone else, to teach you ethics or morals and expect these to guide you throughout your adolescence and young adult years. You have to want them.

YOU are the steward of your own body and your attractions, desires, and leanings. YOU are the one responsible for your actions – to others and to the Lord. Your actual thoughts and feelings are data points, but the next step — taking action — is fully within your control.

Celibate single adults face an uphill battle. It requires an extremely honest assessment of God's Word and the risks and consequences of your choices. YOU always have a choice. Right now, I want to help prepare you for the feelings, desires, and lusts that will pull at you from all directions. How? **By making you aware of them so you can always choose – consciously, not just react.**

Have you seen a commercial for a car out of your price range that makes you want it? I hope you know that one trick up their sleeve is the idea that – **you "deserve" it!**

If we are not careful, we buy into the lie that we deserve just about anything.

Do we, though? What we believe about this will motivate many of our choices, desires, and lusts. Be aware.

The truth is that we only deserve punishment for our sins, but God sent His son Jesus to this Earth to die for you and for me. We deserve nothing good in the strictest definition of the word. **Rich Mullins** wrote a song called ***"Doubly Good to You."***[73] A line from the song says:

> **"If you find someone that is faithful, if you find someone that's true, thank the Lord. He's been doubly good to you."**

And the truth is that sex is good. Nudity is amazing! Our bodies are works of art. If you can say that and believe it, you can see that the stewardship God expects of us is not there to limit us, but to free us, and protect us from ourselves. When we believe this, we are free from worry about those things and can eagerly live full abundant lives.

Sex outside of God's design invites bondage, fear, and worry.

The Relationship Continuum

In their book, *Soul Virgins,* **Dr. Doug Rosenau**[74] and **Michael Todd Wilson**[75] present a way to look at dating and courtship that completely revolutionizes the conversation. "Dating" and "courtship" are almost meaningless words in conversation because their definitions vary so much from person to person. By introducing new terminology to you here, I hope to set you free. I hope you will feel empowered and encouraged. I want you to navigate relationships in a very different way than most. I want a lot of the stress and angst to disappear – and for this to free you up for great success.

I know this may seem too early, but if your goal is to have a successful, vibrant, and happy marriage one day, then this is for you – NOW – TODAY!

Here it is:

Picture yourself walking down a path that starts with you single and unattached and ends happily married to your best friend. Do you want to walk down this path with multiple people, only to lose each other in the woods, or would it be wiser to choose only a few or even just one to walk with you, even if you eventually choose different forks in the path?

Not every love story begins with friendship, but I hope that they end up becoming the best of friends along the way, making **friendship** foundational to the relationship. Through our interactions in the world, we are constantly **CONNECTING**.

CONNECTING provides you with the data you need to know to determine what you like and dislike, your standards, and your ideals for a life partner. The danger in this stage is that one can set impossible standards that no one can meet.

As you are **CONNECTING**, you will find yourself in conversations that last longer with a few people. Then, eventually, you find those few narrowed down to one.

This is **COUPLING**.

Some of these relationships will last for a longer season than others. The danger during this stage is that you get too physical – so the physical must be stewarded intentionally and carefully. The goal of **COUPLING** is to move with one person towards **COVENANTING** – in marriage.

The vocabulary presented here from ***Soul Virgins***[76] makes it easy to see the stages of relational life.

CONNECTING is what you do with everyone in your circle — from close friends, to acquaintances, to strangers on the street.

COUPLING is the pairing up that you will do – traditionally defined as dating or courting.

COVENANTING is marriage, and it is a lifetime commitment.

Now, imagine steppingstones that move you from **CONNECTING** to **COUPLING** and then **COVENANTING**:

The first steppingstone is **FRIENDSHIP**. This is an amazing place to begin. This is vital for future health and growth.

A friend that piques your interest and that you decide to go out with is one that you are **CONSIDERING**. This person has now piqued your curiosity. This step involves evaluation and requires time, energy, investment, and conversations. The physical aspect of the relationship should be reined in, so it does not cloud your judgment. If this person makes the cut, you will then move into an "engaged-to-be-engaged" step called **CONFIRMING**.

At this step, you **CONFIRM** that you ***both*** feel certain about continuing to walk down this path together. A ring, future plans, and dreams are discussed in more detail.

The ring should follow soon – and this is the **COMMITTING** stage. This is engagement and should be as short as possible. The time here is spent intentionally preparing for marriage. It is important to remember that this is ONLY THE BEGINNING — the beginning of a beautiful life together in MARRIAGE.

This **Relationship Continuum**[77] provides you with a broader range of words that allows you to better identify where you are at in your relationship. The boundaries of physical intimacy are different at each stage. Obviously, very minimal physical involvement would be experienced in the **CONNECTING** stage with friends and with those we are **CONSIDERING**.

Intercourse and all genital focused experiences ought to be reserved for the **COVENANTING** stage of marriage.

I like to say that **dating is like marketing**, but it needs to be in its rightful place. Many use the term "dating" to say they are "exclusive." Going out on a date should be something you can do with one person tonight and a different person tomorrow night without being hurtful.

How can that happen? This can only happen if those in the **CONNECTING** stage have a boundary of no physical touch and have not indulged in long, soul-baring conversations. If this time is used to get to know one another (evaluation), it can be an experience that allows someone to see what kind of person they enjoy hanging out with. This is best done in groups – but can be one on one if more boundaries are in place.

Courtship is a traditional change of status from "single" to "taken." It is exclusive. This person is not seeing anyone else, and the young man has asked the young lady's father for permission, though this is considered by many to be archaic (it is NOT – because it is the gentlemanly thing to do. It honors her family. It honors her. This is still important today). **Courtship** would include the **CONFIRMING** and **COMMITTING** stages of the **Relationship Continuum** (This is part of the **COUPLING** stage).

Why does this matter?

YOU must be proactive in preparing for what's ahead. There will be pressures from every side regarding what you should do, who you should be, and what risks you ought to take. **If you decide who you will listen to ahead of time, the temptation to succumb to immediate gratification and feelings has much less power over you.**

If you are educated with a game plan and the right vocabulary, you will have the tools to be able to navigate relationships and enter marriage with as little baggage as possible. I hope you can see that. It is a wonderful goal, even if you can't see it yet. You are young. There is no hurry to get into this life stage.

Choices

Now is the time to be deliberate in deciding **your sexual ethic**. The weight of your future is on YOUR shoulders – at every age. What you do at a friend's house or when you are alone is all on you.

What will you do when some buddies enter an older sister's room to catch her in various stages of undress, or even naked?

It is up to you to decide what to do when someone at school asks for nude pictures.

It is up to you to walk away when your group of friends huddle around a screen looking at pornography.

In the end, the responsibility is on YOU – the weight of YOUR CHOICES and CONSEQUENCES.

* * *

Working Questions – Now it is YOUR TURN:

So, what's your plan? Do you have one? Do you have an approach for healthy dating and relationship building that you plan to use to protect your heart?

___

___

Did you know that a PLAN can protect you from your worst enemy - YOURSELF?

___

___

You are a teenager and think you are ready to date. Are you prepared to steward that kind of responsibility?

___

___

Define dating.

Define courtship.

How can you make wise decisions in your adolescent and young adult years?

Describe the Relationship Continuum with all seven words.

Decide now whether you will play Russian roulette with the possibility of bringing babies into this world prematurely or contracting and spreading sexually transmitted infections — that can be fatal. Will you? Or will you draw a line and say "NO!"

___

___

| 20 |

HELP! - What About the "M" Word?

The "M" Word?

I am guessing that you may start with this chapter – just a hunch. If not, this is still a relevant and touchy subject – pun intended! The "M" word — masturbation — is a controversial practice and a word many people cannot even bring themselves to say. I get it. I don't like this word either. It carries shame with it for many. I actually prefer to use the term self-stimulation in my counseling practice. Most men and women that self-stimulate do so unconsciously. It is not a conscious decision. So, what should we do?

Is it wrong? Can it go wrong?

Why has the church (at times) used this behavior as 'evidence' of someone's commitment to the Christian faith? Have you heard this? I know way too many young men shamed into thinking they must not be a Christian since they cannot stop this behavior on their own. This is sad, isn't it?

Self-stimulation is a private matter that most lie about, but it should be taken out of the shadows and discussed.

I have a process that I take young men and women through to help them **consciously choose** whether this is good for them, and if it is contributing to getting them where they want to go. I will share some of these steps throughout this section.

Medical and Cultural Claims

For well over a decade now, I have been teaching an undergraduate level course on Human Sexuality. Every year it grows in attendance. The content of the class includes topics and issues that I believe parents should address in and before middle school, which is why I wrote this book for you.

During one of my classes, I present a "Theology of Masturbation." Interesting, I know. I do not enter this topic lightly, as I know this issue is one many students struggle with and are confused about – and many also have strong opinions on it. In my course I spend the first hour presenting research, the positions held by the medical community, and cultural opinions. Let's begin now with the **medical and cultural claims.**

The medical community states there is no harm caused by self-stimulation. They assert that it is the best way for young people (and children) to learn how their bodies work and what feels good. They view it as the best alternative for release, since it does not include another person and has zero side effects. The medical community outlines the health benefits that regular orgasms have for men and women. Some benefits include hay fever relief, a lessening of menstrual cramps and pain, lowering the chances of prostate cancer, and aiding vascular health.

Cultural opinion is also positive, though it is still mainly viewed as a private matter. If it involves no one else, then the sentiment is "no harm, no foul." Go for it. Indulge. Enjoy! Our culture champions self-gratification, and so self-stimulation aligns with their ethical considerations.

The Church's Response

The church has held strong beliefs about masturbation. They include, but not limited to, "If you do this, you are not a Christian,", "It is just bad for you," and, "It's a sin." They allow no conversations. There is just a warning or a threat not to go there. This has proven to be an ineffective strategy.

For many young men and women, they have had the act of self-stimulation tied to their salvation, and they are living in shame and guilt - often silently. I have counseled and been in conversations with men and women on the verge of walking away from a call into the ministry — and even their faith — because of the hold that self-stimulation has on their behavior. **I have a very simple solution, but I warn you in advance that this solution is counter intuitive.** Many of you will stop reading, but I ask you to hang on. Read all the way to the end. I have seen incredible success and lives transformed by using the approach proposed below.

Do not shame anyone. We know that Satan loves to work in secrecy and in the dark.

I want you to find someone safe to talk this through with so you can better understand who you want to be and what limits you want to live by. **Getting your behavior out of your unconscious and into words is life changing for your habits.**

This is one of those topics that needs adult help, through ***micro-conversations,*** to bring your habits out of your unconscious operating system and into the forefront of your thinking. This will allow you to make a conscious choice about what is best.

My Personal Approach – An Alternative – A Different Lens

Steven walks into my office. He is twenty years old and feels trapped. He was taught that masturbation is sin and is bad for him. As we begin, I open our conversation to this embarrassing topic through disarming comments that aim to teach and educate. First, I compare the things he knows about self-stimulation to medical research. I ask him questions like, "So what? What's the big deal? Does anyone know or care? Why does this stress you out to the point of depression or frustration?" I am hoping to move him towards a new view of his choice to stimulate himself to orgasm. I find most men and women fall into these habits unconsciously. I want to bring it to his conscious reasoning. Why does he (or she) do this? What is the purpose? What payoff does he (or she) get out of it?

After he is more relaxed about the topic, I lead him down a path towards viewing self-stimulation as amoral and, without question, NOT sinful. Perhaps even acceptable. Why do I do this? I do this because I want HIM to determine the impact it is having on his life. It does not work for me, or anyone else, to tell him it is harmful, if he does not accept it and chooses to live with that truth. So, as I walk him towards it being one hundred percent okay, I begin to drop hints that suggest a new narrative:

What if self-stimulation is actually moving you further away from what you say you truly want? What if, when you self-stimulate while thinking about a person you just met at church, school, or the grocery store, this activity is taking you further away from getting to know them and building a real relationship with them? Maybe this is not such a good idea after all (a conscious choice). At this point, I look for their greater goal in life and relationships. I want them to come to a point of consciously choosing NOT to engage in this behavior, but I cannot go there immediately and achieve this outcome.

When I talk to some people about masturbation, I tell them to stop stressing about it and enjoy it. (Yikes, I know). It is a longer conversation than that, but I am blown away at how many come back a few weeks later and report that by being given permission to enjoy it, but also realizing the potential impact this can have on real relationships, they were less tempted or chose not engage in that behavior any longer. This is a powerful testimony to the importance of honest conversation.

You and I do not react well to rules, laws, and regulations that make no sense to us. However, most of us will comply with a boundary when we understand why it is there. I pray that the Lord will bless you as you head into the difficult conversations you need.

* * *

Working Questions – Now it is YOUR TURN:

What approach have your parents taken in discussing masturbation with you?

____

____

Will you take the medical approach, the stereotypical punitive Church approach, or another one?

____

____

What do you feel is missing here in the explanation, or defense of, and criticism of masturbation?

____

____

What Scripture would you go to that can help you make a wise decision?

____

____

| 21 |

Bullying, Social Media, Smartphones, and TV and Movies

Are you a bully or being bullied?

I know that these are not the only two options, but it often seems like the case.

It might be better to ask, "Are you a leader or a follower?"

If you are a leader, where are you leading others — towards good or evil?

If you are a follower, are you careful WHO you follow and what YOU do? No one wants to be bullied and most of us would never choose to be a bully. Bullying shows weakness and immaturity. It is important to be discerning in both who you follow and in how you lead others.

I hope you will become a defender of the weak and voiceless, so that you will stand up for what is right, speak out against evil, and be a change agent for good. Based on how you manage social media, smartphones, and entertainment, we can get a pretty good assessment on how you will handle this responsibility.

Your role models are key in your personal development as a leader or follower.

How did your parents respond when a coach didn't treat you the way you thought they should?

Did they become belligerent and aggressive?

Did they speak critically of other children, adults, or teachers in your life? Do you mimic their disrespectful tone and stance?

Have you picked up on their prejudice towards minorities? Have you followed their example?

I hope you see the dilemma. Most parents are shocked to find that the behavior of their children away from home or online differs greatly from what they portray to their parents. Shocking, I know!

I hope you choose wisely. May you never become "that" person. Do not let yourself believe that you would never bully someone else.

I hope you are not being bullied either. If you are, PLEASE reach out for help.

Social Media

Do you have social media?

First off, you do not NEED it. It is a WANT! Facebook and Instagram are tools. Tik-Tok and Snapchat are potentially dangerous. Beware! They suck you in. These tools are meant to keep you hooked, trapped, and coming back for more. Most people use one or more social media accounts. However, some are opting out of having any social media accounts. Many fail to use these tools appropriately. For way too many people, it is a venue for posting lies, comparing experiences, and feeling jealousy and hatred towards themselves and others.

Social media etiquette and ethics need to be taught before giving kids any access to these tools. You need to know what is ok to post, and what is questionable. It is important to distinguish between what is true and what might be a lie. You need to know how social media can be misused, abused, and part of illegal activity.

Did you know that naked pictures of yourself when you are under the age of eighteen is child pornography? Period! It is prosecutable. Both the sender and the recipient may be liable for having these pictures on their device. It is critical that you know this beforehand, so you do not have to deal with the consequences after the fact.

It is imperative that you know that anything you post online or send via email or text is public and can come back to haunt you in the future.

A sad truth is that many kids, preteens, and teens have killed themselves over what others have posted about them publicly or sent to them privately via social media. Social media can become another venue that a bully uses to harass others. Think about the persona you are portraying online. Why are you doing this?

Be on the lookout for others who are being bullied and be the young man or woman that stands up for them. **Use social media as a convenient tool to communicate, to connect with friends, and to share fun pics and videos. HAVE BOUNDARIES though as to what you post, share, and like.**

Did you know that this can also hurt your job options in the future? They will look you up and check out your posts to see who you are and what you stand for.

Social media can serve as an extension of a face-to-face community where friends can share funny things. Keep it light. Learn to be careful about what you share — both in personal matters and about hot topics. A lot of false information is available online, and if you will be a part of that world, you need to be wise about how it works.

Smartphones

Do you have a smartphone? It is another device you DO NOT NEED. I know this is extremely counter-cultural. It is a tool. Use it wisely. Most adults, teens, and an increasing number of children have smartphones. **I wonder if parents realize the power of the device they are entrusting to you.** The computer behind the smartphone is more powerful than ALL the computers used in 1969 to get us to the moon. Isn't that mind-boggling?

So, what have they entrusted to you besides a $200–$1500 device? You have access to everything — the world is at your fingertips. That is a scary proposition.

I call smartphones "porn portals."

On a smartphone, you can open Safari, click on Google, type in "porn," or "boobs," or "sex," click again, and you will find text-based results. At the top of the screen are two additional choices that, if chosen, will alter your life forever. The choices: "images" and "videos." (Please don't do this. I give you this information only so you will be aware of how close the danger is to you and your friends.)

Do you truly realize the implications of what you are carrying in your pocket? The access? The temptation? The world?

I will be the first to say that this is NOT about keeping you from everything — and I say this as a homeschool dad! This is ALL about teaching you, training you, and permitting you to steward some choices for yourself. The earlier you are taught to do this, the greater the chance you will have a strong ETHOS as you enter adulthood.

There is NO right time to receive a smartphone. It is about maturity and responsibility for the power and impact of this "tool." Most research today is screaming that we should delay access to screens like smartphones and tables until late teen years. The reason? The misuse of this "tool" is having a serious impact on lives and society.

I have seen too many families shelter their children and then be surprised when their child goes around filters, seeks for videos and images they shouldn't see, and deliberately disobeys family rules. Many teens have not been allowed to steward small things and once they are older, and MUST be prepared to steward greater things, they aren't ready.

Smartphones are not bad — they allow us to keep in touch with friends and family and are a great tool for many things. They allow you to contact a parent or friend if you are in need or danger. They can give you a sense of security. They are great for taking pictures and sharing memories with friends. **They are not evil — they are a "tool."** This "tool" requires and demands boundaries. Alcohol is not evil either, but if either of these are not stewarded well, both smartphones and alcohol are dangerous to the user, and society at large.

Have you been educated about the dangers of smartphones and social media? Are you sick of what you hear? Do you believe that YOU will steward this tool better than others have?

You may be like all those people that play the lottery thinking that a win would change their life and they will be different in how they would handle the big windfall. However, the extreme majority lose friends, harm relationships, and they quickly lose the new financial gain. Sometimes it is lost within the year. You may be ready for the responsibility. But why take the risk earlier than needed?

Have you ever driven a car on a farm? It's easy. There aren't too many hazards. But driving on a highway in traffic and with traffic laws is a different ballgame from driving in the pasture and on paths on a farm. **Driving a car and having a smartphone both require you to exhibit stewardship.**

T.V. and Movies

Stewardship is also critical with T.V., movies, and YouTube because of the overwhelming choices you have before you. For preteens and teens with tight rules and limited access at home, it is tempting to look for media elsewhere in ways that are more harmful. This is difficult terrain for every family to navigate, and one that changes daily. **How should your family manage the tension between free rein and a total lockdown?**

This is tough. Are you more trustworthy than a sibling or some of your friends? This is impossible to measure accurately. It involves risk.

I hope you have examples of others that have good boundaries so you can watch them and follow their examples.

Do you have good, healthy conversations with others that help you highlight potential blind spots, and help you set limits for yourself regarding what you will or will not watch? You need these conversations.

I took my kids to see a movie recently that had a few scenes that were subtly sexual. I talked separately with each of my kids about those scenes. I was surprised by what they noticed.

My twelve-year-old son noticed the sexual parts and was uncomfortable.

My ten-year-old son just laughed and focused on the guy that was hit in the crotch.

My eight-year-old daughter thought the girl's dress was beautiful.

Each of us will have different things we notice based on our age, experience, and temptations. That is what makes this so difficult.

What did you think about that scene in the last movie or TV show you watched as a family?

I don't know; I wasn't there. You were thinking something, though! It is SO important to talk it out and not just let it sit in your operating system, your unconscious. I hope you have a safe space to have those conversations. These can be with a youth pastor, a friend's parents or family, a trusted older friend, or your own parents. Use specific scenes to engage in conversations about how someone was treated, modesty, strength, power, friendship, and sacrifice. Use scenes to create dialogues about who you hope to be when you grow up, or what you would do if you were in that situation.

If I were talking to your parents, I would highlight the importance of THEM starting these conversations as you are viewing various shows or movies. **(I do this in my book "I Can't Say That! Going Beyond 'The Talk'" (2019)).**[78] But this book is for you, the preteen or teenager. So, I say to you – Be Assertive. Be ahead of the game. Seek out these conversations since they will shape you and your decisions more than you can imagine. Use cartoons and commercials to ask questions, to find out what others might do in a situation, or to discover what they believe about a sensitive topic. Always keep the posture of learning. This will serve you well. I promise.

Speaking of tv shows and movies – a powerful influence for many of us are the stars and celebrities we see. This also includes music idols and sport heroes. **How do you relate to these? What about your parents and/or family? How do they relate to their heroes, stars, or celebrities?**

* * *

Working Questions – Now it is YOUR TURN:

Are you being bullied?

____

____

Are you a bully?

____

____

Would you describe any of the adults around you as a bully?

____

____

Are you a leader or a follower?

____

____

If you are a leader, are you leading others towards good or evil – towards impacting the world with hope, or selfish endeavors?

____

____

If you are a follower, are there limits to what you will do, or where you will go? Do you follow blindly?

____

____

What are some of your big life goals?

____

____

How are you stewarding social media for yourself?

____

____

Do you see adults modeling good stewardship of social media? How are they doing that? And how are they NOT?

____

____

What boundaries and rules do you have in place for porn-portals – I mean, smartphones?

____

____

(Knowing your peers – in general) What sorts of issues or problems can arise when children or teenagers have access to a smartphone?

____

____

What are your family's boundaries and rules for T.V. shows and movies? Does anything need to change?

____

____

Read **Galatians 5:17**

The sinful nature wants to do evil, which is just the opposite of what the Spirit wants. And the Spirit gives us desires that are the opposite of what the sinful nature desires. These two forces are constantly fighting each other, so you are not free to carry out your good intentions (NLT).

What two forces are mentioned in this passage?

____

____

| 22 |

Influences, Idols and Boundaries

Who are your biggest influences and idols? Who do you put up on a pedestal? Who do you admire? Who do you want to be? Who do you look up to? Who do you let entertain you?

As you know, people outside your family can be powerful influences, especially as you enter your teen years. You are probably beginning to care more about what others think and less of what your parents think, but this isn't always the case. It is normal to grab onto role models as you think more seriously about what you want to do in the future. Do you feel pressure to stand out? Or are you hoping to just go unnoticed? The comparison factor can be scary. Looks. Talent. Status. Position. Clothing. Devices. This is the reality you live with in school, youth group, sports teams, band, and almost anywhere else you can imagine. It really is inescapable.

So, what can you do to be proactive and stay ahead of the curve?

My advice continues to come down to the *micro-conversations* on these subjects, acknowledging the daily pressures you are facing. Be aware of those you look up to, why you look up to them, and what you do with that pressure. This can impact the decisions you make as you relate to others.

From my observation of families over the past twenty years as a family counselor, most families are not intentionally discipling their children — shaping them to live and love more like Christ. Has yours? How do you feel about your own spiritual growth and development? This is probably a struggle for all families. We cannot emphasize having a relationship with God enough. So, it falls on you to make an effort yourself to grow more like Christ. Why am I putting this here? **Because I see the replacement of discipleship with a different kind of worship** - one that places another human in a place they were never meant to be. It is one thing to look up to someone. It is another thing to take that a step further into idolatry.

While one extreme of parenting today places too much weight on academic and/or athletic success, the other extreme is neglect. This is heartbreaking and can be very damaging. If this is your reality, who do you look up to? You may embrace the same heroes and idols as your parents or primary caregivers' heroes, or you may reject them. There is almost no middle ground, depending on whether you deem your examples as sane. You might think this is crazy, but you can easily become mini versions of your parents. You can also, just as easily, reject everything they stand for as parents and as a family. It is YOUR choice.

The key area I observe that influences how we handle "stars," is whether we have a healthy community that purposefully models saying "no" and living with boundaries, especially when those boundaries are unpopular.

Stars and Idols

How do you relate to celebrities? Are you star-struck and cannot contain your worship? What does your family invest most of their time in watching and consuming? If we are not careful, this mutates into **worship**. The culture that you have in your home is all you knew at first. Now it is expanding.

How do you talk about celebrities, sports, heroes, singers, politicians, and YouTube personalities?

When does admiring someone for their skill or talent move into **idolatry**?

A key indicator is if we choose games, concerts, and screen time OVER real face-to-face interactions. **Do you? If so, you need to make some changes.**

I grew up in Chile, South America. The culture there is very different from the United States. When my family moved back to the US, I became aware of an obsession with sports in the United States that has always felt strange to me. It took me years to be able to find any good in sports at all, since all I saw was it negatively impacting so many friends and families.

I finally saw that there was a crucial difference between families. There are those that **worship** a team or a sport and it keeps them from forming deep, real relationships. And there are families that use sports to further relationships with others by laughing, playing, relaxing, and enjoying time with friends. This is the critical line. This is for your consideration.

How does your relationship with stars and idols impact you — both in time and in money? Had you thought about it much before? If you are now, what would you change?

How do these impact other relationships when you think about the example you are passing on to others?

A Lack of Community

Why does this matter? **Too many of us lack community.**

Galatians 6:2 reminds us we must:

> *"Share each other's burdens, and in this way obey the law of Christ" (NLT).*

I believe that most of us do not know what this would even look like. We attend church and we go to various events, but we are actually friendless. Please be aware of this tendency and do NOT let it take root early. Be intentional about your relationships.

Who are the other adults speaking into your life and into your future?

Young men — do you have a band of brothers? I don't mean a group of buddies you spend so much time with that you neglect responsibility. I mean other guys you look up to and that you could call on, day or night, if you were in need.

Young ladies — do you have relationships that encourage you and friends you could call on if you were in need?

When I speak of community, I am thinking of the people whom you invest in, and they in turn invest in you. You should carefully evaluate the communities you are invested in.

An influential teacher or coach can lead you in an opposite direction from one you would choose for yourself if you thought about it for very long. They can also come alongside you and be a voice you listen to because they offer great advice when you don't want to listen to your mom or dad - and yes, this is normal.

Which people or groups do you spend the majority of your time with?

This may seem inconsequential now, but I assure you it is not. You are developing habits today that you will carry with you for the rest of your life. These habits are hard to change in your adult years. Are you active on a sports team, school group, or club? Are you active and involved in church events or civic groups?

Have you intentionally thought through the impact of those relationships on who YOU are? Do their values line up with what you value? Is that coach, teacher, or mentor leading you in a direction you want to go, or are they subtly leading you where ***they*** want to go?

Here is an odd question - but an important one: **How can you expand or limit those who have influence over you?** What do I mean? You have the final say on whom you let speak into your life. This includes podcasts, movies, tv shows, youtubers, and friends. If you can do this now, you will more than likely be able to do this more efficiently and intentionally in your adult years. This is critical at every age of our lives. It is an important skill for your future success.

What might need to change?

Is there anyone that you should limit spending time with because they drag you down?

Is there anyone that you should invest more time in because they are an encouragement?

Now let's flip this around —

Do you bring people down when they're around you?

Are you a source of encouragement to your friends?

Be extremely intentional with your community. I have seen families choose a community because of the interests of their children (YOU) that destroyed their family as it pulled them in different directions. They were just trying to make everyone happy and instead, they pulled their family away from a faith community that could have spoken words of wisdom to them.

The fact is that today's average family is overworked and stressed out. Choose how you spend your time wisely. Leave yourself time to rest. Be attentive that you don't push yourself in a direction you think is best, but that leads you to resent yourself and the direction you chose.

A word of warning: just because you badly want to do something, it doesn't mean that it is a wise investment for your time, energy, or family's money.

Time is NOT an unlimited resource. Prioritize your time and give preference to those things that build up your family and your faith.

Proverbs 18:24 says:

"There are 'friends' who destroy each other, but a real friend sticks closer than a brother" (NLT).

Be that second friend mentioned here to others, modeling for others in all you do.

Proverbs 17:17 says:

"A friend is always loyal, and a brother is born to help in time of need" (NLT).

John 15:13 says:

"There is no greater love than to lay down one's life for one's friends" (NLT).

Reasons to Say "No" and Live With Boundaries

Did you know that boundaries are good, necessary, and an expression of love? Do you perceive these as unloving or uncaring? They are not. I hope you can see that.

As a preteen and teenager, there is an important muscle you will need to exercise. **Can you say "NO" to things, or do you struggle with over-committing?** This impacts you and your view of work, Church, and others in need.

There are so many needs right in front of us, and it seems impossible to say "NO" to anything. Let Jesus' example encourage you. Jesus, in His few years of ministry, exemplified boundaries. He took time away from the crowds and spent that saved time in prayer with His Father. He invested heavily into His disciples — His closest friends.

Do you do this?

Or do you live and act as if you are above this kind of need? Yikes!

If Jesus needed boundaries, how much more do we? We need game nights and barbeques with friends, but we also need quiet evenings with just our family - or even just time alone. We need to spend time in ministry — and time in a hammock. We must take care of ourselves and those we love.

The amount of sleep you get each night matters and impacts everyone around you. Your body also uses this time to heal and file memories away into your long-term memory.

Your time with God is vital to your overall health.

Your time with family and friends can be life giving.

Rest is rejuvenating. Somehow, these times that are life altering have been demoted for busyness and overcommitment - even when they are good things!

I believe that a contributing factor to the increase in mental and physical health issues is a lack of boundaries. What do I mean when I say boundaries?

To eat well, you must take the time to prepare a healthy meal. You can't pick up fast food on the way to ball practice every evening and expect to be healthy. You must carve out space — a boundary — into your schedule that allows you to take care of your health needs. **To find rest and rejuvenation, you must set aside time and protect it in your schedule.**

I heard once of a leader that had a business meeting scheduled on his calendar daily from 5 to 6pm. When someone was trying to schedule a meeting with him, they were frustrated that he would not consider moving this appointment and asked him what was so important. His reply was, **"Dinner with my family.** When I put 'dinner with family' on the calendar, it kept getting shuffled and seen as a lesser priority. This way I keep it protected." What a great example. Are you setting up boundaries?

Boundaries encourage and invite freedom!

They create an ecosystem of health and wellness in relationships and spiritual renewal.

Philippians 3:5–6 describes how Paul was "all in" and committed to his interpretation of the law. This led him to persecute Christians and to live his version of perfection. Verses 7–9 show the **shift in his priorities:**

> *"I once thought these things were valuable, but now I consider them worthless because of what Christ has done. Yes, everything else is worthless when compared with the infinite value of knowing Christ Jesus my Lord. For his sake, I have discarded everything else, counting it all as garbage, so that I could gain Christ and become one with him. I no longer count on my own righteousness through obeying the law; rather I become righteous through faith in Christ" (NLT).*

We live for Him. If you recognize this now and make it a priority, I promise it will change your future.

* * *

Working Questions – Now it is YOUR TURN:

Who are your biggest influences and idols? Who do you put up on a pedestal? Who do you admire? Who do you want to be? Who do you look up to? Who do you let entertain you?

____

____

How do you talk about celebrities, sports, heroes, singers, politicians, and YouTube personalities?

____

____

When does someone that has become an idol, cross a line into an unhealthy place?

____

____

How does your relationship with the stars and idols impact your family, both in time and in money?

____

____

Have you intentionally thought through the impact of those relationships on who YOU are? How?

____

____

How can you expand or limit those influencing your family? What needs to change?

____

____

Is there anyone that you should limit your time with because they make you more cynical or depressed?

____

____

Who should you be investing more time in because they are an encouragement and a true friend?

____

____

Are you a downer to be around and therefore others ought to avoid you?

____

Are you a source of joy, encouragement, and challenge — a true friend?

____

____

Read **Galatians 6:2.** This passage reminds us that we must,

"Share each other's burdens, and in this way obey the law of Christ" (NLT).

Most of us do not know what this actually looks like. We attend a church, and we go to this or that event, but in truth we are friendless. Who shares your burdens?

____

____

Read **Proverbs 18:24**

There are "friends" who destroy each other,
but a real friend sticks closer than a brother (NLT).

Proverbs 17:17

A friend is always loyal,
and a brother is born to help in time of need (NLT).

John 15:13

There is no greater love than to lay down one's life for one's friends (NLT).

Your friends matter. Who are your friends? Name them here. What kind of influence do they have on you?

____

____

____

____

Can you say, "No," to things, or do you struggle with over-committing?

____

____

Do you live with boundaries? Are they healthy? Unhealthy? Rigid? Flexible?

____

____

Do you go beyond self-care in putting yourself first? Do others come before you or your family to an unhealthy extent?

____

____

Read **Philippians 3:7–9**

I once thought these things were valuable, but now I consider them worthless because of what Christ has done. Yes, everything else is worthless when compared with the infinite value of knowing Christ Jesus my Lord. For his sake I have discarded everything else, counting it all as garbage, so that I could gain Christ and become one with him. I no longer count on my own righteousness through obeying the law; rather, I become righteous through faith in Christ. For God's way of making us right with himself depends on faith (NLT).

Are you all in? Have you put your faith in Christ? If not, contact me and let's talk, or go to your church and talk with your pastor or an elder. Make this real in your life! It will change everything.

____

____

| 23 |

The New You!

My hope for you by now is that you desire to live by a Biblical Sexual Ethic. There are many other aspects of our lives that matter, but they are beyond the scope of this book. **Being sexually healthy requires a commitment to a specific ETHOS – a belief system – a way of living – within boundaries.** It also requires that you learn to listen to a different drummer than most people around you. This is where the challenge lies.

Along your journey ahead – and for some of you maybe even today - you will find a key piece of the puzzle for success will be found in how you manage your own personal hurts, failures, and disappointments. **Shame traps too many people**. Breaking the bonds that keep you trapped leads you to true freedom. Here, you have the opportunity to experience true joy. Then, once you have found this freedom and joy and peace, what I ask of you – is that you pass it on.

Imagine looking at your own adult children one day and recognizing that they have made thoughtful, informed decisions that they can defend rather than emotional and impulsive ones. Imagine being proud of the young man or woman they have become. Imagine a sense of gratitude for the adults God entrusted to them who have decided to be godly change agents in the world.

It might be easier to envision yourself. Can you picture your life in a few years, living life on your own, and you see a confident, competent man or woman that loves God, sees life through a Biblical lens, and acts based on a Biblical worldview? Can you imagine acting in response to being grounded in God's Word and not reacting emotionally?

It Begins Today – in YOU

Jared and **Kendra** knew that they had rough lives growing up, and they wanted something different for their children. With the birth of their first son, they began teaching him about his body, sexuality, dating, and marriage. They continued as they added five more siblings to the family. They invited the hard (and weird!) questions from their children and answered them the best they could. Because of their honesty about their own failings, their stories of childhood abuse, and the role God played in their story, their six children avoided a lot of the pain and heartache that many face today. Their children did not all arrive at adulthood without drama or mistakes, but **none of them had the excuse of ignorance or naivete**. As each of them walked through their adolescent years, they encountered struggles with pornography and dating when they were too young because of peer pressure. They knew, without a doubt though, what their parents believed, what their parents' expectations were for them, and that they were responsible for their own actions before God.

All six of **Jared** and **Kendra's** children eventually married, and they were all joyous occasions. All six of them remain faithful in their pursuit of God in their adult lives, passing the same down to their own children. Even though they didn't have one hundred percent success in all of their choices, they each knew their parents loved them. They knew that God loved them enough to die for them. And they knew that they could choose. Through the knowledge given to them by their parents, they were better positioned to make their own choices. They could clearly see the destination each choice might lead to, and they could choose with wisdom. What a beautiful picture.

Do you want that for yourself?

Your parents may not have had these conversations with you when you were younger. That is out of your control. **Start today, by learning to live from a different worldview**. Begin by intentionally crafting your own Biblical Sexual Ethic — your ETHOS.

Your ETHOS

So now what? How do we pull all of this together? What are my next action steps?

Jeff is a seventeen-year-old young man whose parents prepared him to live by a Biblical Sexual Ethic.

He is respectful of authority.

He honors women and avoids areas of temptation.

He has struggled with pornography, but he has chosen to die to those desires and fill his life with better things.

He has a great relationship with his parents and his siblings.

He has great relationships with girls his age and hasn't dated.

He has a healthy view of marriage, thanks to years of ***micro-conversations***.

Recently, his parents have had longer conversations about the reality of marriage, its struggles, and its joys. **Jeff** is eager to leave home, see the world, and have new adventures. He has decided on a degree from a college that will set him up to have an income that will allow him to support missionaries, invest in ministries that change the world, and support the family he hopes to have one day.

Jennifer is a twenty-one-year-old young woman living on her own. She is watching her friends get in and out of sexual relationships, mocking marriage, and spending money like there is no tomorrow while they mooch off their parents to pay for their cell phone bill, car insurance, and miscellaneous purchases.

She remembers all the uncomfortable conversations with her mom and dad that helped inform her about her body, her health, God's design for sex, marriage, parenting, and friendships. She is very thankful that she can easily reject the world that her friends are asking her to join.

She wants a peaceful life with less heartbreak, without fears of a sexually transmitted infection, and without worries about getting pregnant. She has financial stability and is willing to wait for a husband who will treat her with respect and as an equal partner in marriage.

These scenarios are possible because of the daily and weekly investments into their ETHOS. Since you are reading this book, it is on you to find those that can help you do this well. I want you to have your future paved to be a confident, resilient, young adult.

Will this always yield positive results? NO. Not all of those who had parents invest in them chose to live it out. You have the free will to reject everything I am presenting to you in this book. You choose!

You have free will and can reject everything you have been taught. Your parents and I ultimately have to entrust you to God and to your own decisions, since you are ultimately responsible for yourself. That is hard for me to grasp, believe, and live out as a parent myself. Your parents probably blame themselves for every bad decision you make, even those they had no control over. No parent is perfect. You aren't perfect. Be honest with yourself in this process. You will be a better person because of it.

Don't Wait on the Adults in Your Life To Reach Out – You Can "Go There!"

This is a tall order. I am asking you to trust me. I know that many people have invested in you. Every teacher, daycare worker, coach, AWANA teacher, babysitter, pastor, family friend, and family have stock in who you become. They have planted seeds - something I have mentioned throughout this book as ***micro-conversations*. These are not lectures. Sometimes they are a conversation and at other times just a few sentences to plant an idea or perspective into your heart and mind.**

The advice I give parents is NOT to wait on YOU, the preteen or teen, to ask a question.

But – my advice to YOU - as a preteen or teen is NOT to wait on the adults in your life to "go there" on any subject you are curious about or have questions about. I encourage everyone to be

the one willing to open the dialogue and get the conversation started.

But – a word of caution! Some adults are just not ready or safe to talk to about hard subjects. Be selective. Be wise. Be careful. But "go there!"

Based on my years of research and counseling, the norm in most homes is to have zero conversations about these topics because the children and teens are not bringing them up on their own. It's crazy that this is left up to you! **Be abnormal and "go there." Be abnormal and initiate those hard conversations.** This is for you! Don't wait.

Do not wait until you have a boy over and they ask if you two can go up to your room to study and close the door. Know what is wise and have a plan. Have conversations ahead of time about the wisdom, temptations, and implication of such a decision. (And FYI - this is a bad idea!)

Do not wait until you are sixteen years old and want to go out on a date with someone to decide whether this is wise. Establish parameters, guidelines and steps that you need to take beforehand. Have these conversations early and often — staying ahead of these crossroads where so many teenagers and their parents collide. Stay ahead of this with ***micro-conversations*** that ultimately leave the decisions in YOUR hands as you grow up. Your parents and others will not always be there. These earlier conversations create a foundation that will guide later choices, options, temptations, attractions, and desires.

Colossians 3:23 is a stern reminder to:

> *"Work willingly at whatever you do, as though you were working for the Lord rather than for people" (NLT).*

That is how I want you to look at growing up - it is WORK! Work — for the Lord. It is about a bigger picture than just you, your freedom, and your immediate emotions and desires.

Your Mentors, Examples, and Life Leaders

Some have the opportunity to invest in you – even just a little. You can probably think of a few – a coach, a teacher, a family member, or a friend. Others come along and get to do what I call **"watering the seeds."** As you go about your days, further conversations with peers and other adults are all building on previous seeds that were planted. You have probably heard that pornography is dangerous; it sucks you in and is bad for you. Build on this as you listen to a sermon that dives deeper and addresses your heart, temptation, attraction, and the power of **desire**. Carefully entrust your life journey to a select few mentors where you can unpack what it feels like to walk past the fifty-foot breast in the window of Victoria's Secret in the mall and discuss its appropriateness there – in a sober, healthy manner – not in jest. What are they advertising? Who are they advertising to? How does it impact women? How does it impact men?

Use scenes in movies and T.V. shows to open dialogue that leads into **further discussions**. Use news stories to discuss perpetrators and victims. To discuss harm. To discuss shame. Use these to talk about being aware of your surroundings and what you should do if you are ever in a similar circumstance. Consider acting it out carefully, so you automatically respond rather than freezing if you are ever in that situation.

Use family drama and the pain your friends experience to learn about compassion, patience, and caring for another in a difficult situation. This is important at all ages and stages of life. Listen to differing perspectives. This is healthy. Be curious. Be teachable.

Be willing to be challenged. Invite disagreement. Learn now, in the company of others, so you can leave your home confident, compassionate, and eager to be a positive force in the lives of others, without compromising the gospel, Scripture, or your faith.

Can you commit to Colossians 3:23 and see developing a biblical sexual ethic as work?

> *"Work willingly at whatever you do, as though you were working for the Lord rather than for people"* (NLT).

Boundaries and Choices

A critical dimension of your sexuality and sexual development are boundaries and choices.

If these aren't well established, you are at the mercy of your feelings, desires, and peer pressure. To live within boundaries requires you to step back, recognize the difference that results from living within these, and be thankful for their protection. **Ironically, it is these boundaries that give us freedom.**

When I graduated from seminary and began my life as a Licensed Professional Counselor, I was a single twenty-five-year-old male in a female-dominated field. Ninety-nine percent of my clients were women, and most of my friends were female. It terrified me. I had an ETHOS drilled into me from my family and my training regarding the importance of boundaries. I also knew of cases where one accusation of wrongdoing had destroyed a person's reputation and career. I set up incredibly strict boundaries. **These boundaries were for my freedom.** Within these boundaries, I had less to worry about. Later, I was working at a college and was told I needed to loosen my boundaries if I was going to work with college students. It surprised me, and I wondered if I should loosen up. I quickly realized though that I had more freedom by using these boundaries, and so I added more! One example of a boundary I set was never eating alone with a woman who was not my wife.

Boundaries (or the lack thereof) are entrenched into your ETHOS at an early age as we learn from our families and absorb their **energy** and **culture**. As we play that out in our lives, we free ourselves, adopting some constraints put on us by our families and dispensing with others.

You have the freedom to choose. Our culture continually speaks out of both sides of its mouth. On one hand, you are told to be free and choose for yourself whatever you want. But, on the other hand, if someone chooses to act with reservation, wisdom, or within a Biblical Sexual Ethic, they could ridicule you for making the "wrong" choice. **Find freedom in boundaries, your freedom of choice, and in saying, "NO."**

How To Say "No"

Learning to say, "NO," is a crucial skill. We are always saying, "NO." In effect, **every time we say, "Yes," to something — we are, in turn, saying, "NO," to something else**.

Learn to say, "NO" readily.

It is crucial that you gain the vocal and internal ability to stand up for yourself and live within boundaries. Are you familiar with the concept of **fight or flight**? If you get into a sticky situation, you have a release of adrenaline and are, in a sense, forced to spend that energy by fighting, or fleeing. However, there is another response that isn't talked about often — freezing — that has serious consequences since the energy built up by adrenaline and angst rarely gets resolved.

When men and women that have been abused or violated tell their stories, they usually regret not having spoken up, fighting, or running away. Instead, they froze. However, despite — or maybe because of — freezing, they survived. They made it through. Many people remain stuck at this traumatic event because the built-up energy needs a place to go. It needs to be released. From this experience, they learned to remain small and silent. Their ability to say, "NO," diminishes. Their power diminishes. Their freedom diminishes.

An Example

Lisa and **Brett** have invested in their children with a vision for their children's future success. They started young, teaching and training their children in a **Biblical Sexual Ethic.** As they progressed through each year of life with their children, they also knew that part of the bargain was trusting God. They have hope in things unseen. Their faith is in God and His work in the lives of their family.

Hope breeds a peace that passes all understanding. Hope expects great things.

Hope for the best things for your future.

What is the most important goal in your growing up and launching?

Dr. George Barna speaks of this goal in his book *Revolutionary Parenting.*[79]

What should your parents' primary goal be? Dr. Barna's research found a specific goal I think we ought to keep in mind. It is mine right now in writing this for you! And with this primary goal in view, all other parental priorities will work themselves out.

Dr. Barna found the most important goal was to raise and launch **"Champions for Christ."**[80] — this ought to be our top goal.

Hope for great things! Expect more - from yourself and from those you follow!

* * *

Working Questions – Now it is YOUR TURN:

Can you commit to Colossians 3:23 and see developing a Biblical Sexual Ethic as work?

"Work willingly at whatever you do, as though you were working for the Lord rather than for people" (NLT).

____

Yes or No?:

I commit to the skill of saying, "No."

____

I have a vision for myself and my future?

____

I have hope that I will be a "Champion for Christ." (It can start today!)

____

| 24 |

What Do I Do With My Hurts, Failures, and Disappointments?

Bad things happen. I know you know that. It is not fair. The chance that you are reading this and have not experienced some sort of sexual shame or harm is very small. I say, again, that I am so, so sorry. This is not how it is supposed to be. I want you to know though that there is HOPE! There is a path to freedom - freedom from shame, from self-hatred, and from the need to live a lie.

Paul is a twenty-two-year-old who was taught a Biblical Sexual Ethic but chose to take his own path. He decided he had to try everything out for himself. Learning the hard way is a reality for many people. Those that love people like Paul grieve over their choices. We love them. We pursue relationships with them. But we must also remember that these are HIS choices.

Julianna is eighteen and a survivor. She grew up in a great home with a loving, single mom that talked with her early and consistently about these things, used *micro-conversations* often, and built into her daughter a solid sense of identity, strength, and passion to live by a Biblical Sexual Ethic. Her ETHOS was unshakeable. Well, it was unshakeable until her first boyfriend. She met a young man in college, and they began dating. By the end of their first year together, she was a different person. He seemed to be sweet and caring and said and did all the right things. But he had slowly nibbled away at her soul with demeaning comments that said she was not good enough. He would criticize her appearance, weight, intelligence, and decisions. Eventually, she had no resolve left and when he pushed on her physical boundaries, she had no fight left in her. She surrendered to his desires without a fight or a care. She did not realize what had been happening until it was too late.

I have heard this story too many times from young women. The behavior of these "men" is disgusting and heartbreaking. This is grooming, leading to rape, even though there was no fight, and no one said, "NO."

Jill grew up with a dad that loved her and she was a strong, confident twenty-five-year-old even though her mom had left them years ago. Her dad was proactive, engaging, funny, and raised his little girl the best he could. She had a strong Biblical Sexual Ethic — an ETHOS — and excelled in all areas of her life as a teenager. However, she went to a party one night and had something to drink that had been tampered with. She woke up the next morning in a lot of pain and bleeding. She had been "roughed up," and was unaware of what had truly happened at the party the night before. Now, at age twenty-five, she has grown in strength and resolve to help other girls never find themselves in a situation like that. She has a passion and calling that, when combined with her story, has propelled her to make a difference in a way that only someone in her shoes could do.

Freedom from Shame

Shame steals everything — life, joy, desire, and your future. For many of us, our default setting is to stay here — to let it take up residence and settle down. My hope and desire for you is that you can find freedom from shame in your own story. I want you to see that **when shame enters; it is only there to steal, kill, and destroy.** Sound familiar? The marvelous truth is that **God is a redeemer.** Rest in this. Believe this. Live this out. Face the shame. Recognize that it only sucks you into a spiral of self-hatred and hatred of others. Realize that it only steals your joy and any desire you might have left.

Dr. Dan Allender[81] explains in his speaking and writing how to overcome shame. The unlikely source of joy is **found in being broken**. When you allow yourself to feel **sorrow** and **grief,** your loss allows you to find yourself in a place of **gratitude.** There is no room left for contempt or hatred. You can now **dance** for joy. What does this dance look like? This freedom? This joy?

It is being truly broken and then, as Proverbs 31:25 says:

What a beautiful picture of strength, grace, peace, and fearlessness. You can laugh at the devil's schemes as you rest in God's perfect plan for your life.

So, what is the task for you now?

First, you must address your story. Confront it. Share it with a trusted helper.

What are you holding on to? Where does this enemy keep you tied up?

You can usually find this as you review your story.

We all have places in our story that need attention, care, and honesty.

> ***"She is clothed with strength and dignity; she can laugh at the days to come" (NIV).***

Forgiveness Frees YOU!

Paul had to try everything. He made his own way. One of his biggest hurdles will be **forgiving** himself for the pain he caused his family, himself, and others.

Julianna did nothing wrong. She knows that in her head, but she doesn't feel it in her heart. She will need to **forgive** herself for trusting him, even though there was no way she could have known what he would become. She faces the insurmountable hurdle of forgiving her ex-boyfriend.

Jill beats herself up for going to that party and touching that drink. She has found **forgiveness** for the guys that raped her, even in the vagueness of some memories.

Forgiveness is never saying it was okay.

Forgiveness is loving someone in the way that God does — not giving them what they deserve for their actions or hearts.

Truthfully, we all deserve one thing — hell. By the grace of God, we are offered free, eternal life. **Forgiveness** is not something we do once we feel like it. It is a conscious choice of our own personal freedom. It is cutting the ties with someone that harmed us and still has a hold on us. This is difficult for our emotions to grasp, which, if we are not careful, can keep us captive.

Forgiveness is freedom. Be free!

Growth and Your Joy

What comes from relieving ourselves of the burden of shame and resting in God's forgiveness?

We grow. We truly experience joy. We find freedom. We become who God created us to be — worshipers.

Let's look at this from another angle. It is crucial that YOU learn about this process. You need to understand about the real world. You do not need your family only for shelter. The adults in your life ought to prepare you.

Do you feel prepared for the hurts and disappointments that will inevitably come? You need key figures in your life to teach you to stand up for yourself - and for others.

I was driving home from a movie recently with my oldest son and talking to him about the difficulty of going against the grain with friends — standing up for someone that is being picked on or calling out dirty jokes and conversations that are disrespectful of women or others as unacceptable. **It starts with one person. YOU can be that one.**

Listen to others' stories about their successes and their failures. Learn from them. Listen and ask questions. You will probably learn more from others' failures than from lectures - or even a book like this.

Face YOUR OWN shame over past actions.

Face YOUR OWN fears of being found out and being unloved.

Find healthy models - not perfect ones - redeemed ones with stories.

Share YOUR story when appropriate.

Speak up, say "NO," - and flee when necessary.

Who are the most influential people in your life from birth to around the age of 10? Your parents. Listen to their stories, use them to teach and guide you.

Around the age of eleven, everything changes. Remember, your teenage years do not have to be the nightmare that so many go through. YOU need to take more risks. **You MUST learn how to fail gracefully.** May you learn this while you are young so you can learn from smaller mistakes and get back up and try again.

Prepare to fail. And get back up.

Prepare yourself to face disappointment with a faith in God that brings you back to life; but know that this doesn't happen overnight.

Prepare yourself to face heartache with a trust that God has all those details worked out for your good. He is a gracious God.

Rest in these truths.

Live by the *"peace that passes all understanding"* (Philippians 4:7, NKJV).

* * *

Working Questions – Now it is YOUR TURN:

So what is the task for you? First, you must address your story. What are you holding onto? Where are you all tied up by the enemy? Usually this can be found as you review your story. We all have places in our story that need this attention, care, intimacy, and grace. What have you found so far?

____

____

Is shame ruling how you interact with your family or friends?

____

____

Do you hate yourself or others? Does contempt live in your heart? Gratitude and contempt cannot coexist in the same heart.

____

____

What are you grateful for?

____

____

____

Do you put on a mask and act fake around others? Are you unable to be honest with those close to you?

____

____

Do you have areas in your story where you need to forgive and let go?

____

____

I commit to growth and JOY!

Read **Proverbs 31:25**

She is clothed with strength and dignity, and she laughs without fear of the future (NLT).

This passage refers to **strength**, **dignity**, and **laughter** for tomorrow. What do these mean to you?

____

____

Read **Philippians** 4:7

Then you will experience God's peace, which exceeds anything we can understand. His peace will guard your hearts and minds as you live in Christ Jesus (NLT).

Do you have that peace?

____

____

| 25 |

Steps to Freedom by Addressing Past Trauma

Earlier, we discussed the impact trauma has on us, and how shame devolves into hate, or contempt, and how this is a path of death. I hope you are one of the few that does NOT have hard stuff that you already need to work through. But, we live in the real world. Most of you reading this have already experienced trauma, whether you acknowledge it or not. You should have been protected at all costs, but this is an impossible task. It is good in theory. Parents cannot do this in reality. **To expect that your parents or anyone else can always protect you is a setup for failure and disappointment.** This is why preparation is SO important. Yes, some of you will need what is in this chapter to process what you have already been through, but the rest of you will have stuff that is coming. I want you to be prepared so you can minimize the effects as much as possible.

Most parents believe that their child is free of sexual thoughts and that if they can just keep them from being "exposed" to something, they will be protected. However, in my counseling experience, I see over and over again that the child who was "protected" looked for pornography, or they began experimenting sexually with their friends or siblings and now border on being labeled as a perpetrator. This is avoidable.

This is where I tell parents that THEY are responsible for preparing you. Some of them gave you this book – excellent job! Others, though, err on the side of too little, too late. So, I get to be the one to help prepare you. YOU must be proactive and open to learning throughout your life.

The statistics on exposure to pornography and engagement in first sexual experiences are a wake-up call. My hope for you is that you want more for your life than just a fling, a one-night stand, or the lie and tease of nude videos online. Be prepared to say "NO."

Do you have a tight rein on your use of technology? If so, this is a good thing, even if it does not feel like it. There is a reason we place restrictions on the age to drive a car. Do you have the capability to drive at a younger age? Absolutely. But is it wise? Same with technology. I do not see complete isolation from technology as preparation. You need to learn to steward the tools available to you. **The scariest reality in this is how others now have access to your heart, and your mind.** How? Via text, email, and a variety of social media channels. This is leading to more and more kids and teens killing themselves. This ought to terrify most parents. I want you to see it as a concern as well - for you, and for your friends. When harm has occurred to someone, those closest to them rarely know anything about it.

No one can control your actions when you are outside of your home, away from parents, at a friend's house, on a friend's device, or even when you just switch to a neighbor's internet access point. YOU have the responsibility to be WISE!

This also extends into preparing to leave home and face different views, beliefs, gender issues, bullying, and more.

When you joined the sports team, were you prepared for the locker room talk, comparison, and possibility of not being the best?

Whether you are in a private, public, or homeschool setting, preparation is key. Many of the stories I hear are of abuse and lines crossed at a church camp or at a fellow Christian's home with their "protected" kids. Everyone has the potential to become curious, but that curiosity needs guidance. An excellent resource I recommend to parents is **Dr. Peter Levine's** *Trauma-Proofing Your Kids.*[82] I have my college students read it also, even though most are not married and do not have kids. It is packed full of great tools and resources to build resilience. This is a key for success in the face of potential trauma.

Building Resilience

Dr. Levine suggests that trauma is magnified in a person by the level of shutdown in a terrifying experience. We know traumatic events such as a lack of love, touch, safety and nourishment affect babies. This trauma is stored — trapped — in the body. It remains there throughout a lifetime. We call learning to minimize its power and effect **"trauma-proofing."**[83]

This can be accomplished by **"building resilience"** at an early age — even as young as infancy.

The recipe for building resilience is the **level of know-how in fighting or fleeing, rather than freezing.**[84]

Fighting and fleeing spend the adrenaline and physical energy pent up in response to a threat or potential trauma, regardless of our age.

Freezing is a survival mechanism that gets us through an experience, but that energy remains pent up inside our physical body. This energy penetrates throughout our bodies, which manifests itself in physical and mental health difficulties throughout our lives.

So, **what is "building resilience?"** This is your ability to "rebound" after something activates the fight/flight/freeze mechanism. Think of an event — whether it is an actual threat, or a perceived one, — as knocking you off balance. Your equilibrium is lost. The quicker that you can return to your baseline, the better off you will be. The goal is to learn how to do this for yourself. To find yourself able to respond to an event with ease and without excessive reaction is an empowering feeling. Not everyone will get to this point, but the goal is to **be more self-aware** of how you respond.

Knowing that no matter how freaked out you get, your body will calm down eventually can make the worst situation tolerable because you know that you will naturally calm down in a moment or two. This is a powerful truth to learn.

Think about it this way: your nervous system is always communicating to others' nervous systems. That sounds weird, doesn't it? What happened when you fell as a child? You probably looked at your parent to find out how you should react. If your parent freaked out, you freaked out. If they were calm, you were more likely to be calm. Many parents make small issues huge by their reaction, or better said, their over-reaction. It is good to calm yourself, but **it is even better if you can experience something uncomfortable and not let it get the best of you.**

A concept I love from Dr. Levine and other authors on healing trauma, is that of the **"felt sense."**[85] We have thoughts and feelings about a situation. We also have physical sensations with each experience. Putting words to these physical reactions can be powerful, empowering, and freeing. You may freak out but **choose** to not overreact. You may feel something, but, based on your physical sensations, reinterpret what you felt. You can think something and, based on the physical sensations, change your relationship with the event itself. This is powerful stuff.

Building resilience includes a calming presence from trusted adults. This is a big deal if your parents are not willing or able. YOU need these key people in your life just as much as I do. We ALL do. You will look to those individuals for their reactions and how they react to you, almost intuitively. Our brains are complex and include the ability to feel, think, and use the felt sense in a way that better informs our bodies as to the reality of an event. This allows us to regain equilibrium more quickly, or maintain control in the face of potential threats, hurt, fear, or pain.[86]

What Do I Do In The Face Of Potential Harm?

Jenny stresses out over an upcoming test. She remembers that she has a choice over how far she lets this train run away in her head. She assesses the worst-case scenarios, notices her body sensations, and considers her thoughts and feelings. She sees her reaction as valid because of the lack of time she spent studying. She recognizes that the speed of her heart rate is an overreaction, and that catastrophizing is unhelpful. Almost immediately, she finds her physical body calming down. She has averted a panic attack, similar to dozens of others she used to have. She has learned to be resilient. She has learned to stay inquisitive and curious about her responses, rather than over-reacting and adding fuel to the fire, which only encouraged a full-blown panic response in the past.

Ken is a police officer who has found himself in tough moments when fear and panic entered his system. He has learned how to respond. He begins by noticing his body and its reactions first. He then assesses the situation as to the validity of his initial reaction to the potential threat. Is it real or only perceived? He then reassesses his physical reactions, and if they are unnecessary, calms down quickly. However, if they are valid, he finds himself able to shift in his reaction towards the situation and respond appropriately rather than having his physiology take over. This is resilience. He maintains control more often than not. He can think more clearly in those moments. He finds himself more calm in the face of danger, whether real or imagined.

What do YOU do? You can learn to tap into this innate ability. You are wired to respond to danger. You also have the ability to perform under stress.

The key is to allow situations to occur so you can learn after each one how to better interpret the moment's data, keep things in the conscious choice part of your brain, and respond intuitively and intentionally. Each time you can exercise this muscle, it will serve you better throughout your life.

Discussing your reactions, the data, and even the failures is important whenever it is possible. My goal is that you learn you have more choices than you realize when it feels like your body or brain is being hijacked and you feel out of control. This does not have to be the default. Success breeds success. The next time you will be more likely to regain control and choose well in less time. **Listening and paying attention to your physical sensations is a critical skill.**

Another critical aspect for mental and physical health is **REST**. It is empowering to learn how to put language to your experiences, feelings, and physical reactions. **Rest is critical.** Processing your reactions in a safe place after the fact becomes a learning experience. I hope you can find a trusted adult in your life to help you. Giving yourself the space and freedom to feel is priceless.

If you have experienced trauma, another helpful tool is the **intentional use of play.** It is much easier to process what you've experienced by playing it out. You can do this via art, music, toys, games, etc. You can use these tools to draw out your own feelings and reactions to a situation.

As I mentioned earlier in this book, one approach that we took with our children when they were young was to talk with them after they had been with a babysitter. We would ask them if their babysitter had touched them in their private areas or asked them to do anything that they thought was weird. We were not expecting an honest response, as those experiences often bring on shame and silence. **We were looking for a different physical reaction to the question than the previous thirty times we asked them.** (We also communicated to our sitters that we always asked these questions, so they would not feel singled out and to hopefully prevent anything from happening). We attempted to pay attention to whether they paused, averted their eyes, or squirmed in coming up with their response. This was us, as parents, learning to use the data before us wisely. Yes, it is uncomfortable, but it was our way of saying that we were choosing to be a safe place to share this information.

Being Prepared

From birth to age five, you were absorbing the **ENERGY** that was put out by your reactions, passions, and emotional and spiritual health.

This time of life is all about a child's safety and letting them know they have people they can trust. Most children are overwhelmingly trusting. We, as parents, want to preserve that by being a trusted, stable presence in your life.

Between the ages of six and ten, you are absorbing the **CULTURE** of your home. A child is already beginning to separate from their parents a bit. They want — and need — opportunities for freedom. They need to experience pain, pleasure, loss, fear, joy — the range of human emotions. **They learn to worship what their parents worship,** see the world through their parents' eyes, and react to their interpretation of the world in tangible ways over the following years.

The ages of eleven to seventeen welcome the peak of sexual interest and curiosity. How does that sound? Interesting and intriguing? Or gross and scary? This stage of development also brings along a stronger separation from caregivers and a struggle with your identity. Does this sound familiar yet? If not, it will most likely arrive soon enough. Many ask questions like:

"Who am I?"

"What do I stand for?" and

"Where am I going?"

The TEEN years are a time that most begin to date. This provides even more reason for the incredible need for stewardship and a strong Biblical Sexual Ethic — an ETHOS. **Parents that decide to have "the talk" now will find it almost useless at this point.**

When does harm enter the story? Unfortunately, it can be present at any of these ages. **Preparation** is the key. **Resilience** and the ability NOT to freeze is crucial.

It is imperative that you have the skills you need for self-regulation and knowing how to fight or to flee. It is up to you in moments of decision and temptation to choose well and steward yourself, your body, and your mind well.

My desire is that you know that knowledge is the start of preparation. Education will give you a much greater chance for success.

Be Prepared.

Be a Good Steward.

May you become wiser than your years.

* * *

Working Questions – Now it is YOUR TURN:

Were you prepared when you started middle school or high school for all that you would face?

____

____

Fight, flight, and _______________?

Explain how each of these can be a response to trauma.

____

____

What is building resilience?

____

____

From birth to 5, children are absorbing a family's ___________.
Explain.

____

____

Between ages 6 and 10, children are absorbing a family's ___________.

Explain.

____

____

Between the ages of 11 to 17, our children are entering the peak of their sexual interest and curiosity — have your parents prepared you? How did they do this? Do you think they should have done something differently?

____

____

| 26 |

What This Looks Like - Practically Speaking

You've taken in a lot of information as you've read this book!

The next step is the pruning process as you examine why you believe — or don't believe — certain things. You will find that you are cementing some beliefs or behaviors and letting others go. You are adding information, challenging old assumptions, and allowing *"iron to sharpen iron"* (Proverbs 27:17, NLT).

A word of caution is necessary though: **be discerning of who you listen to and who you elevate as an authority** — myself included. In this chapter, I want you to put some of these things down in writing. So, grab a notebook or journal and jot down some of your thoughts. This will help you tremendously in exercising wisdom and discernment in your choices in the present and future.

A Biblical Sexual Ethic — your ETHOS — must include a theology of sex, marriage, gender, and what this means for you.

I want you to BE A LEADER - to be an EXAMPLE! If you believe that being a leader means that you have the ultimate authority in all things, but you are not sensitive to the needs, opinions, and view of others, your life will bear the fruit from this approach. If, on the other hand, you don't have the confidence to believe that you can understand Truth as you read it from God's Word, then your beliefs will not carry weight. If you allow fear to keep you from speaking up or fighting for something, your legacy will bear these fruits. **I want you to LEAD!**

I hope that you will commit to think through these issues, study God's Word, and be able to articulate what you believe and why you believe it to others. Commit to living by your Biblical Sexual Ethic, and lead by example with confidence.

Ecclesiastes 3:22 puts our work into perspective:

> *"So I saw that there is nothing better for people than to be happy in their work. That is our lot in life. And no one can bring us back to see what happens after we die" (NLT).*

Invest in your most important job - strengthening your heart, character, and integrity so you can be strong, courageous, and a change agent in this world.

This is YOUR WORK. Be happy in YOUR WORK – now, today.

Your Personal ETHOS

Your Personal ETHOS — or belief system — must have a foundation. **Your first step will be deciding if that will be tradition, your personal experiences, or God's Word.** Your actions will prove which one guides you at any given moment or decision point.

Are you guided more by what others think of you?

Are you motivated by fear because of your own experiences of traumatic events?

Deciding to make God's Word your foundation will require that you make difficult decisions. Some of these will be unpopular — not only to others in your friend group, but even to strangers or acquaintances. This is part of the reason I am so adamant that seeds be planted in YOUR life at a younger age than most families think is necessary. This provides a greater chance that YOU will adopt a Biblical Sexual Ethic as your own and makes it less likely that you will choose current cultural stances or personal experiences as your foundation.

You will have a much easier transition into your teen years and adulthood if you settle many of these questions in your heart now. I want your adolescent years to be a time of relationship and adventure with your family and friends as you carefully and intentionally prepare yourself to launch into the adult world.

This MUST be the goal - To launch into adulthood well.

You cannot stay a kid forever.

You need independence.

You need room to spread your wings, fly, fall, and get up again.

I believe that your priorities regarding dating, sex, and marriage must be addressed when you are in your formative years.

You can do this! And you are not alone.

Living Out Your Ethos

As you process all that you have read so far, where are some places where you feel stuck?

What are some questions that emerge?

As you think about dating, having sex (hopefully not soon!), marrying, being a spouse, and becoming a parent, what are some concerns you have?

Can you clearly see a path for yourself that is full of joy, strength of character, and healthy relationships? Or does the path ahead look painful?

I wish I could spare you from any pain or trauma. The truth, though, is that I cannot. I can only prepare you. I want to describe the road before you so you will avoid pitfalls and side trails and choose, on your own, to stay on the path.

If your foundation is Scripture — God's Word — you can find clarity on many issues. This will not be without difficulty, as you navigate issues and questions that are not clearly detailed in Scripture. Let's review:

Gender:

Scripture is clear about God creating humans as male and female. Scripture is clear about the Lord calling them to come together and multiply (Genesis 1:27-28; 1:15-24). Unless you were born with ambiguous genitalia, also known as intersex, you are either male or female. Remember, you are unique in your design as a male or female. Many of the battles that people are facing today are not actually against their gender, but against what society has said a man or woman should look like or act like.

Pornography:

Research shows that pornography is damaging to the heart, the head, and relationships. It also exploits the men and women in the videos and images. Scripture is clear on this one. Recent studies show an increase of men in their twenties with erectile dysfunction because of pornography use. WOW! This is avoidable. There is no place for it inside or outside of marriage. If you want your marriage to thrive, say NO! If you want to be married and stay married one day, say NO! If you are content being single, but desire to treat others with respect, then say NO![87]

Dating:

When should you date? Great question. If we look to Scripture, you will see that it does not address dating. A rule of thumb is to remember the admonition of Scripture:

> "there must not be even a hint of sexual immorality, or of any kind of impurity, or of greed, because these are improper for God's holy people" (Ephesians 5:3, NIV).

There is no magic age, but dating should wait until you can bear the weight of another person's heart and be responsible for the outcomes of a physical relationship. You are NOT at an age to marry yet, unless you are out of high school. It is my opinion that you are playing with fire. We discussed this in greater depth in chapter 19.

Marriage:

The Lord says:

> *"Give honor to marriage, and remain faithful to one another in marriage. God will surely judge people who are immoral and those who commit adultery" (Hebrews 13:4, NLT).*

Scripture is also clear that this covenant is between a man and a woman (Genesis 1:18-25; Matthew 19:1-9; 1 Corinthians 7). The purpose of marriage and family is the raising up of the next generation to know God and honor Him (Psalms 18:5-7).

Marriage is hard, but it is an incredible blessing to walk through life with someone - especially if they are a best friend. What great care God has for us! Yes, we live in a broken world that has led many into more than one marriage after the dissolution of a previous marriage. God is a God of grace. He restores. He renews. Sexuality is to be stewarded in marriage, just as it is during your single days. Marriage is the only setting in which intercourse should be experienced since it has the potential to bring life into the world. Does that mean all other sexual activity is acceptable outside of marriage? The Lord says:

> *"God's will is for you to be holy, so stay away from all sexual sin. Then each of you will control his own body and live in holiness and honor—not in lustful passion like the pagans who do not know God and his ways. Never harm or cheat a fellow believer in this matter by violating his wife, for the Lord avenges all such sins, as we have solemnly warned you before" (1 Thessalonians 4:3-6, NLT).*

The only place for sexual intimacy is within marriage.

Sex:

Sex (intercourse) is primarily meant to serve as the place where the sperm and egg come together to create new life. Thankfully, that doesn't happen every time a man and woman come together! Sex — and by that I mean genital play — is also meant to be a pleasure enjoyed by a man and woman within the safety and boundaries of marriage. Research shows that those in a monogamous relationship, whether or not they are married are exponentially more likely NOT to worry about sexually transmitted infections. Sex is meant to be beautiful. Sex is meant to be holy, a sacrament. Sex is also meant to be a regular part of marriage. This serves as a protection against the temptations that abound. It is an incredible source of pleasure as well. Procreation is a natural result, but waits for God's timing. The 3 P's.

Technology:

These tools need to be stewarded. They are not expensive toys! Know they are tools. It is critical to know what is appropriate to view and post online. The tools are not the enemy, but Satan sure knows how to use them. Be aware and careful with cyberbullying and internet safety.

Idols:

Be careful who or what you put on a pedestal and worship. There is to be ONLY ONE GOD. Be intentional. Be cognizant of what could become an idol. Do not let it distract you from the One who truly deserves our worship or your involvement in a local church, which is the Body and Bride of Christ (Hebrews 10:23-25; 1 Corinthians 12). You need the Body of Christ, and the Body needs you.

* * *

Your Assignment

Now, it is your turn to make this YOURS.

Start with the Scripture passages highlighted here and examine them for yourself.

Pray that the Lord will instruct you in both the meaning of the Scriptures, and how to live them out.

* * *

Working Questions – Now it is YOUR TURN:

Proverbs 27:17 says that
As iron sharpens iron,
so a friend sharpens a friend (NLT).

It is in the fellowship with others that we grow. What does this mean?

____

____

Define ETHOS.

____

____

As you process all that we have covered, what are some questions that emerge?

Can you clearly see the path ahead? Does it threaten pain and damaging relationships, or joy and healthy relationships?

Spend some time writing out a list of areas you would like to discuss with your parents.

Why is it so important for us to "go there?"

Your Living ETHOS — Use this space to write out YOUR personal beliefs and strategies for these topics:

Gender

____

____

Pornography

____

____

Dating

____

____

Marriage

____

____

Sex

____

____

Technology

____

____

Idols

____

____

Now it is your turn to make this YOURS. The next steps may involve research and prayer.

Look this one up:
You are to *"... be happy in your ________________"* (**Ecclesiastes 3:22**).

Are the adults around you happy in their work? Are you (which is school and growing in your own personal ETHOS?)

____

____

Read **Genesis 1:15–24.**

Let these lights in the sky shine down on the earth." And that is what happened. God made two great lights — the larger one to govern the day, and the smaller one to govern the night. He also made the stars. God set these lights in the sky to light the earth, to govern the day and night, and to separate the light from the darkness. And God saw that it was good.

And evening passed and morning came, marking the fourth day.

Then God said, "Let the waters swarm with fish and other life. Let the skies be filled with birds of every kind." So God created great sea creatures and every living thing that scurries and swarms in the water, and every sort of bird—each producing offspring of the same kind. And God saw that it was good. Then God blessed them, saying, "Be fruitful and multiply. Let the fish fill the seas, and let the birds multiply on the earth."

And evening passed and morning came, marking the fifth day.

Then God said, "Let the earth produce every sort of animal, each producing offspring of the same kind— livestock, small animals that scurry along the ground, and wild animals." And that is what happened (NLT).

Verses 27-28:

So God created human beings in his own image. In the image of God he created them;
male and female he created them.

Then God blessed them and said, "Be fruitful and multiply. Fill the earth and govern it. Reign over the fish in the sea, the birds in the sky, and all the animals that scurry along the ground" (NLT).

This passage reminds us of God's perfect design. What is His design for marriage and children?

____

____

| 27 |

Your Plan of Action

A few months ago, my twelve-year-old son asked me, "So, when can I date?"

My response to him was:

> "Remember when we went through '***Passport to Purity***'?[88] You signed over that decision to me, and I told you that the best time is your junior or senior year of college. Do you remember why?"

He did remember. Can he be responsible for her heart? Can he drive? Can he afford dinner and a movie? Can he afford a ring? Is he ready to have a baby within a few years of beginning dating?

He already knew my answer, though. We have been discussing this for years and he attends many of my college classes and teachings at churches on the subject. He needed some affirmation. Why? He hears a very different message around him, and he also has internal drives and desires he is learning to steward.

I continued, "This is the time to have amazing relationships without getting hung up on titles. Get to know a lot of different young ladies, learn what you like and dislike. Have fun with friends, grow, mature, have more fun, and live by boundaries. Then, when you are older, you can walk into a relationship and have little to no baggage to carry into marriage."

He got it! Why? We have had this discussion multiple times.

We go back to it. We expand on it.

He has new questions about it.

This is a beautiful exchange. Remember who is responsible, though, for these decisions to steward his dating, sexual, and relational self?

He is. YOU are. Not your parents, not me, no one else.

My Theology of Sex - Owning it

Is sex (intercourse) okay between two consenting adults?

A better question is whether this is wise. Another question is whether this is something that will separate us from God. That's a wild one. I want you to be able to answer questions like these. You are preparing yourself to navigate difficult questions in a challenging world that lives by a different ethic.

Just being told, "NO," or, "It's bad," is not helpful. Sometimes it is abusive. Sex and sexuality are beautiful parts of all of us, single and married alike. I want you to make wise decisions with your body, with what you look at, and how you live in community with others.

Write out Scripture and other ideas and resources that inform your ETHOS on Sex.

Further questions are at the end of each chapter. Please don't skip those.

Do you have questions? Write them down. Think through them. Wrestle with them. When you come to a conclusion, you can be confident because you know you have done the work of prayerfully studying Scripture to understand the picture of God's design.

Be careful that your own experience is not the only thing forming your beliefs. Listen to what others say but be careful who you listen to. Some are truly seeking to understand and apply Scripture. Others are looking out for their own good. Some are neutral and deserve our attention as we filter them through Scripture and God's desire for our best.

My Theology of Marriage - Owning it

Marriage is not a right. **Marriage is a sacred commitment** and a privilege that you should NOT enter into lightly. It is hard. It doubles both your joy and your burdens. Companionship is an incredible gift, which helps explain why there is such a large push in our culture to redefine marriage.

Marriage is two broken people choosing to bind their lives, souls, and bodies to go through life together. Marriage is give and take. It is FULL of dying to yourself. It is NOT for the faint of heart. Marriage is a place to wrestle with hard things, disagree, fight, make up, forgive, hurt, and heal. It is a safe place for couples as they go through both beautiful and difficult times. It is also the only place where children truly thrive.

The more we learn about human development, the more we recognize the importance of engaged parents, the role of the father, and models of both masculinity and femininity. It is where children first learn about leadership, cooperation, forgiveness, and grace.

There are troubling teachings in some churches regarding headship and authority, submission, and the roles of a husband and wife in marriage. As I study Scripture, I see no sign of a husband dominating his wife to the point where she has no voice and must obey as what Jesus intends for marriage to look like. His example is one of putting His bride before Himself.

What is your theology of marriage? Write out the beliefs you have about marriage.

What is your framework based on?

Does your framework consider the totality of Scripture, or are they cherry-picked to make you more comfortable?

Are you a cynic? A romantic? Are you grounded in the truth?

What are some questions that come to mind as you think about marriage?

What has been your experience with marriage in your family?

What are your fears?

Write them down and prayerfully wrestle with them. Apply Scripture to your situation. Again, be aware of the sexual ethic and respect for Scripture that others have as you decide who to listen to for advice on marriage.

Self-Leadership and Leading Others

One belief I hold after over 20 years of counseling practice and teaching, is that most single parents, regardless of whether they are the mother or father, believe that they must be both mom and dad in their children's lives. I have found this to be a dangerous place to live. This can cause more damage to their children. Did you grow up in a single parent home? How was it?

I believe that what kids and teens need most from their single parent is for them to be the best mom or dad that they can be. They are NOT and never will be the other parent. It is so important for them to stop pretending they can be all things to their children.

Hang with me here. Think about it. It is important that a single mom get her children around a healthy male influence. A single dad needs to get his children around a healthy female influence. There is already an irreplaceable loss here. It can be very helpful to acknowledge that loss and help them grieve. It is a powerful gift to their children to be proactive and intentional, to put positive influences in their children's lives. This is where the Body of Christ can come alongside families when they make their needs known.

This is also true for families with two parents. **As men and women, your parents fall short of who they should be in your life.** We need community. For some families, they put their kids in school, a sport, or an extra-curricular activity and call it good — influence in place. Check. I want to advise you and your parents not to do this blindly.

Think about the importance of these questions: What is the worldview of those running these activities? Are they leading you well? Are they healthy, quality examples?

I hear testimonies from students that there were many key influencers — both for good and for bad — in their developmental years. Outside of parents, they mention coaches, youth pastors, and teachers most often. I want you to see that you have great power in **CHOOSING** whom you let influence you. **Build your OWN band of influencers** now. Choose well. Be deliberate and thoughtful.

Interestingly, my wife and I have built this with our children via Boy Scouts with our sons, and American Heritage Girls with our daughter. I am honored that other parents invite me into their lives to become an influence in their sons' lives. I often tell my sons that if they have a question or problem that they don't want to talk to me about, I hope they will go to one of the other dads in our Scout troop. I also tell them they will sometimes find themselves jealous because I am helping, correcting, and encouraging another boy. I want them to know that I am doing what I want other parents to do for them.

At our seven-day summer camp out last year, I only spoke with my son about four times. I was present, but I kept my distance. I had several conversations with other boys. I was also building relationships with the other dads, which is critical for my own health and well-being. I was there when my son had a breakdown, but quickly removed myself again after calming him down, **so he could figure out a solution on his own.** Do you see the importance of raising up men and women that have the grit, strength, and security to march to a different drum?

I want my children to know how to face adversity and not back down. I also want them to have the wisdom to look at potential conflict and walk away. This is what I want for you. This is where you take the wheel and lead. It is up to you to do this for yourself if your parents are not already curating some of these influences for you. **This turns a corner as YOU lead your peers in a better direction.**

Be an influencer with your peers. Be an example. Stand firm in what you believe. Live by convictions. Live strong. Be strong. Be courageous. Be intentional. Be firm. Change the world around you.

Can a parent be there for each crisis, question, and event? NOPE! But the teaching, training, and preparation of those that invested in you will be there, whether it was intentional or not. Your leadership as a teen or preteen is real. Lead your peers with integrity, with strength, and with gentleness. Remember, you ARE a leader! Lead confidently. Lead with integrity.

Lead by Example

Okay, that was a lot! **Leadership is a difficult - and worthy task.** Leading others in a purposeful direction can change lives. It may be difficult to establish boundaries from which to say "NO!" Here are some examples:

Every young preteen lady needs someone to teach her and prepare her for her period. Your menstrual cycle could begin when you are ten or eleven years old. I don't want you to be surprised and think you are dying. Be prepared.

Every young man will experience an erection and, after realizing what the trigger was, almost always feels embarrassment and shame. He needs someone to educate and encourage him.

I am a resource to you if you are ever stuck. Do not hesitate to reach out to me, your pastor, or another Christian counselor.

After all that you have read here and the work you completed at the end of each chapter, **YOU ARE READY TO LEAD!** Be open to talking about things and be honest about how hard it is. Carefully share your mistakes, heartaches, and pains. Be vulnerable. Many of your peers are uncommunicative, uninformed, or misinformed because they won't trust reputable sources with their questions. I know it takes a lot of courage to open your heart to someone else. Remember that you have access to be the Body of Christ. **You are not alone.**

I have a unique passion, training, and expertise that allows me to partner with you and help you enter these hard conversations. Be an example to others of what you want them to be. You are an example already, whether you want to be or not, so you should be intentional and thoughtful as you guide others into rewarding relationships, a life with boundaries, and calculated risks. **Even more important to me is guiding others into a relationship with Christ.**

Lead with Assertiveness

When my son first asked about babies at age 6 or 7, we got a book off the shelf on that subject and read it. He ran off, and it seemed to make no impact on him, but it did. A few months later, he asked a more pointed question, and my wife passed the conversation off to me. I got the same book out and the sex part registered. Suddenly, he understood that the penis had to go inside the girl for the sperm and egg to meet. His response was, "GROSSSS!", and five seconds later he was playing with Legos and in another world. He wasn't though, and neither were you. Many people find this realization to be traumatizing - especially if they are older when they get "the talk". **Every preteen and teen is processing what they see and hear.** With my son, a few more weeks passed and our next conversations — *micro-conversations* — went deeper fast.

He showed me he was ready, and we needed to talk about it. It was earlier than I expected to have this conversation. **By giving him this information, I was giving him the responsibility to steward it wisely.**

Have you seen the kid at school that takes this information to school and shares it with everyone? That is a valid concern for parents. It is important to have discernment and to be careful where and with whom you discuss these things. But, if we do not prepare ourselves (and others), they can misuse this information. We need wisdom.

Go there. Lead. Prepare. Be gracious. Be patient. And remember — ***micro-conversations***, not lectures!

Lead with Confidence

You can lead with confidence.

What gives you confidence? **Knowing what you believe, and why you believe it.**

Should you date at sixteen-years-old?

What do you believe? You need to know.

You can do this. You never need to have all the answers. It is so important to remain teachable throughout your life. Be assertive in leading yourself and friends towards wisdom, discernment, and boundaries.

* * *

Working Questions – Now it is YOUR TURN:

Write out Scripture and other ideas and resources that help inform your ETHOS on sex.

____

____

____

____

Why should I wait until marriage to have genital contact with another person?

____

____

What is my theology of oral sex? Everyone seems to say it is okay, but is it really? Is it healthy or unhealthy? Is it gross or sick? Is it an acceptable part of healthy sexual play within marriage?

____

____

Is it okay to have a third person in a sexual relationship? Why not?

____

____

Is sex (intercourse) okay between two consenting adults?

What do I do with my sex drive as a single adult with raging hormones? This feels like a cruel punishment from God.

What do I desire in a healthy sexual relationship in marriage one day? If I desire my spouse to be pure, what am I doing to keep the same commitment?

Do you have more questions? Write them here. Wrestle with them as you seek an answer in Scripture and seek wise counsel.

What is your theology of marriage? Write out the beliefs you have about marriage — whether they are crazy, funny, wild, anything! Ponder on your beliefs. Are they biblical? Do they line up with what God's Word says?

____

____

____

____

Am I a cynic who needs to lighten up or am I a hopeless romantic and I need to wise up?

____

____

Should a believer marry an unbeliever?

____

____

Is marriage designed to be between a man and woman? What have your parents taught you? Does the Word of God inform your beliefs or popular culture?

____

____

Are there requirements for marriage?

____

____

What does it mean to be "sexually compatible"? Is this important? How do you know?

____

____

Do you believe that the Lord would call a couple in two different directions? What should you do if you believe you are being led down different paths?

____

____

Is friendship a foundation for a great marriage? If we do not have that, can we ever find it?

____

____

What role does forgiveness play in marriage?

____

____

What are some other questions that come to mind as you think about marriage? What are your fears, hang-ups, and struggles?

____

____

| 28 |

You Are a Gift to Others

Phil and **Seth** are best friends. They have known each other since they were in elementary school. They are now in high school and dealing with the pressure to date and lose their virginity. Phil comes from a great home that prepared him to live from a Biblical Sexual Ethic. Seth lives in a home where he sometimes wonders if they will have food. Seth has never heard his parents say "I love you" to him or to each other. He witnesses fighting and anger and violence. Phil and Seth could not be more different. They are responding to the pressures of their teen years and peer pressure in drastically different ways. The difference has been Phil's confidence to lead. Phil has watched Seth get into relationships and even face a pregnancy scare. Phil has always been a patient friend. His faithfulness through some dark times has resulted in Seth listening as Phil has shared with him a very different ETHOS for sexuality and boundaries that is countercultural. Now, after lots of heartache on Seth's journey, he is listening to Phil and ignoring the pressure of peers and other girls. He has banded together with Phil to raise the bar on the kind of girl - or better said woman - he will consider going out with, let alone consider marrying. Seth has a new ETHOS because of a friend who led with confidence and boldness, but also with tact and care. **THIS IS COMMUNITY.**

Kenny is 17 and is thankful for the men in his life. He happened upon a scout meeting at a nearby school where he was able to connect with boys and dads that showed him the kind of man he could choose to be. He is choosing that now more than ever. Even more importantly, he came to know Christ as his Savior because of the faithfulness of the families in that Scout troop. The most influential person was not one of the adults. It was a boy a year older than him that he thought was cool. He saw something different in him and wanted what he had. Over the years and through a bunch of campouts and adventures, he followed this friend and these dads to the decision to be a Christ-follower. Isn't that inspiring and exciting? I hope it is to you. YOU could be that influential friend - even now.

Ken and Jill are parents that began their journey when their son, who was not yet a teenager, began acting out sexually, and they came in for counseling. I had the honor of walking with this young man through much of the material presented in this book. I talked with him about pornography, the "M" word, and helped him develop a Biblical Sexual Ethic. The purpose of these conversations was to empower him to consciously choose what he would do in all situations, rather than acting unconsciously. I also walked with his parents through this process, so they were equipped to lead their other children toward a Biblical Sexual Ethic. They need to have their own personal ETHOS that is grounded in God's Word and realistic about preparing them for the world outside their home.

Sam and Carolina are parents that have grown children but saw them make unwise decisions when they were in their teens and their twenties. Now, their children are all married, and they have the honor of being Grammy and Pappy. They realized that since they had not talked with their grown children about issues surrounding sexuality, their now grown children were now following in their footsteps and not talking with their grandchildren. Sam and Carolina began to have micro-conversations with their children as they encountered various situations, and this planted seeds in their hearts and minds. This led their married children to ask hard questions leading them to examine their own sexual ethic — their ETHOS — and what they lacked when they were growing up. They empowered themselves as adults with knowledge and followed the example of Grammy and Pappy. They were grateful that their parents cared enough to get involved and motivated them to talk with their children. They were prepared when they had to walk through some traumatic incidents and experiences that their children encountered. Their parents, Sam and Carolina, took a risk for their grandkids' sake and it paid off greatly.

As you are reading, I hope you are being transformed.

I hope you have been encouraged and motivated to raise the bar for the man or woman you desire to be as an adult. The people you listen to and allow around you can absolutely change the course of your life and future forever. I do not make this statement lightly.

YOU are engaging in a battle today at school, in your home, online, and in person. There is so much out there that is intent on grabbing your attention and distracting you from doing the healthy or wise thing. It is either telling you that you are not good enough, or that you can do anything. Let's get grounded in God's Word and KNOW who and whose we are.

You will face heartache and heartbreak. You will experience love and loss. This is life. How you handle these can be life changing in a positive or negative way.

My Final Plea to You – Do Not DO Life Alone!

If you are "doing this alone" – PLEASE STOP!

Life was never meant to be a solo sport. Growing up into a young man or woman that honors God and makes confident, wise decisions is done in community. Please do your best to find a community within your church that will come alongside you to pray for you and influence you. Also, may YOU be that person to others in your peer group as well.

Does God play games or make mistakes?

No, He doesn't. **Can you trust that He placed you into your family with a purpose – even if you cannot see it?** Can you see that God has your life in His hands and has a purpose for everything you go through - even the things you wish you could undo or never experience? This is tough. This really becomes difficult when dealing with trauma. We must remember that Satan is alive and active. He is out to steal, kill, and destroy. May you always challenge that story. May you live a life aimed at thwarting the devil's schemes. I promise it is a great way to live. It is hard, but it is very rewarding.

Saying, "NO" today to a temporary pleasure or high because you can see the rewards down the road allows you to live with TRUE FREEDOM. Live that way!

It Is All About Stewardship

Jeffrey is a handful. He is loud and eager to answer. He is energetic and funny. He is curious and wild. He gets himself into trouble with his impulsivity. He is a gift to this world. The man he will become depends on many factors. What if YOU are the influence that changes his life through your friendship?

Sarah is a shy, quiet young lady. She does not engage with others. She retreats from relationships. She struggles with her thoughts but does not let anyone know. Sarah is a gift to this world. What if you are the one to help her believe that and find her voice? What if you are the one that leads her to the Cross?

You are a gift from God. Your uniqueness and idiosyncrasies are part of God's design. He does NOT make mistakes. You, as a preteen or teenager, will make mistakes in every role you play. Our God does not. Growing and learning about yourself, your personality, and your gifting is part of the journey. Your emotions and behavior can be overwhelming. Trust that God made you in His image. Yes, we live in a fallen world - take that into account - and live with grace for yourself, and for others. Live with Truth, boundaries, and HOPE.

What if you now carry the title of perpetrator or molester? You need community, hope, grace and forgiveness. This does not discount the need for discipline for the evil done towards another. You still need to bear the responsibility, but you also need to know that you are still lovable — to those in your life and to God — and have hope for the future.

What if you were molested? You need community, hope, grace, open arms, and a listening and safe ear. You need to BE BELIEVED.

You need to know how to process what has happened and that you are worth fighting for. You need to know that you still have a bright future.

How do you steward your own sexuality, gender, and temptations?

How you manage these will impact how you are able to be there for others and encourage them in times of need. If you are struggling in this area, please get help. The best gift that you can give yourself is honesty regarding your mistakes and then asking for other's forgiveness and/or getting the help you need. **DO NOT DO THIS ALONE.**

My guess is that you probably need to see confession, repentance, and forgiveness modeled more than you need a perfect parent or leader or friend. It is usually in our times of greatest need that we see God. We see Him in others and how they love us and support us. However, this help often depends on US reaching out and asking for help – or confessing. **GO THERE!** And, yes, some do not handle things well. Move on to someone that will. These will be YOUR TRUE COMMUNITY. Be sure though that they are leading you in a healthy, God-honoring direction.

This is all about stewardship. Of our stories. Of our power. Of our friendships. Of our vulnerability.

Your Responsibility and Being Proactive

What you have read is ALL about preparing you for battle. This a battle for you and your friends' hearts – and **who you will worship and serve.**

Are you responsible for your friend's decisions?

No, you are not. They have free will. They are their own person. You will each grow up, face temptations, and make your own decisions. As you enter different life stages and the struggles that come with each, you will be accountable for your own decisions. It is hard not to feel responsible for a friend's decisions because you think you didn't do enough or prevent them from going out with that person or making that poor choice. It is important to remember that part of our job to pray for them. It is NOT about making anyone behave. You are only responsible for YOU and your own personal decisions!

So, my question to you is, do you feel prepared? If not, keep studying. I hope you are honest and say NO. These pages are a foundation for you to build on as you prepare for all God has before you, but it is not the end.

Did you know that stranger danger is preparing for the nine percent chance of abuse from a stranger? Most harm comes from within - from those we know and trust. May you learn to say, "NO," and stand up for yourself if a sibling, uncle, babysitter, or family friend asks you to take your clothes off or do something sexual. Boundaries. This is tough. This takes grit. This takes training. So, I am planting the seed for you to know that saying "NO" IS the loving thing. Exercise that muscle.

I often hear from parents, "But I had those conversations with my child!" However, when I have then talked to their children, they say they did not have these conversations. What is the disconnect? The disconnect comes from the form of "the talk" which usually comes (if at all) way too late. "The talk" is usually an information dump given too late to have a meaningful impact on building their child's sexual ethic — their ETHOS.

You are more prepared than most. May you be an example to those in your life. When my son was at school one day he got frustrated with his peers and their flirting and subtle sexual banter - both from the boys and the girls. He thought that they were talking about boyfriends and girlfriends at too young of an age. **He called a meeting at lunch and gave them a long lecture about dating, boundaries, sexual ethics, and what to do and what not to do.** I was so proud of him. Where did he get this? From me. His primary example. And this was leadership. This was standing up for health and truth and what is helpful - not what is popular. I love this. I want this to be you in your community and friend groups - even if they laugh at you, shun you, or ridicule you. STAND UP FOR HEALTH. Stand up for protecting others, integrity and for keeping things age appropriate.

It is being proactive when you drop truths into others' lives that they can then choose to pick up. What if you are the only one in their life that shows you care? **BE THAT PERSON - BE THAT FRIEND!**

Being Confident

A key part of being confident is knowledge. There aren't many people that love reading books about marriage, trauma, parenting, sexuality, and shame. You each have your own passions, interests, skills, and areas of expertise. Share these with others by helping them. Help someone fix something if you are great at fixing things. Help someone plan something if that is your skill set. This book is my attempt to share my skill set and knowledge with you. I want to help as many preteens, teens, and families as possible change their future and their family tree.

* * *

Working Questions – Now it is YOUR TURN:

Do you feel like your parents have failed you? There is always hope. Even parents that might get this part right will miss other things their children need. What are areas beyond sexuality that need their (or another trusted adults) attention and investment?

____

____

____

____

Did your parents discuss stranger danger and prepare you for the 9% chance of abuse from a stranger – but never prepared you to say "NO" and stand up for yourself when a sibling, uncle, or family friend asks you to take their clothes off or do something sexual?

____

____

Write out John 15:13

____

____

____

How does this verse impact you?

____

____

____

| 29 |

The Power And Importance of Community

Community

Sam and Kelly have found themselves struggling with their sixteen-year-old son. The battles, stress, and tears are devastating to them both. The impact it has had on their marriage has been earth shattering. Their saving grace has been their community. They attend a large church where they were lost in the crowd for a long time. But now, within that community, they have formed friendships that have become their lifeline as they now have peers to bounce ideas off of and shoulders to cry on. Two families in their group have been through similar struggles with their own children and have been a tremendous source of encouragement as they share the tools they have picked up over the years.

YOU need this as a teenager also. It matters who you choose to hang out with and WHO you let influence you!

My wife and I have seen the power of community throughout our lives, even before we were married. Before I met my wife, people from my Sunday School class would pick me up and take me to doctors' appointments when I was battling with my health. Throughout our marriage, our church community and friends have been an incredible support through health scares, loneliness, the births of our children, and when we had to make hard decisions. For me, my biker (motorcycle) friends have been a source of friendship, spiritual encouragement, and an example of how to live as imperfect men of God. Our life stage now finds our community coming from the relationships we have with parents of our children's friends at our church's Boy Scout and American Heritage Girls troops.

Think about it — who do you spend the most time around?

What are their beliefs and values?

Do you want to be like them?

Be intentional about community NOW and it will impact your whole life. Too many adults are lacking good, healthy communities in their lives. Many times they were also missing out on community when they were young.

THIS IS SO IMPORTANT: This means you will need to be very thoughtful about what you commit to, how much time it will take, and the impact it will have on your family, money, faith, and heart. You do not have to say yes to everything. You actually cannot. And a "YES" to one thing is a "NO" to another. Be intentional and work with your family if they are safe. If they are not - meet with a friend's parents, youth pastor, or coach who can be an asset to you.

YOU Were Never Meant To Do This Alone

I am humbled when I see single moms bearing the weight day in and day out of too much on their plate – with the kids, and work, and bills, and – well, everything. We are stubborn people. We struggle to ask for and receive help. We all have pride issues. Some of us have servant issues. We do not receive well — and some of us do not give well. Where are you on that spectrum?

Marriage was not meant to be two people banding together and then disappearing from the world. I know you are not here yet, but the seeds of your future marriage are already planted through examples and your perspective on what marriage is supposed to be. Every marriage needs input and challenge from friends and others to grow. (You may or may not have seen the importance of this in your family.)

Men — you need godly men in your life of all ages. I am writing this while on a camp-out with my oldest son's Boy Scouts troop. There are three other dads here that I love spending time with whenever I get the chance. I love that my son will feel comfortable going to them if he is struggling and that their sons might come to me.

That is community — that is the Body of Christ.

Ladies of all ages — you need women in your life. You need someone that can encourage you today as a preteen, as a teen, as a student, and one day as a wife, mom, and in your career aspirations and priorities. We ALL need mentors and mentees.

Be intentional to build relationships in which you are serving others. There is always someone that can benefit from knowing you and learning from your experiences and what the Lord is teaching you.

Times of crisis will reveal who your friends are like nothing else. Many years ago, I was lying in a hospital bed following a motorcycle wreck. A car had pulled out in front of me and I t-boned it with my six-year-old son on the seat behind me. Thankfully, he wasn't hurt at all — not even a bruise! I remember looking at the three men standing there in my hospital room, who had taken care of my wife, kids, and bike, before they were there with me. I said, "Man, it stinks to have to have this happen to be reminded of those that love us." My band of brothers.

Seek Out Community

The first place that I would recommend you look for community is in a local faith community. What characteristic is the most important to you in bonding to another person or group of people? Is it personality, a common hobby, faith, life stage? These can be the glue that holds a beginning friendship together.

Picture this: Think about a group of parents that gather together to cheer on their son or daughter in their sport. The common thread that unites these parents is usually the age of their kids and their children's mutual interest in that sport. There is often not much else. This is unfortunate, and it is often an unhealthy community. Often, groups like this bond together when they are trying to get a coach fired, or they are focused on a common problem and they feed each other's negativity. Relationships like this will not help you when you are in a crisis. However, a group of parents can also realize that while they may have initially met through their children's sport, they share many other things in common and they can be a source of encouragement to their kids, each other, their teams, and bring the light of Christ where it may not have been seen before.

I recently went on a motorcycle trip with a group of men from a local church. I knew a few of them from a previous trip five years earlier. The excuse to get together was our love and enthusiasm for motorcycles. The real reason for our excursion over the Cascade mountains and into the high desert of Eastern Oregon was a shared faith, a time of Bible Study, fellowship, and the deepening of friendships!

The youth group or other amenities may heavily influence your choice of a faith community as you consider what they offer. I would ask that a main priority be that they offer more than fun and games. The fun and games are important, but I want you grounded in God's Word. This is the most important aspect of any ministry. Be sure you know your priorities.

Years ago, my wife and I began attending a smaller church in a storefront that had the senior pastor's messages piped in via satellite. Neither of us had ever thought we would attend a church like that. What we quickly found were faithful friends, a community, and, yes, several bikers in attendance! They became very close to us in some huge times of health crises I went through.

As a teenager, FINDING community is essential.

FIND IT! You can also build into the community through serving. This will depend on your own spiritual growth and what you can handle at this time in your life. It is NOT healthy to always be the receiver.

Be Community to Others

Being a community is the other side of this equation. Serve a peer that has a special need. Follow your interests and see who else enjoys these same activities. You may find yourself building an incredible community where you are serving younger kids that do not have parents. If music is a passion, be a part of a musical group of like-minded people — this is community. Serve in the nursery. This was a place I started and learned to love. The intentionality you show here will shape how tomorrow goes. Life happens. Life can even fall apart. KEEP SERVING! Make it part of your DNA and ETHOS.

Who is in your corner?

Are you in someone else's corner as their world crumbles?

My family does not do Boy Scouts primarily for the skills that can be learned there. We do it for fellowship and community, with the parents that have grown over the years to become our go-to community. Some have gone through crises and we have been there to love them and serve them. When we have been in need, these families have stepped up to serve us. Yes, there is fun at the campouts and accomplishment as you complete a merit badge, but in the end, the best part is the community of friends.

Find a quilting group. Join the choir. Start a board games club. Seek things that will invite relationship, conversations, and vulnerability. It is amazing what we share at night, in the dark, around a campfire. Most men do not open up, but many will in this environment. I love that. Being a counselor, I love to talk deeply about life and will naturally seek this out everywhere, but for many others it is difficult to trust people enough to share.

Galatians 6:2 reminds us to:

> *"Carry each other's burdens, and in this way, you will fulfill the law of Christ"* (NIV).

I have met regularly with a friend, or a couple of friends, over the years and I always look forward to the time when we can get together. Regardless of whether it is over lunch or taking a walk, we can pray together and challenge one another. Most adults do not do this. **So, I CHALLENGE YOU to set this as a priority now so that it will be one for you as an adult.**

Find, build, and be in community.

Times of crises will reveal how well you have done this.

* * *

Working Questions – Now it is YOUR TURN:

Who is in your community?

____

____

____

____

Who can you call at a moment's notice for help, to talk, to cry, to vent—or to go to a movie, laugh with, and spend quality time with?

____

____

Who, outside of your family, do you spend the most time with? What are those people's beliefs and values? Do you want to be like them?

____

____

How are you SEEKING community in your life? Where is it based in?

____

____

How are you BEING community for others? To whom?

____

____

Write out Galatians 6:2 as a reminder.

____

____

* * *

What's Next?

Kevin, age 16, has a solid foundation from a Biblical Worldview on gender and sexuality, who he wants to be as a young man, and on the kind of woman he hopes to marry one day. What else does he need? He needs you and I. He needs support and encouragement. For many, it will be difficult to be vulnerable. Please do. Take risks - especially relational risks. These are hard. Community is difficult - especially when there is conflict. I hope Kevin will become the leader he can be. I hope he can stand firm against temptations and follow the bigger picture for his future that helps him laugh at temptations, short-lived highs, and experiences.

Sally, age 21, also has a solid foundation in God's Word and a Biblical Sexual Ethic. What else does she need? She needs you and I. She needs support and encouragement. She also has a clear picture of the kind of woman she desires to be. This makes her choice of community and influencers imperative. Where she works matters. Who she hangs around and listens to and follows matters. She is in a vulnerable place.

I hope both **Kevin and Sally** can find answers, encouragement, and community from those in their life. But, when these are not safe, or are not providing what we need for what we are going through, there are other options available. Professional, experienced advice is available.

I have been in private practice as a Licensed Professional Counselor since 2000. A recurring theme I see in families, singles, and couples is that **they wait to seek help because it embarrasses them to talk about that area of their life and they pull away from all community.**

I personally believe that most people's counseling needs could be handled among mature, fellow believers within the Body of Christ. We need to be the body and reach out and serve others with our gifts, friendliness, and a listening ear.

Professional Services

We are fortunate to live in a day and age with so many resources available to help you if you are struggling. For generations, people struggled silently and alone. Some continue to do so - but it is not because of a lack of available help. Families kept mental illness, depression, addictions, and abuse under cover to protect themselves and those they loved. Though we still have a long way to go in removing the stigma of mental illness, it has entered the national conversation and I hope that we will see even more changes in the years ahead. **Please know that if you find yourself struggling, you do not have to walk this path alone.** There are professionals across the world with training that can come alongside you if you find yourself in need. As you look for a professional to meet with, you will need to consider both their professional training and if they will be supportive of your beliefs, values, and goals. If they are not a good fit, please don't give up your search for help. Call someone else. Keep calling until you find someone that is a fit for you and where you are at in your life.

I am humbled every time I sit with an individual or family and that they trust me with difficult parts of their stories. I work with teenagers and children who are dealing with sexual issues.

This book is just the beginning because we all know that a book won't do the work for us. YOU must get up, learn the skills, and implement new strategies. **YOU are the biggest hurdle standing in your way.**

If you desire to dive deeper into these issues and be part of an online community that is learning, sharing, and growing together, I invite you to join me online at

http://wwww.HealingLives.com

Contact me at **www.drcoreygilbert.com** for professional counseling, coaching services, and courses to help you along the way. It is an honor to serve.

Access more resources including video trainings and more content for free that go along with this book at **teenbook.healinglives.com**

| 30 |

Bibliography

Allender, Dr. Dan. *The Wounded Heart.* U.S.A.: The Allender Center, Audio training, 2012.

Allender, Dr. Dan. *The Wounded Heart: Hope for Adult Victims of Childhood Sexual Abuse.* U.S.A.: NavPress, 2018.

Amen, Dr. Daniel. https://www.amenclinics.com

Amen, Dr. Daniel. *Healing ADD.* U.S.A.: Berkley, 2013.

Amen, Dr. Daniel. *The Brain in Love.* U.S.A.: Harmony, 2009.

Amen, Dr. Daniel. *Sex on the Brain.* U.S.A.: Harmony, 2007.

Amen, Dr. Daniel. *Unleash the Power of the Female Brain.* U.S.A.: Harmony, 2013.

American Board of Christian Sex Therapists. http://www.abcst.sexualwholeness.com

AWANA. https://www.awana.org

Barna, Dr. George. *Revolutionary Parenting.* U.S.A.: BarnaBooks, 2007.

DeMoss, Nancy Leigh. *Lies Women Believe.* U.S.A.: Moody, 2001.

Gilbert, Dr. Corey. *I Can't Say That: Going Beyond That Talk.* HealingLives, 2019.

Gilbert, Dr. Corey. www.drcoreygilbert.com

Hill, Dr. Wesley. https://spiritualfriendship.org

Institute for Sexual Wholeness. http://www.sexualwholeness.com

Kennedy, Gillian. "The Effect of Sexual Arousal on Risky Decision Making - Thesis." University of Lethbridge, 2010. https://www.uleth.ca/dspace/bitstream/handle/10133/3056/kennedy%2C%20gillian.pdf?sequence=1&isAllowed=y

Leaf, Dr. Carolyn. *Switch on Your Brain: The Key to Peak Happiness, Thinking, and Health.* U.S.A.: Baker Books, 2015.

Levine, Dr. Peter. *Trauma and Memory.* U.S.A.: North Atlantic Books, 2015.

Levine. Dr. Peter, & M. Kline. *Trauma-Proofing Your Kids.* U.S.A.: North Atlantic Books, 2008.

McDowell, Dr. Sean. Transgender Identities, the Church, and Scripture. https://www.youtube.com/watch?v=1sJeC3Hlvio, 2020.

Mullins, Rich. "Doubly Good to You." Song recorded by Amy Grant on album Straight Ahead. U.S.A.: Myrrh, 1984.

Parler, Branson. (n.d.). The Center for Faith, Sexuality & Gender. Pastoral paper: The Bible, Polyamory, and Monogamy. www.centerforfaith.com

Pearcey, Dr. Nancy. *Love Thy Body.* U.S.A.: Baker Books, 2018.

Penner, Dr. Clifford and Joyce Penner. https://passionatecommitment.com

Pope John Paul II. *Theology of the Body.* Lectures. Vatican City: 1979–1984.

Rainey, Dennis and Barbara. *Passport 2 Purity Getaway Kit.* FamilyLife, 2012.

Rosenau, Dr. Doug. https://sexualwholeness.com

Rosenau, Dr. Doug. *A Celebration of Sex: A Guide to Enjoying God's Gift of Sexual Intimacy.* U.S.A.: Thomas Nelson, 2002.

Rosenau, Dr. Doug, and Wilson, Michael Todd. *Soul Virgins.* U.S.A.: Sexual Wholeness Resources, 2012.

Santinelli, J., MA. Ott, M. Lyon, J. Rogers, D. Summers, R. Schliefer. "Abstinence and abstinence-only education: a review of U.S. policies and programs." *PubMed.gov.* January 2006. https://www.ncbi.nlm.nih.gov/pubmed/16387256.

Sax, Dr. Leonard. *Boys Adrift.* U.S.A.: Basic Books, 2007.

Sax, Dr. Leonard. *Why Gender Matters* (2nd edition). U.S.A.: Harmony, 2017.

Selmys, Melinda. Quote from Dr. Mark Yarhouse's book *Understanding Gender Dysphoria*, 2015.

"Sexual Risk Behaviours: HIV, STD, and teen pregnancy prevention." *Center for Disease Control (cdc.gov)*. 2015. https://www.cdc.gov/healthyyouth/sexualbehaviors/

Sprinkle, Dr. Preston. *Embodied: Transgender Identities, The Church, and What the Bible Has to Say*. David C. Cook, 2020.

Sprinkle, Dr. Preston. https://www.prestonsprinkle.com

Travers, Ann. *The Trans Generation: How Trans Kids (and Their Parents) Are Creating a Gender Revolution*. NYU Press, 2019.

Tripp, Paul David. *Age of Opportunity: A Biblical Guide to Parenting Teens (2nd edition)*. U.S.A.: P & R Publishing, 2001.

West, Christopher. *Fill These Hearts: God, Sex, and the Universal Longing*. U.S.A.: Image Publishing, 2013.

West, Christopher. *Heaven's Song: Sexual Love as it was Meant to Be*. U.S.A.: Ascension Press, 2008.

West, Christopher. T*heology of the Body for Beginners: A Basic Introduction to Pope John Paul II's Sexual Revolution (revised edition)*. U.S.A.: Ascension Press, 2008.

Wilson, Gary. *Your Brain on Porn: Internet Pornography and the Emerging Science of Addiction*. U.S.A.: Commonwealth Publishing, 2015.

Yarhouse, Dr. Mark. https://sexualidentityinstitute.org

Yarhouse, Dr. Mark. and L. Bukett. *Homosexuality and the Christian: A Guide for Parents, Pastors, and Friends.* U.S.A.: Bethany House Publishers, 2010.

Yarhouse, Dr. Mark. and L. Bukett. *Sexual Identity: A Guide for Living in the Time Between the Times.* U.S.A.: Bethany House Publishers, 2003.

Yarhouse, Dr. Mark. *Understanding Gender Dysphoria: Navigating Transgender Issues in a Changing Culture.* IVP Academic, 2015.

Zimbardo, Dr. Philip. *The Demise of Guys.* U.S.A.: Amazon, 2012.

"#EvolveTheDefinition" (advertisement), *Bonobos,* 2018. https://bonobos.com.

| 31 |

Endnotes

1. ^ Gilbert, Dr. Corey. www.drcoreygilbert.com
2. ^ Barna, Dr. George. *Revolutionary Parenting.* U.S.A.: Barna-Books, 2007.
3. ^ AWANA. https://www.awana.org
4. ^ Leaf, Dr. Carolyn. *Switch on Your Brain: The Key to Peak Happiness, Thinking, and Health.* U.S.A.: Baker Books, 2015.
5. ^ Ibid.
6. ^ Pearcey, Dr. Nancy. *Love Thy Body.* U.S.A.: Baker Books, 2018.
7. ^ Ibid.
8. ^ Ibid.
9. ^ Pope John Paul II. *Theology of the Body.* Lectures. Vatican City: 1979–1984.
10. ^ West, Christopher. T*heology of the Body for Beginners: A Basic Introduction to Pope John Paul II's Sexual Revolution (revised edition).* U.S.A.: Ascension Press, 2008.
11. ^ West, Christopher. *Fill These Hearts: God, Sex, and the Universal Longing.* U.S.A.: Image Publishing, 2013.
12. ^ Ibid.
13. ^ West, Christopher. *Heaven's Song: Sexual Love as it was Meant to Be.* U.S.A.: Ascension Press, 2008.

14. ^ "Sexual Risk Behaviours: HIV, STD, and teen pregnancy prevention." *Center for Disease Control (cdc.gov).* 2015. https://www.cdc.gov/healthyyouth/sexualbehaviors/
15. ^ Penner, Dr. Clifford and Joyce Penner. https://passionatecommitment.com
16. ^ Rosenau, Dr. Doug. https://sexualwholeness.com
17. ^ Amen, Dr. Daniel. *The Brain in Love.* U.S.A.: Harmony, 2009.
18. ^ Ibid.
19. ^ Ibid.
20. ^ Ibid.
21. ^ Ibid.
22. ^ Ibid.
23. ^ Ibid.
24. ^ Ibid.
25. ^ Amen, Dr. Daniel. https://www.amenclinics.com
26. ^ Amen, Dr. Daniel. https://www.amenclinics.com
27. ^ Kennedy, Gillian. "The Effect of Sexual Arousal on Risky Decision Making - Thesis." University of Lethbridge, 2010. https://www.uleth.ca/dspace/bitstream/handle/10133/3056/kennedy%2C%20gillian.pdf?sequence=1&isAllowed=y
28. ^ Amen, Dr. Daniel. *Sex on the Brain.* U.S.A.: Harmony, 2007.
29. ^ Ibid.
30. ^ Amen, Dr. Daniel. *The Brain in Love.* U.S.A.: Harmony, 2009.
31. ^ Institute for Sexual Wholeness. http://www.sexualwholeness.com
32. ^ Allender, Dr. Dan. *The Wounded Heart.* U.S.A.: The Allender Center, Audio training, 2012.
33. ^ Allender, Dr. Dan. *The Wounded Heart.* U.S.A.: The Allender Center, Audio training, 2012.
34. ^ Yarhouse, Dr. Mark. https://sexualidentityinstitute.org
35. ^ Sprinkle, Dr. Preston. https://www.prestonsprinkle.com
36. ^ Hill, Dr. Wesley. https://spiritualfriendship.org

37. ^ Tripp, Paul David. *Age of Opportunity: A Biblical Guide to Parenting Teens (2nd edition).* U.S.A.: P & R Publishing, 2001.
38. ^ "#EvolveTheDefinition" (advertisement), *Bonobos,* 2018. https://bonobos.com.
39. ^ Sax, Dr. Leonard. *Boys Adrift.* U.S.A.: Basic Books, 2007.
40. ^ Ibid.
41. ^ Amen, Dr. Daniel. *Healing ADD.* U.S.A.: Berkley, 2013.
42. ^ "#EvolveTheDefinition" (advertisement), *Bonobos,* 2018. https://bonobos.com.
43. ^ Zimbardo, Dr. Philip. *The Demise of Guys.* U.S.A.: Amazon, 2012.
44. ^ DeMoss, Nancy Leigh. *Lies Women Believe.* U.S.A.: Moody, 2001.
45. ^ Amen, Dr. Daniel. *Unleash the Power of the Female Brain.* U.S.A.: Harmony, 2013.
46. ^ Sax, Dr. Leonard. *Why Gender Matters* (2nd edition). U.S.A.: Harmony, 2017.
47. ^ McDowell, Dr. Sean. Transgender Identities, the Church, and Scripture. https://www.youtube.com/watch?v=1sJeC3Hlvio, 2020.
48. ^ Travers, Ann. *The Trans Generation: How Trans Kids (and Their Parents) Are Creating a Gender Revolution.* NYU Press, 2019.
49. ^ Ibid.
50. ^ Sprinkle, Dr. Preston. *Embodied: Transgender Identities, The Church, and What the Bible Has to Say.* David C. Cook, 2020.
51. ^ Ibid.
52. ^ Ibid.
53. ^ Ibid.
54. ^ Ibid.
55. ^ Yarhouse, Dr. Mark. *Understanding Gender Dysphoria: Navigating Transgender Issues in a Changing Culture.* IVP Academic, 2015.
56. ^ Ibid.

57. ^ Ibid.
58. ^ Ibid.
59. ^ Ibid.
60. ^ Selmys, Melinda. Quote from Dr. Mark Yarhouse's book *Understanding Gender Dysphoria*, 2015.
61. ^ Yarhouse, Dr. Mark. *Understanding Gender Dysphoria: Navigating Transgender Issues in a Changing Culture.* IVP Academic, 2015.
62. ^ Yarhouse, Dr. Mark. https://sexualidentityinstitute.org
63. ^ Yarhouse, Dr. Mark. https://sexualidentityinstitute.org
64. ^ Sprinkle, Dr. Preston. https://www.prestonsprinkle.com
65. ^ Allender, Dr. Dan. *The Wounded Heart.* U.S.A.: The Allender Center, Audio training, 2012.
66. ^ Yarhouse, Dr. Mark. and L. Bukett. *Sexual Identity: A Guide for Living in the Time Between the Times.* U.S.A.: Bethany House Publishers, 2003.
67. ^ Parler, Branson. (n.d.). The Center for Faith, Sexuality & Gender. Pastoral paper: The Bible, Polyamory, and Monogamy. www.centerforfaith.com
68. ^ Ibid.
69. ^ Ibid.
70. ^ Ibid.
71. ^ Ibid.
72. ^ Ibid.
73. ^ Mullins, Rich. "Doubly Good to You." Song recorded by Amy Grant on album Straight Ahead. U.S.A.: Myrrh, 1984.
74. ^ Rosenau, Dr. Doug. *A Celebration of Sex: A Guide to Enjoying God's Gift of Sexual Intimacy.* U.S.A.: Thomas Nelson, 2002.
75. ^ Rosenau, Dr. Doug, and Wilson, Michael Todd. *Soul Virgins.* U.S.A.: Sexual Wholeness Resources, 2012.
76. ^ Ibid.
77. ^ Ibid.
78. ^ Gilbert, Dr. Corey. *I Can't Say That: Going Beyond That Talk.* HealingLives, 2019.

79. ^ Barna, Dr. George. *Revolutionary Parenting.* U.S.A.: Barna-Books, 2007.
80. ^ Ibid.
81. ^ Allender, Dr. Dan. *The Wounded Heart: Hope for Adult Victims of Childhood Sexual Abuse.* U.S.A.: NavPress, 2018.
82. ^ Levine. Dr. Peter, & M. Kline. *Trauma-Proofing Your Kids.* U.S.A.: North Atlantic Books, 2008.
83. ^ Ibid.
84. ^ Levine, Dr. Peter. *Trauma and Memory.* U.S.A.: North Atlantic Books, 2015.
85. ^ Ibid.
86. ^ Ibid.
87. ^ Wilson, Gary. *Your Brain on Porn: Internet Pornography and the Emerging Science of Addiction.* U.S.A.: Commonwealth Publishing, 2015.
88. ^ Rainey, Dennis and Barbara. *Passport 2 Purity Getaway Kit.* FamilyLife, 2012.

About the Author

Dr. Gilbert is a dad, husband, University professor, counselor, scoutmaster, an avid backpacker, skier, camper, and motorcyclist.

He spends his days investing in families, counseling, and teaching on healthy sexuality from a Biblical worldview, trauma, the importance of the local church and God's design for marriage.

PODCAST
He hosts a podcast called the "FAMILY FEATURES PODCAST" - Check it out.

SPEAKING
Book Dr. Gilbert to come to your next event by going to his website below and completing the Speaker Request Form. He LOVES to come to you and invest in you and your families.

COACHING
Get help yourself - for you personally, to face your past and dream again, for your marriage, and/or for your family. Book a FREE consult with Dr G by going to his website below.

COURSES
Join one of Dr. Gilbert's courses on "Love, Sex, Dating, and Marriage" aimed at the teen through any age single adult that wants a biblical design for dating, courting, and marrying well.

COUNSELING
For those local to Oregon I am honored to walk along side you in person. Contac' me for more information.

Find out more about Dr. Gilbert's other courses and trainings on his website.

It is an honor to serve.

Find out more at **www.drcoreygilbert.c**

CENTER FOR SEX & TRAUMA EDUCATION AND TRANSFORMATION

HealingLives, LLC
www.drcoreygilbert.com

om